Hiking T

Fifth Edition

by
Evan Means

edited by
Bob Brown

Old Saybrook, Connecticut

The Globe Pequot Press assumes no liability for accidents happening to, or injuries sustained by, readers who engage in the activities described in this book.

Library of Congress Cataloging-in-Publication Data is available

ISBN 0-7627-0225-7

Manufactured in the United States of America
Fifth Edition/First Printing

Contents

* indicates a handicapped-accessible trail

List of Maps

Help Us Keep This Guide Up to Date

Every effort has been made by the author and editors to make this guide as accurate and useful as possible. However, many things can change after a guide is published—establishments close, phone numbers change, hiking trails are rerouted, facilities come under new management, etc.

We would love to hear from you concerning your experiences with this guide and how you feel it could be made better and be kept up to date. While we may not be able to respond to all comments and suggestions, we'll take them to heart, and we'll also make certain to share them with the author. Please send your comments and suggestions to the following address:

The Globe Pequot Press
Reader Response/Editorial Department
P.O. Box 833
Old Saybrook, CT 06475

Or you may e-mail us at:

editorial@globe-pequot.com

Thanks for your input, and happy travels!

Acknowledgments

This book could not have been produced without the help and encouragement of many people. We express our sincere thanks to those who made this effort possible: to Grimes Slaughter, a past president of Tennessee Trails Association, who needled contributors to get their assignments done and whose topographical maps were indispensable; to the other officers of TTA and the members who contributed; and to Chancellor Bob Brandt and Joe Gaines, who furnished background material.

We could not have completed this project without the support and cooperation of the U.S. Forest Service, the Tennessee Valley Authority, and the Tennessee Department of Conservation. State trails system administrator Harry Williamson and trail coordinators Mike Dahl, Bob Richards, and David Shupe all went out of their way to help. We thank David Stidham, recreation planner for the U.S. Army Corps of Engineers and chairman of the Nashville Chapter of TTA, for handing out assignments and keeping his group working.

Special thanks to Clarence Streetmand and David Rhyne of Bowater Southern Paper Corporation for their encouragement. Thanks also to Molly Killingsworth for her excellent editing job. A pause in memory for those old-timers Paul Fink and Paul Adams, and special thanks to B. W. Chumney, who provided historical information about Cherokee National Forest. The author appreciates the help of the TTA people who assisted in bringing this book up to date, including Bob Barnett, president; Bob Brown, whose enthusiasm inspired me to start the first edition; and the folks in the Memphis, Murfeesboro, and Nashville chapters. Thanks to state parks personnel and the staffs of the Big South Fork and the Cherokee National Forests.

Editor's Acknowledgments

The editor wishes to thank those individuals who contributed trail descriptions for the current and previous editions of this work; whose names appear at the ends of their contributions.

Grateful acknowledgment is also given to those who revised existing trail descriptions or provided new information for this edition: Mack Prichard, Sam Powell, Bob Richards, Alison Brayton, Steve Hendricks, Clayton Pannell, Nick Fielder, Alan Wasik, John Howell, Billy Glenn Smith, Stuart Carroll, Billy Martin, Kenny Daniel, Bill Troup, Sam Reed, Jim Nash, Jim Harrison, Tom Shouse, Roy Harkness, Jack Collier, Charles Spearman, Jim Leeson, Jack Coleman, Jerry Conley, Monika Mayr, Howard Ray Duncan, Kevin Hamend, David Taylor, Bo Townsend, Bobbie Bennett, Linda Hixson, Tim Netsch, Starlene Shackleford, Joyce Haarson, Janice Scott, John D. Ross, Sally Lee, Stan Malone, and Bob Anderson.

The editor is also grateful to Alan Stokes for the significant improvement to the maps in the 4th edition, redrawing each with clarity and detail. For this edition he revised maps where necessary and added excellent maps for four segments of the Cumberland State Scenic Trail.

On behalf of the members of the Tennessee Trails Association special thanks go to Mack Prichard, Tennessee's "Conservation conscience" for almost four decades and the catalyst for TTA's formation and its advocacy for a statewide system of scenic trails, and to Kathleen Williams, who early in this decade was the pioneering advocate for a statewide system of greenways.

Finally, it was an honor to be asked by Evan Means to revise this little volume, his labor of love for almost two decades.

Preface

Hiking in Tennessee is rewarding for the scenery alone. The state's highly differentiated topography stairsteps generally downhill from east to west across nine distinct physiographic provinces, drained by three major river systems and underlain by extensive case systems:

- In East Tennessee the Unaka Mountains (or Blue Ridge), the Valley and Ridge, and the eastern parts of the Cumberland Mountains and Cumberland plateau lie in the watershed of the upper Tennessee River.
- In Middle Tennessee the northwestern parts of the Cumberland Mountains and Cumberland Plateau, most of the Eastern Highland Rim and the Central Basin, and the northeastern part of the Western Highland Rim lie in the Cumberland River watershed.
- In West Tennessee most of the Western Highland Rim and all of the Southern Coastal Plain drain into the lower Tennessee River, while the Loess Plain and the Mississippi Alluvial Plain drain into the Mississippi River.

More than enthralling views of landforms, streams, and caverns, however, some of the most memorable experiences of hiking Tennessee trails are the sights, sounds, smells, and other sensations of the forests that cover about half the state's surface. They are predominantly of native hardwoods types, much recovered from heavy logging early in the twentieth century but newly threatened by clear-cutting and replacement with planted pine monoculture. These indigenous forest types include:

- spruce-fir (an Ice Age relict catastrophically reduced just since the 1960s by blight and air pollution) and northern hardwoods on the highest mountain tops of the Blue Ridge;

- oak-pine on the mid-slopes of the Blue Ridge and the Cumberland mountains;
- cove hardwoods and mixed mesophytic in the deep coves of the Blue Ridge, the gulfs and gorges of the Cumberland Plateau, and the rich hollows of both Highland Rims;
- oak-hickory in most of the Valley and Ridge, Cumberland Plateau, Highland Rims, Central Basin, and Loess Plain;
- red cedar in some of the Valley and Ridge and much of the Central Basin;
- oak-hickory-pine on the Southern Coastal Plain; and
- bottomland hardwoods on the alluvial floodplains of the Mississippi and its tributaries.

Consistent with its diverse physiography and forest cover, Tennessee is one of ten states with the greatest diversity of plant and animal species. Its streams have more species of freshwater fish, crayfish, and snails than any other state and more species of mussels than anywhere else in the world. Unfortunately, Tennessee is one of four states with the highest percentage of imperiled aquatic species, and it possesses globally important ecosystems in more than 200 sites now threatened with degradation or destruction.

Though still blessed with great scenery and biodiversity, the state has lost much, and what remains is vulnerable:

> . . . Before Europeans came to Tennessee, a large Native American population mostly lived in harmony with the land and its fruits. Thus, the immigrants found boundless forests that were sometimes interspersed with prairie-like openings and glades, abundant underground resources, and free-flowing streams. Two hundred years later, however, population growth with subsequent pollution and urban and suburban development is rampant. There are few virgin forests, prairies are almost totally under tilth, and the landscape is frequently marred from mining operations. High dams on the Tennessee and

Cumberland rivers and their tributaries, and chan-
nelization of many West Tennessee streams, have
permanently altered these watercourses. Overall, entire forest types and communities are gone, and
many species are extirpated, and numerous others
hang on precariously. Meanwhile, disturbed areas
provide a fertile ground for introduced, often unde-
sirable, species.
—*Atlas of Tennessee Vascular Plants,* Vol. I, 1993

Wherever you hike in Tennessee you walk in the footsteps of
American Indians. The state is one of the richest in Native American habitation, burial, and ceremonial sites, particularly those of
the Woodland and Mississippian traditions. Virtually every major
stream valley is archeologically significant almost from source to
mouth. Unfortunately, long a target of pothunters, many of these
sites continue to be degraded or lost before they can be preserved
or even seriously studied by anthropologists.

For more than a century after its first settlement by Europeans,
Tennessee was an agricultural state populated by farm families. By
the mid 1800s the landscape of much of East and West Tennessee
and most of Middle Tennessee was agrarian. Today, farm families
constitute only a small part of the state's population, but agriculture remains a major part of both its economy and its uniquely
beautiful scenery. Sadly, much of the state's most productive and
scenic farmland is succumbing to encroaching freeways and residential or commercial development.

Today's hiking trails were the Indian paths of prehistory, later
followed by the longhunters and then by settlers pushing westward through "the wilderness." Many routes follow old horse trails
and wagon roads that connected forts and stations, farms,
churches, mills, mines, quarries, furnaces, foundries, boat landings,
villages, and towns. Some lie along the routes of army marches
during the American Revolution, the War of 1812, the Creek War,
or the War Between the States. Tennessee is second only to Vir-

ginia in the number and importance of Civil War engagements fought on her soil.

Tennessee trails, then, are paths to the geological, ecological, and cultural history of the state. Chapter I tells of the footpaths used by Native Americans and the adoption and improvement of their ancient routes by the Europeans who displaced them.

Chapter 2 tells how hiking trails evolved in Tennessee during the twentieth century, starting with those built by the Civilian Conservation Corps during the Great Depression. Especially noteworthy was the formation of the Tennessee Trails Association (TTA) in 1968 to promote a statewide system of hiking trails and to work toward conservation of the rapidly disappearing natural and cultural resources within those proposed trail corridors. Passage of the Tennessee Trails System Act in 1971 led to a multiple expansion of hiking trail mileage by the state's Department of Conservation working with local governments, private companies, the TTA, and many other volunteers.

Since 1987 most trail development in Tennessee has been in the form of local greenway projects, and this has resulted in a multiple expansion in the number and total mileage of multi-use trails and trails accessible to those with disabilities. Recent public/private initiatives have sought to coordinate these grass-roots efforts and encourage linkages among local greenways to create a statewide greenway system.

Each of Chapters 3 through 10 describes a set of trails with a common theme or some common management philosophy. The individual trail descriptions in each chapter highlight significant natural or cultural features of the trail, and those in Chapter 4, State Scenic Trails, are supplemented by somewhat detailed historical notes.

Chapter 11 profiles private citizens' organizations that have been important preservers of Tennessee's natural and cultural heritage and providers of outstanding hiking opportunities. Each of these groups offers a program of organized hikes and conservation work trips. Among their members are many experienced hikers who can advise where, when, and how to enjoy our trails. Many of the trail descriptions in this book were written by these folks.

Finally, Evan Means has assigned all royalties from the sale of this book to the TTA, an active partner in the creation and maintenance of Tennessee's trails and greenways. The author, editor, and all the contributors to this fifth edition hope it will help you experience an hour or two, or a lifetime, of joy, wonder, and friendship hiking Tennessee trails.

Trails for People with Disabilities

While previous editions of this book grouped the *trails accessible to those with disabilities* in a separate chapter, the greatly increased number of such trails in Tennessee suggests that another arrangement would be more useful to the reader. Therefore, in this edition each such trail description is included in the chapter that contains descriptions of other trails in the same park or preserve where the accessible trail is located. Every trail accessible to the disabled is noted in the Table of Contents and in the text by a ⑤ icon, and the majority of them are described in the newly titled Chapter 9, Urban Trails and Greenways.

In 1990 an interim draft of a *Design Guide for Accessible Recreation* was published by the National Forest Service and National Park Service. It estimated that as much as 57 percent of our population has some degree of disability: 37 percent of us with significant long-term physical, mental, or emotional limitations; 10 percent who are elderly or have invisible disabilities such as cardiac or respiratory problems; and 10 percent with temporary disabilities such as broken limbs.

The N.F.S./N.P.S. interim design guide uses three accessibility levels to classify outdoor recreation facilities:

- Accessible—Generally, these sites are usable without assistance by all but the most severely disabled.
- Challenge Level 1—These sites are more difficult for those with limited mobility, and some disabled persons may need assistance.

- Challenge Level 2—These sites are usable by the more athletic disabled person without assistance, but those with limited mobility will probably need assistance, while use by the severely disabled without assistance is not recommended

A few of the standards for trails and pathways suggested by the guide, and used in rating the trails visited by the editor and described in this volume, are as follows:

	Accessible	Challenge Level 1	Challenge Level 2
Grade	5% max.	8.3% max.	12.5% max. not to exceed 200 ft.
Width 1-way 2-way	4 ft. 5 ft.	32-in. min.	32-in. min.
Cross Slope	2% max.	2% max.	3% max.
Surface	Hard	Very firm, compacted	Natural, passable by wheelchair
Distance Between Rest Areas	200–300 ft. max.	100–200 ft. max. where grade greater than 5%	200–300 ft. min. using natural level places where possible

The trails for the disabled are each rated as to overall accessibility based on the above standards for *grade, width, surface,* and *distance between rest areas*. Almost all these trails exceed the 3 percent maximum *cross slope* cited in these standards, at least for short distances in turns. Cross slopes of up to 13 percent are encountered on many of them, and this is noted in the relevant trail descriptions. Each trail surface is also rated as *smooth, fairly smooth,* or *rough.*

All these trails are unobstructed. Most of them have no curbs but are railed at danger spots and on all bridges and elevated boardwalks. The permitted use of each trail, besides wheelchair, is indicated as either *foot* or *multi-use*. The latter includes traffic by foot, bicycle, possibly skateboard and in-line skate, but not horse.

Although selected primarily as suitable for persons with disabilities, all these trails are interesting and enjoyable for anyone. Some are great jogging trails, and many are particularly attractive for family walks with children.

Introduction to the First Edition

Before we completed the inventory for this volume, we had a dream of including all the trails in Tennessee in one volume. When the count reached 283 outside the Smokies and we were still counting, it became apparent that our dream was impractical. We have tried to describe the best hiking trails, distributed from east to west, since that is the direction taken by the explorers and settlers who crossed the Appalachian Mountains from Virginia and the Carolinas. The Appalachian Trail and Great Smoky Mountains National Park are not included in this guide, since a large number of guidebooks cover those areas. We recommend *Hiking in the Great Smokies* by Carson Brewer, available at park visitor's centers, and *Hiking the Great Smoky Mountains* by R. and P. Albright (from The Globe Pequot Press). Guidebooks for the Appalachian Trail area are available from the Appalachian Trail Conference, P.O. Box 807, Harpers Ferry, West Virginia, 25425; the Sierra Club also has some excellent guidebooks.

There are more than a hundred hiking trails listed on the map "Trails of the Cherokee National Forest" (now outdated and out-of-print; see Chapter 3). These range in length from 0.2-mi. interpretive trails in recreation areas to 138 miles of the Appalachian Trail. Hikers also have access, at their risk, to fourteen motorcycle, thirteen horse, and six bicycle trails. Obviously, we couldn't include all of them, so we have picked out some of the best. There are many good trails in state parks, but again, we selected a few good trails and left out some of equal quality.

We had many pleasant experiences while doing field research. We walked through Cumberland Gap with Daniel Boone and followed his footsteps along Walden Ridge. We followed the paths of the Indians along the crest of the Appalachians and camped beside tumbling mountain streams. In our mind's eye, we followed David

Crockett on bear hunts in the canebrakes along Tennessee rivers and carried corn to his gristmill at Crockett Falls on Shoal Creek in Lawrence County. We watched squirrels romp in a hollow oak tree, then climbed Big Ridge, where Indians ambushed and scalped the pioneer Peter Graves in 1794. We marveled at the views of the great "gulfs" carved by nature from the Cumberland Plateau and rested in rock houses, great overhanging rock formations that have sheltered hunters and hikers for centuries. We hope that the reader will share these experiences with us and find other adventures on Tennessee trails.

There is very little flat land in Tennessee, and most of the trails are rocky to a certain extent. We recommend sturdy hiking shoes that protect the ankles. A light staff is essential to maintain balance on precipitous paths, aid in climbing and descending steep slopes, and serve as a probe when crossing logs and rocks that might harbor dangerous snakes. Temperatures vary widely over a twenty-four-hour period, so plan your clothing accordingly. The clothing layers peeled as you climb a mountain slope will feel good when put back on at the top. Nights are cool in the mountains, so arrange to sleep warmly. We assume that most readers have reference material on camping and backpacking equipment, so we shall not bore you with further instructions. Good hiking!

—Evan Means, 1979

1. Historical Background

Most of Tennessee in the mid 1700s was heavily populated with the American bison, our "buffalo." There is evidence that prior to 1500, for many centuries at least, the buffalo was absent east of the Mississippi, excluded by the Amerindians' intensive cultivation of the river bottoms and their heavy hunting pressure. With the natives' depopulation by epidemics of smallpox and measles progressing rapidly inland from the Atlantic and Gulf coasts in the 1500s, their fields returned quickly to prairie, oldfield pines and cedars, and canebrakes now open to a bison invasion from the west. The bison's abundance in Tennessee in the late 1600s and early 1700s, especially at salt licks, attracted the French and English hunters who slaughtered them for their hides and as a food source, often for their tongues alone. Between 1770 and 1790 bison were hunted almost to extinction in the Central Basin and much of East Tennessee. The network of "buffalo roads" throughout the state, however, remained the highest, driest, and easiest overland routes of travel for the Indians as well as the longhunters and the settlers who followed them.

When they crossed the Appalachians into the upper Tennessee Valley in the middle of the sixteenth century, Hernando de Soto, and later Juan de Pardo, found and utilized an elaborate system of trails established by Indian traders from the Ohio Valley to Florida and the lower Mississippi River. A party that penetrated the Cherokee country from Virginia in 1673 found Spanish trade goods, even though they were the first white men most of the Indians had seen. Along the northern border of Tennessee, buffalo trails (or traces) provided pathways for the explorers and early settlers.

De Soto's party in 1540 is now thought to have crossed the Blue Ridge along the Nolichucky and French Broad rivers and then to have followed the route of the Great Indian Warpath, down the

1

Tennessee Valley through Cherokee towns near the junction of the Hiwassee and Ocoee rivers then south along Conasauga River into northeast Georgia. No doubt, de Soto followed Indian trade routes from north Mississippi to the fourth Chickasaw Bluff, now Memphis, and the towns of the Chickasaws. Marquette and Joliet visited the Chickasaws in 1673, followed by La Salle in 1682, but they followed the rivers and made little use of trails.

Gabriel Arthur accompanied a party of Cherokees through Cumberland Gap in 1673, and Virginia's Governor Spotswood and his "Knights of the Golden Horseshoe" found the Gap in 1716 while exploring the upper Shenandoah Valley, but this important pass had been used by Indian raiders and traders for centuries. Dr. Thomas Walker named it, and the river beyond, for William the Duke of Cumberland in 1750 as he scouted for 800,000 acres of transmontane lands for his Loyal Land Company of Virginia. Daniel Boone, John Finley, and four others traveled from the Yadkin Valley in North Carolina in 1769 and followed the Warriors Path through Cumberland Gap.

Daniel Boone's reports of the land beyond the great mountain barrier prompted the first attempt to migrate from the Yadkin Valley to Kentucky in 1773, but it was turned back by hostile Indians near the Gap. After Colonel Richard Henderson's "Transylvania Purchase" of the Cumberland River watershed from the Cherokee in 1775 (repudiated by both Virginia and North Carolina), a growing stream of settlers poured through the Gap along a route opened by Boone and thirty axemen into Kentucky. Though hostility of the Cherokee had diminished, attacks by the Shawnee and white highwaymen increased. This route became known as the Wilderness Road. A faction of the Cherokee bitterly opposed to the "sale" to Henderson broke away and settled in towns around the mouths of North and South Chickamauga creeks in the Chattanooga area. For the next two decades these "Chickamaugas" made travel by the more southerly routes into Middle Tennessee highly dangerous.

Trails connected the Overhill Cherokee towns of Chota, Talassee, and Tellico along the Little Tennessee and Tellico rivers with

2

their Valley settlements along the upper Hiwassee River, with Middle settlements on the headwaters of the Little Tennessee and the Tuskaseegee, and with Lower settlements on the Tugaloo River in north Georgia and the Keowee River in South Carolina. The Black Fox Trail ran from the lower Hiwassee settlements past a salt lick in present Rhea County, past Indian mounds east of Pikeville, across the Cumberland Plateau, across the Collins River, past Short Mountain, and on to Black Fox spring at present Murfreesboro.

In volume 1 of *Tennessee, The Volunteer State* (1923), John Trotwood Moore and Austin P. Foster tell of a branch of the Indian War Trail crossing Chilhowee Mountain at Millstone, Georgia, from Fort McTeer to the Cherokee town of Tuckaleechee.

Another trail ran from the Old Creek Crossing, near present Bridgeport, Alabama, up Sequatchie Valley past many prehistoric townsites, past mounds at present Pikeville, out the head-of-Sequatchie, and on to Crab Orchard Cove. Early settlers in the 1790s used this trail south from the Crab Orchard to enter Grassy Cove and the Sequatchie Valley.

The Chickamauga Path began in the North Georgia and Chattanooga settlements, crossed the Tennessee River at the Old Creek Crossing, and then crossed the Cumberland Plateau to Beersheba Springs. From there it went to the site of the present town of Rock Island, crossed the Caney Fork River, and passed a little west of the present town of Sparta, branching out at a fortified town on Cherry Creek. One fork went to the settlements of the Cherokees at Officer's Mounds near Algood and then to Carthage on the Cumberland River. The other fork went to the present site of Mayland and on beyond Jamestown. An important trail ran between the present towns of Monterey and Sparta, connected with the Chickamauga Path near the junction of the Cumberland, White, and Putnam county lines in the present community of Yankeetown. Settlers used this trail to move into the Calfkiller River Valley.

North of the Cumberland River, buffalo paths connected salt licks and provided trails for the settlers who moved from upper East Tennessee to French Lick, now Nashville. The buffalo disap-

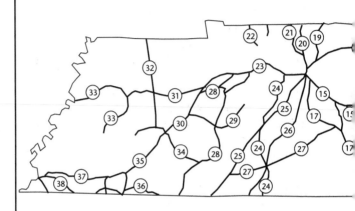

1. The Old Cherokee Path to Virginia
2. The Chesapeake Branch of the Great Indian Warpath
3. Boone's Trail from the Yadkin River to Boonesborough
4. The Great Indian Warpath
5. The Catawba Trail
6. Holston Trace (Emory Road)
7. The Clinch River and Cumberland Gap Trail
8. The East and West Trail
9. The Tennessee River, Ohio, and Great Lakes Trail
10. The Chickamauga Path
11. The Cumberland Trace
12. The Black Fox Trail
13. The Unicoi Turnpike
14. Tuchaloochee and Southeastern Trail
15. The Cisco and St. Augustine Trail
16. The Sequatchie Trail
17. The Great South Trail
18. The Nickajack Trail
19. The Cumberland and Great Lakes Trail

Tennessee Indian Trails

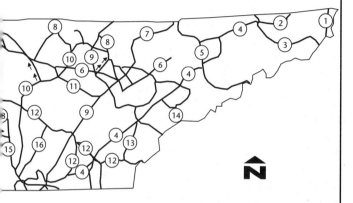

20. The Cumberland and Ohio Falls Trail
21. The Nashville–Saine River Trail
22. The Palmyra-Princeton Trail
23. The Lover Harpeth and West Tennessee Trail
24. Route of General Jackson's expedition against the Indians in 1787
25. The Natchez Trace or the Middle Tennessee Chickasaw Trace
26. General Jackson's Old Military Road
27. The Oki Waterloo Road
28. The Duck River and Northeast Mississippi Trail
29. Trail between Duck River and Beach River, Tennessee
30. The Cisco and Middle Tennessee River Trail
31. The Mississippi and Tennessee River Trail
32. Massac Trail
33. The Brownsville Fort Ridge and Hale's Point Trail
34. The Cisco and Savannah Trail
35. The West Tennessee Chickasaw Trail
36. The Cherokee Trace
37. The Bolivar and Memphis Trail
38. The Memphis-Pontotoc Trail

peared from Middle and East Tennessee around the end of the seventeenth century, apparently because of excess hunting and, possibly, the rapid conversion to farmland of grassy uplands and rich bottomland forests and canebrakes.

The Natchez Trace, which provided a return route for flatboaters from Natchez back to Nashville, was called the Chickasaw Trace by the first settlers at Fort Nashborough, and it was often traveled by James Robertson to and from the Chickasaw towns in north Mississippi as he negotiated with this friendly Indian nation. The Natchez Trace Parkway follows the general route of this historic trail. Another Chickasaw Trace ran from the vicinity of the Pinson Mounds southwest to towns around present Bolivar, where a branch went west to the fourth Chickasaw Bluff, now Memphis, and the main trail, south to the north Mississippi towns. Another Chickasaw trail, the Massac Trace, passed through Madison County, where College Street in Jackson was laid out along it, north to Fort Massac in Massac County, Illinois. Other trails in Middle Tennessee ran from French Lick and from numerous ancient towns around Palymyra northwest and north, respectively, to major salt deposits along the Saline River in Illinois.

Captain James Robertson led a party overland from the Holston country to French Lick in 1779, following buffalo paths from the Wilderness Road at Cumberland Gap westward through the Kentucky country and down the Cumberland River to their destination. Meanwhile, the Donelson Party floated down the Holston and the Tennessee to the Ohio, then pushed back up the Cumberland River. The river trip to French Lick was the more hazardous, running through Chickamauga territory and through treacherous eddies and rapids. The settlement's name was changed from French Lick to Nashborough, and later to Nashville.

With the surge to settle the country west of the Appalachians, road building was emphasized. On November 6, 1786, Colonel James Robertson was empowered to enlist 201 men to protect the inhabitants of the Nashville settlement and to cut a road from the Clinch River to Nashville. This clearing work began in August of

1787 at Clinch Mountain and proceeded along the route of an old Indian trail, the Holston Trace, up Crooked Fork and Emory River, across the Cumberland Plateau and Highland Rim to the Cumberland River at Flynn's Creek and on to Nashville by September 1788.

This North Carolina Military Trace was improved by William Emory in 1792 and the route changed on the eastern end to pass through Southwest Point (Kingston), from which a better road to White's Fort (Knoxville) was already in general use. Also increasingly in use by more daring travelers was a more southerly route, an old Indian Trail—The Cherokee or Cumberland Trace—from Southwest Point across lands claimed by the Cherokee through Crab Orchard to the Standing Stone at Monterey where it intersected the Military Trace. In 1802, after a new agreement with the Cherokee, the Cumberland Turnpike Company opened a new, much improved road along this route to present Monterey and then across the Highland Rim past present Cookeville to William Walton's Ferry at present Carthage, from which a road already ran to Nashville. Commonly known as the Walton Road, this soon became the major route westward from the Carolinas, Virginia, and Pennsylvania.

Around 1787, Glover's Trace was opened, mostly along the route of another Chickasaw Trace. It ran from Nashville through Charlotte down Trace Creek and across the Tennessee River, then south through west Tennessee to the Chickasaw towns in north Mississippi with a branch going southwest to the fourth Chickasaw Bluff. John F. Brevard advocated opening Glover's Trace for boatmen returning from New Orleans. Brevard's interest in opening Glover's Trace may have resulted from the activities of highwaymen who waylaid travelers on the Natchez Trace, robbing them of the proceeds from the sale of their goods and boats in New Orleans. Travelers on the Wilderness Road through Cumberland Gap suffered similar indignities. William Cocke arranged with the Chickasaws in 1815 to open Glover's Trace, but the U.S. government refused to bear any of the expense.

A map of 1817 shows a network of about 1,500 miles of roads, almost entirely along old Indian trails and traces and all located in East and Middle Tennessee. Roads developed more slowly west of Nashville since most settlers went down the Tennessee, Cumberland, Ohio, and Mississippi rivers and into the interior via their tributaries, the Big Sandy, the Obion, the Forked Deer, the Hatchie, and the Wolf rivers, and most of the commerce and communication went the same way. Also, roads were difficult to build across the wide and swampy bottoms of all these streams.

The Tennessee Territory, ceded to the federal government by North Carolina in 1790, became a state in 1796. By 1804 county courts were permitted to build roads and to establish ferries. By a series of treaties between 1791 and 1819, the Cherokees relinquished all their lands except in the southeast corner of Tennessee. The Chickasaw territory in West Tennessee was purchased in 1818. The development of a young state called for mass means of moving goods and raw materials, and again an emphasis was placed on road building. Many of the old Indian trails became wagon roads, and eventually, the fast highways of today.

In Northwest Tennessee David Crockett used a few remaining trails to hunt bear and deer. Old Indian trails remained in use in the Great Smoky Mountains, and some of them are still in use in the national park as recreation trails. Today, it appears that U.S. 11W follows the Great Indian Warpath from Bristol and Kingsport down the Holston Valley to Knoxville. U.S. 25E follows a pioneer route from Bean Gap through Cumberland Gap. Some early migrants turned down the Powell Valley, following trails that have become TN 63. U.S. 127 follows the ancient route through the Sequatchie Valley. U.S. 41 and I–24 follow the general route of the Nickajack Trace. U.S. 70S traces part of the Chicamauga Path between McMinnville and Sparta, and U.S. 70N follows much of the Walton Road, while TN 84 from Sparta to Monterey follows the Calfkiller River Route described earlier. TN 30 follows the Black Fox Trail. U.S. 41A, TN 269 (through Wartrace), and TN 252 follow much of the route of the Great South Trail, or Creek War Trace, from the Chickasaw Old Fields on the Tennessee River in southeast

Madison County, Alabama, north to French Lick (Nashville).The Natchez Trace has become a national parkway. U.S. 70 follows the old Glover's Trace westward from Nashville to the Tennessee River, while U.S. 64 probably takes the Chickasaw Route from Bolivar to Memphis.

The evolution from trail to wagon road to stagecoach road to automobile highway, along with the advent of the steamboat and the railroad, changed the travel habits of Tennesseans. Game trails remained along the ridges; cattle drovers used a few trails in the Smokies; hunters still roamed the mountains. The most famous hiker of the nineteenth century, John Muir, mostly followed roads, not trails, while crossing Tennessee from Jamestown to the Hiwassee River on his 1,000-mile walk to the Gulf. A new generation in a new era has revived interest in foot trails, however, and that interest means development and expansion of the trails system in Tennessee.

2. Trail Development in the Twentieth Century

At the turn of the century, a few old Indian trails still existed in the Appalachian Mountains, but the Great Warpath and the Indian trade routes had become wagon roads. Hunters used game trails along the crests of the ridges in the Cumberlands; footpaths existed along most of the rivers. Well-defined trails in the Smokies were used by cattlemen who pastured their stock on the high balds in the summertime. The cattle were driven up the mountain in spring and were brought back to lower elevations before the first snowfall. Logging companies built railroads into the mountains, and these were used by the few hunters and fishermen who had time for those pursuits. Few people went hiking for pleasure.

The advent of the Boy Scout movement in 1910, with its emphasis on outdoor skills, including trail marking and hiking, brought a new interest in trails. It was still several years, however, before there was much trail development in Tennessee.

A growing interest in forest conservation influenced the Tennessee General Assembly to pass an enabling act in April 1901 permitting the federal government to purchase land in East Tennessee to establish public forest reservations. After more than forty attempts were made in Congress to pass a forest purchase law, Rep. John Weeks of Massachusetts introduced a successful bill in 1909; it was signed by President William Howard Taft in March 1911. Within two months of the signing of the Weeks Bill, several purchase units were established in Tennessee. Acquisition of private land started immediately. From 1911 to 1936 there were many changes in purchase units and forest boundaries; in 1936 President Franklin D. Roosevelt established the present Cherokee National Forest.

At the time of acquisition, only a few tracts of land were served by permanent road and trail facilities. One of the first jobs of the U.S. Forest Service was to improve access. Trails were a means of getting materials into the mountains for building fire towers and inventorying the newly acquired timber resources. The first trail signs were installed on the Appalachian Trail in 1929 and the first trail guide pamphlets were issued in 1930, but little trail development occurred until the Civilian Conservation Corps (CCC) was created in 1933.

In the early 1920s a group of influential citizens organized the Great Smoky Mountains Conservation Association for the purpose of getting a national park in the Smokies. Dr. Hubert Work, Secretary of the Interior under presidents Harding and Coolidge, had appointed a committee to study national park possibilities in the Southeast. This committee met with the association at the Mountain View Hotel in Gatlinburg on August 6, 1924. Paul Adams and Paul Fink, twentieth-century mountain men from Tennessee, told the group that the most spectacular area in the Southeast centered on Mount Le Conte. The next day Adams, Fink, and Wiley Oakley, a mountain man from Gatlinburg, led the group on a trip to Mount Le Conte. In order to pursue their campaign, the Great Smoky Mountains Conservation Association employed Paul Adams to establish a camp on top of Mount Le Conte. All materials except trees cut on the site were packed in on foot. The camp was started July 13, 1925, and later replaced by Mount Le Conte Lodge, which is still operating. The story of the camp is told in Paul Adams's *Mt. LeConte,* last printed in 1978.

In 1921 Benton MacKaye, of the U.S. Department of Labor and formerly the U.S. Forest Service and Harvard University, wrote a highly visionary article for the *Journal of the American Institute of Architects* titled "An Appalachian Trail: A project in Regional Planning." In it he proposed a series of recreational communities throughout the Appalachians from Maine to Georgia to be connected by a walking trail, all to be created by volunteers working with landowners and government to protect the remaining Appalachian wilderness from uncontrolled urban development. The Appalachian Mountain Club of Massachusetts and New Hampshire, the Green Mountain Club of Vermont, and the New York-New Jersey Trail Conference, already discussing a linking of trails in their areas, quickly adopted the trail part of MacKaye's vision and by 1923 had built 6 miles of it. The Appalachian Trail Conference was formed in 1925, and the entire Appalachian Trail was completed in 1937.

According to its fiftieth-anniversary handbook, a newly formed Smoky Mountains Hiking Club organized in 1924 joined the Appalachian Trail Conference in 1928 and pledged to sponsor construction of the Appalachian Trail through the proposed national park. The Great Smoky Mountains National Park became a reality in 1937, with assistance from the Rockefeller Foundation; many miles of trail have been built since then, adding up to a total of some 900. Many good guidebooks are available on the Smokies and the AT.

The Civilian Conservation Corps, created by the Franklin D. Roosevelt administration during the Great Depression, built many miles of trails in state forests, national forests, the new national park, and in the Tennessee Valley Authority's demonstration parks around the new Norris Reservoir. Those parks—Norris Dam, Big Ridge, and Cove Lake—are now a part of Tennessee's state park system. With the forty-hour workweek spawned by the depression, the people who were lucky enough to be employed found themselves with time to spare. Some of them found their way to the new trails built by the CCC. World War II interrupted nonessential public works, but the recreation boom continued to grow.

In 1958 Congress created the Outdoor Recreation Resources Review Commission (ORRRC) in an effort to determine future recreation needs. In 1962 the ORRRC reported that driving for pleasure was the primary recreational pursuit of the American public and that walking for pleasure ranked second. An updated study in 1967 showed that walking for pleasure had moved into first place. The Tennessee Department of Conservation's Division of State Parks published an inventory of the state's recreation resources in 1962. That report mentioned vacation trails in Standing Stone State Park and only nature trails in others. Only four parks had naturalist-nature trail programs.

In 1965 Congress created the Land and Water Conservation Fund, part of which provided matching grants to each state for acquisition and development of lands for outdoor recreational use. Financed by an annual appropriation, LWCF was Tennessee's major source of funding for outdoor recreation areas, averaging more than $2 million a year in grants until 1980. Since 1980 these grants have averaged less than half a million dollars a year.

In March 1965 the Clinch and Powell River Valley Association (CPRVA) proposed the Cumberland Trail, to follow the crest of Cumberland Mountain from Cumberland Gap to Cove Lake State Park, then Walden Ridge to Oliver Springs, with a connecting trail to Oak Ridge. After a news release in area newspapers, CPRVA received fifteen letters offering help and permission to cross private land. A student intern from the Department of Political Science at the University of Tennessee explored land ownership on the proposed route that summer. But the association changed officers in July 1965, and the project fell by the wayside.

Tennessee Trails Association (TTA) was organized in late 1968 by a small group of people interested in creating a long hiking trail down the line of high mountain crests running generally southwest across the state from Cumberland Gap to the Tennessee River gorge. The group included representatives from the Tennessee Conservation League, Tennessee Scenic Rivers Association, Tennessee Citizens for Wilderness Planning, Tennessee Department of Conservation, TVA, Bowaters Southern Paper Corporation, Cumberland County Chamber of Commerce, and Plateau Properties, Inc. The Cumberland Trail was chosen as a pilot project to prove the feasibility of a statewide system of such scenic trails. (Robert M. Howes, retired director of the Land Between the Lakes National Recreation Area, later informed the author that he had proposed such a trail when he was president of the Smoky Mountains Hiking Club.) At

TTA's first annual meeting, Stan Murray, chairman of the Appalachian Trail Conference, urged that the proposed state trails system be connected to the AT via the Cumberland Trail. He offered a vision of the system as a network of green corridors protected through outright ownership or scenic easements.

TTA and the Department of Conservation sponsored the first state trail symposium at Montgomery Bell State Park, April 11, 1970. State and national agencies and a number of private organizations attended the meeting, and Rep. Robert Bible of the Tennessee General Assembly discussed a proposed state trails system act. It was decided that the TTA would work with Rep. Bible to refine the act for introduction in the 1971 session of the legislature. The Trails System Act, sponsored by Rep. Bible and Sen. Douglas S. Henry, Jr., passed the state legislature and was signed by Governor Winfield Dunn in April, 1971. It designated seven state scenic trails and provided for recreation trails and side, or connecting, trails. The scenic trails were to be primarily foot trails, with provision for some bicycle and horse trails. Tennessee's was the first state trails system act.

An assistant commissioner in the Department of Conservation was responsible for scenic rivers, natural areas, and trails, all under a single administrator, and for state parks. Joe Gaines, a forester who had been working as a state park naturalist, became the first trails system administrator on March 1, 1972. Very little money was available at first, but nine new positions for trails and scenic rivers were approved by the Department of Personnel late in 1973. Supervisors for the Chickasaw Bluffs, Cumberland, and Lonesome Pine trails were employed at the beginning of 1974. Limited funds were budgeted for 1975, and master plans were prepared for the three trails. The Dunn administration asked for $600,000 for trails in the 1976 budget. But Ray Blanton, governor for the term beginning January 1975, impounded the remaining funds in the 1975 budget and withdrew the $600,000 Dunn request.

The Conservation Department had not officially recognized the sections of the Cumberland Trail built by the Tennessee Trails

Association, so in 1976 the TTA became a nonprofit corporation to provide a legal entity for agreements with landowners and to maintain continuity of the scenic trails program. Work continued on the southern end of the Cumberland Trail on public land. The efforts of the state trails system staff were diverted to state parks and to the new South Cumberland Recreation Complex, which includes Grundy Forest, Stone Door, and Savage Gulf State Natural Areas, some TVA land, and private lands in Grundy and Marion counties. The complex is a joint effort of TVA, the state of Tennessee, and the local development district.

TTA's South Cumberland Trail Committee was organized on December 12, 1972, at Signal Mountain. Under the leadership of chairman Sam Powell, the committee, in cooperation with the Division of Forestry and Cumberland Trail coordinator David Shupe, had completed 10 miles of trail from Signal Point to Prentice Cooper State Forest by early 1978.

The trails program was accelerated in state parks and recreation areas in 1976 and 1977. Administrator Gaines reported to the Tennessee Trails Association's annual meeting on November 19, 1977, that more than 200 miles of trails had been constructed during the preceding two years. The trails program received a boost during the 1977 Tennessee legislative session when House Bill 199 was passed, authorizing the Commissioner of Conservation to enter into agreements with nonprofit corporations with regard to recreational and natural areas and facilities, to provide park rangers for such publicly and privately owned areas used by the general public, and to acquire lands adjacent to such areas. Tennessee already had a landowners' liability law, passed in 1963, opening more land for hunting, fishing, and other outdoor recreation. TTA used this law successfully in getting permission to build trails across private land. This law also influenced Bowater Southern Paper Corporation to open its lands for public recreation and to initiate a pocket wilderness program, described in Chapter 10.

The Conservation Department found some extra money in 1977 and launched a cooperative program with TTA to implement sections of the Cumberland Trail and the Trail of the Lonesome Pine. Mrs. Floy Bostic was employed to contact landowners along the latter route, with trail chairman Gordon Newland of Kinsgport coordinating her efforts. They knew the people of the area and were highly successful in getting permission to build the trail across private property. David Shupe worked with TTA on a 22-mile stretch on the north end of the Cumberland Trail. A large industrial landowner, the American Association, gave written permission to develop the trail across its land. The A.P. Huber Company, which acquired this property, has continued the agreement. Mr. And Mrs. Earl Hobson Smith, owners of McClain Rock, gave verbal permission. A Young Adult Conservation Corps (YACC) crew was assigned to this section in the fall of 1978.

The Big South Fork National River and Recreation Area, developed by the U.S. Army Corps of Engineers and managed by the National Park Service, has more than 170 miles of hiking trails. It is located in Fentress, Pickett, Morgan, and Scott counties in Tennessee and McCreary County in Kentucky. The Sheltowee Trace National Recreation Trail has been extended into Pickett County to connect with the John Muir State Scenic Trail, which passes through the Big South Fork. TVA provided labor to help build trails, which were planned by a private contractor for the Corps of Engineers.

During the Carter administration, TVA used YACC labor to build trails on its reservoir properties and to assist state and county agencies with their trail programs, as well as the Big South Fork Project. Labor from the Regional State Prison in Morgan County was also used for trail work. During the 1970s, TVA and the state of Tennessee cooperated in an attempt to convert abandoned railroad beds to trails for hiking, bicycling, and horseback riding. As a result of disputes over land ownership and resentment of abuses by motorcycle riders, the program was dropped.

There was strong interest in trails on the local level also. The North Ridge Trail in Oak Ridge was built by Tennessee Citizens for Wilderness Planning (TCWP). It was designated a National Recreational Trail in 1973, the first within a city to be so named. TCWP still maintains the trail, with the assistance of local scout troops. The Department of Conservation, City of Murfreesboro, Middle Tennessee State University, and Rutherford County cooperated in establishing the Rutherford County Bicycle Touring System in 1975. This was followed by the development of a hiking-horse-back-canoe system in 1977 on lands of the Corps of Engineers J. Percy Priet project. The Corps developed other trails on its projects, some with the assistance of TTA volunteers and scout troops.

Following a precedent set decades earlier by the Smoky Mountains Hiking Club and the Tennessee Eastman Hiking Club (Tennessee's two Appalachian Trail Conference "maintaining clubs" responsible for more than 200 miles of the AT), TTA established an Adopt-a-Trail program in 1982. Other organizations, including TCWP and the Sierra Club, quickly joined in and adopted trails.

Governor Lamar Alexander, who was inaugurated in 1979, supported the trail system and set 1985 as the goal for completion of the Cumberland Trail. By 1986 the Department of Conservation had completed about 100 miles of the Cumberland Trail from Cumberland Gap to Lone Mountain State Forest. It was managed as the state's only linear park by Ranger Bobby Harbin, headquartered at Cove Lake State Park.

In 1986, the Governor's Commission on Tennesseans Outdoors, chaired by Ann Tidwell, made many important prescient recommendations. These included:

- a Cabinet-level task force to coordinate and encourage recreation-related development in four corridors—the Mississippi River, Kentucky Lake, the Cumberland Plateau, and the Appalachian Mountains;
- completion of the State Scenic Trails authorized by the State Trails System Act, with a manager for each trail and increased publicity and promotion by the Departments of Conservation, Transportation, and Tourist Development;
- matching grants to cities to promote open space preservation, greenbelt development, and riverfront planning.

Holdouts used the threat of condemnation to stir resentment among landowners on Clinch Mountain, and the state backed off the Trail of the Lonesome Pine in 1984. The administration of Governor Ned Ray McWherter, faced with budget problems, gave trails a low priority in 1987, and new trail construction came to a halt. The state trails system administrator position was abolished in 1988.

In 1990, as part of the McWherter administration's 10 percent budget cut for all departments of state government, the Department of Conservation completely eliminated operating funds for the Cumberland State Scenic Trail. The department ceased maintaining the sections it had built, but TTA volunteers continued minimal maintenance of the Grassy Cove segment (Section 5), while Tennessee River Gorge Trust members and State Forestry Division personnel kept open the Tennessee River Gorge segment (Section 9).

Despite continuing cutbacks for trails on Tennessee's state and national public lands, the 1990s started on a more positive note. Citizens began organizing local "Friends" groups to support their neglected nearby parks and forming new privately-funded land trusts to save specific threatened natural and cultural areas. Existing land trusts, such as the Tennessee River Gorge Trust and the Southern Appalachian Highlands Conservancy, grew in membership, in the lands they protected, and in the programs they offered.

Most importantly, urban greenway projects, begun in several cities in the 1970s and 1980s, continued to expand into municipal and countywide greenway systems and were being replicated in smaller communities across the state. New greenway trails were typically built in compliance with the federal Americans with Disabilities Act, greatly expanding opportunities for trail users of all ages and abilities.

New legislation was also promising. In 1990 the General Assembly passed the State and Local Parks Partnership Act, an initiative of the Tennessee Recreation and Parks Association. It directed nearly half of an increase in the real estate transfer tax into a Local Parks and Recreation Fund. The LPRF provides matching grants, through an open competitive selection process, to local governments for parks, natural areas, greenways, or other recreational facilities. The Symms National Recreation Trails Fund Act of 1991, in effect, transferred a portion of the federal tax on nonhighway recreational fuel to each state for matching grants to localities to develop trails—30 percent for motorized, 30 percent for nonmotorized, and 40 percent for multi-use trails. The federal Intermodal Transportation Efficiency Act of 1992 directed 10 percent of new surface transportation funds to states for matching grants for state or local "transportation enhancement" projects, including bicycle and pedestrian trails that have alternative transportation potential.

In complaince with the Symms Act, the new Tennessee Department of Environment and Conservation (TDEC) created in 1993 the State Recreation Trails Advisory Board, with two members from each of ten trail-user groups. This board was responsible for awarding the Symms Fund grants.

Also, 1993 saw the first of a series of statewide initiatives to support and coordinate growing grass-roots efforts for parks and greenways. The privately funded Tennessee State Parks Foundation was formed that year to assist state parks' "Friends" groups. In 1995, the Tennessee Greenways Program was created by The Conservation Fund, a non-profit organization based in Washington, D.C., with grants from the Lyndhurst Foundation, TVA, and the State Division of Forestry. Its purpose was to foster creation of a system of greenway corridors across the state.

In 1996, Governor Don Sundquist announced his Bicentennial Greenways and Trails Program, challenging communities to create 200 miles of new or expanded greenways and trails as part of a statewide system, in celebration of the state's two hundredth birthday. He allocated $50,000 for grants of up to $2,500 to be awarded competitively to local communities for planning proposed projects that would best meet his challenge. Grants were made to twenty-five communities statewide, and 207 new miles of greenways and trails were completed in 1996 with an additional 194 miles planned. These planning grants also helped produce good projects for the 1997 round of LPRF grants made to thirteen communities across the state.

Early in 1997 the Tennessee Greenways Program of the Conservation Fund, in partnership with the National Park Service (NPS) and TDEC, conducted workshops across the state to encourage community greenway initiatives. Also in 1997 the Tennessee Greenways Program merged with Tennessee State Parks Foundation to become the Tennessee Parks and Greenways Foundation. One of its goals is to "create a green infrastructure for Tennessee with state parks as the crown jewels."

Late in 1997 Governor Sundquist created the Governor's Council on Greenways and Trails. It replaces the State Recreation Trails Advisory Board, and its voting members represent a broader spectrum of interest groups. One of the council's first tasks is to consider the results of a series of workshops held in early 1998 in each of the state's nine Regional Development Districts pursuant to its development of a statewide greenway plan.

The Tennessee Wildlife Resources Agency has been an active partner in statewide greenway efforts. After a half century of highly successful restoration of game specieis and habitat, TWRA in recent years has been, with minimal direct funding, restoring nongame species' habitats and providing increasing public opportunities, including trails, for "Watchable Wildlife" observation. Much of this work has been done on TWRA Wildlife Management Areas, but much also on other lands in partnership with other public agencies and private organizations such as The Nature Conservancy.

With operating budgets expected to remain tight for our parks and forests, and with the limited new public funds for trails and greenways coming as grants to be matched by the grantees, public/private parnership is, more than ever, essential for trail development. A notable example of such a partnership is the Cumberland Trail Conference (CTC), an initiative of the TTA to revitalize its thirty-year-old vision for the Cumberland Trail. Under the energetic and innovative leadership of its CT Project Manager, Robert Weber, and CT Resource Development person, Arlene Barnett, supported by the TTA Plateau Chapter, eight "Breakaway" students from East Tennessee State University spent a week in March 1996 restoring much of the Eagle Bluff unit of the CT Cumberland Mountain segment. (Breakaway is a nationally recognized program based at Vanderbilt University offering students an alternative spring break emphasizing environmental action.)

In 1997, Weber and Barnett recruited fifty-three Breakaway students from five universities and secured private funding for their three weeks of work completing the Eagle Bluff unit restoration and building the first rugged 2 miles of the new CT Obed Wild and Scenic River segment. This segment along the Obed National Wild and Scenic River through Catoosa State Wildlife Management Area is being built by the CTC in parnership with the National Park Service and TWRA.

With Breakaway as its backbone, the CTC was formally organized as a nonprofit in 1997 and with TDEC now has a formal agreement regarding their respective responsibilities under the Tennessee Trails System Act. Also, in 1997, the CTC partnered with sixty-two clubs of Rotary International's district in East Tennessee for help through its Preserve Planet Earth program in securing local communities' support, landowners' cooperation, and funding for the Breakaway trailwork. Another CTC partner, the Morgan County Regional Correction Facility, provided a team of inmate and two officers several days a week through the summer of 1997 to work on the Obed WSR segment. The result was 2.5 new miles of superb rockwork in difficult canyon terrain.

In March 1998, the CTC recruited fifty-two Breakaway students and thirty-six TTA volunteers and secured private funding for three weeks of work. The first two weeks were spent on the Tennessee River Gorge Segment building a new 72-ft.-long suspension bridge across one mountain stream, completing fifty-nine rock steps out of another gorge, and refurbishing badly degraded steps on the switchbacks below the Signal Point trailhead. The third week, 2 miles of the Cumberland Mountain segment were opened from the Tri-State marker in Cumberland Gap National Historical Park to the park's southern boundary.

CTC's goal is to complete the CT from Cumberland Gap to the Tennessee River Gorge by October 2008, the fortieth anniversary of TTA's founding. With such creative and enthusiastic partnering of citizens' groups and public agencies, surely the broader vision of a statewide network of protected ecologically and culturally significant corridors can also be realized in the next decade.

In June 1998 Governor Sundquist announced the creation of the Cumberland Trail State Park "to be the backbone of Tennessee's expanding system of greenways and trails." He also presented the Governor's Greenways and Trails Stewardship Award to the Cumberland Trail Conference Breakaway Program. Over the next eight to ten years the state will work in partnership with the CTC to develop and maintain the trail, linking it with public and voluntary private lands and encouraging connections to county and city trails.

3. Cherokee National Forest

Cherokee National Forest extends along the eastern border of Tennessee from the Virginia line on the north to Great Smoky Mountains National Park, then from the southern end of the park to the Georgia line. It is surrounded by other national forests in the neighboring states: Jefferson in Virginia, Pisgah and Nantahala in North Carolina, and Chattahoocheee in Georgia. It is divided into six ranger districts, three on each side of the national park. Federal ownership is not continuous within the designated boundaries of the forest. The north end has the greater percentage of its area in private ownership. The Tellico and Ocoee ranger districts in the south end have the most land in public ownership. From the northeast to the southwest, the ranger districts are Watauga, Unaka, Nolichucky, Tellico, Hiwassee, and Ocoee. These were the homelands of the Cherokee Indians, traversed by the rivers that head the Tennessee Valley—the Holston, Watauga, Nolichucky, Little Tennessee, Tellico, Hiwassee, and Ocoee.

Trail maintenance has been limited by tight budgets in recent years, and some damage from 1993 ice storms remains unrepaired. In some areas trail signs may be missing or trail segments overgrown. It is recommended that hikers call or write for current information on any trail they plan to hike and carry a topographic map of the area and a compass.

There are 740 miles of trails in the Cherokee, 587 of which are designated primarily for hikers, 133 for horses, 46 for trailbikes, 24 for all terrain-vehicles, and 60 for bicycles and mountain bikes, with some overlap among uses. For trail information write Cherokee National Forest, P.O. Box 2010, Cleveland, TN 37320, or call (423) 476–9700.

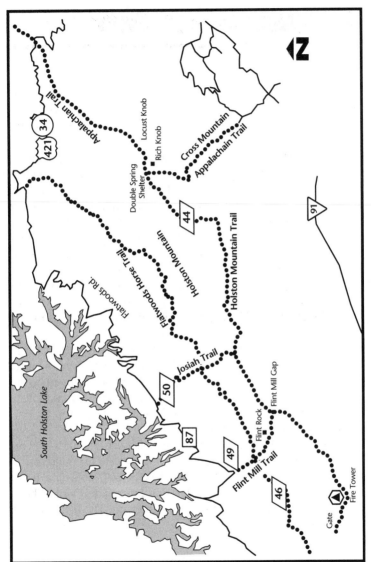

Watauga Ranger District, Holston Mountain Trail

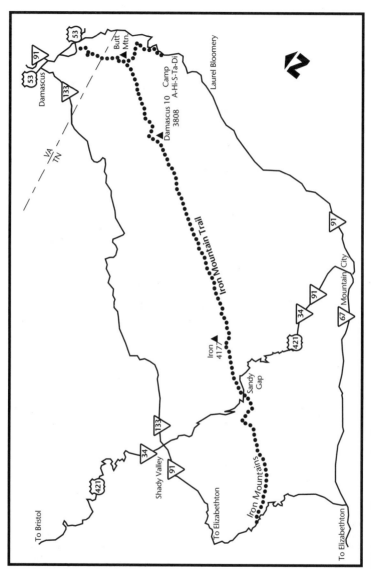

Watauga Ranger District, Iron Mountain Trail

Watauga Ranger District

Headquarters are located at Unicoi Drive, Unicoi, TN 37692. This district has a total of 141 miles in twenty-six trails, including the Appalachian Trail. We describe two trails: an 8-mi. section of the Holston Mountain Trail and the Iron Mountain Trail.

Holston Mountain Trail. Number 44, Carter, Doe, and Shady Valley, USGS quads 207 NE, 214 NW, 213 SW. Length, 8.29 mi. plus road hike of 1 mi.; rating, moderate. From Elizabethton go northeast on TN 91 for about 1.5 mi. past Carter to Panhandle Road (Forest Service Road FR 56) and turn left. Go 4.2 mi. on FR 56 to fork on crest of Holston Mountain (access to crest is limited in winter) where there is a gate and roadside parking at the junction of FR 56 and FR 56A. Walk 1 mil on FR 56A past gate to Holston High Knob lookout tower (no public access to tower), elevation 4,100 ft. The trail runs northeast along the crest of Holston Mountain to Flint Mill Trail, number 49. There are views of South Holston Lake to the west and of the Iron Mountains to the east. The trail swings north and continues along the crest about 4 mi. to the Josiah Trail, number 50 (3,500 ft.), climbs gradually to the Carter-Sullivan county line (3,700 ft.) and follows the ridgetop to the junction with the Appalachian Trail on Rich Knob at 4,247 ft. Double Springs trail shelter is at this junction.

A possible loop hike starts from Holston High Knob, turns left onto the Flint Mill Trail, and drops down the mountain to Flatwoods Horse Trail, number 87. Turn left on the Flatwoods Horse Trail to Short Spur Trail, number 48; go left to FR 202; then left again to Holston High Knob—total distance 8 to 9 mi. Clockwise: Leave car at junction of FR 202 and Short Spur Trail and start down the mountain from there.

Iron Mountain Trail. Number 54, Shady Valley and Laurel Bloomery USGS quads, 213 SW and 213 SE. Length, 18.19 mi.; rating difficult. From Elizabethton, take TN 91 northeast 20 mi. to the top of Cross Mountain. Turn right onto Cross Mountain Road (FR 53) and go 1.5 mi. to the top of Iron Mountain and the trailhead, which is on private land with no permanent access. The elevation at the start is about 3,700 ft. The trail runs east and northeast on the crest of Iron Mountain, 4,000 ft. elevation, with views of Shady Valley and Holston Mountain to the west and Laurel Creek Valley and the mountains along the North Carolina line on the east. It follows the crest at an average elevation of 3,900 ft., crossing Sandy Gap and U.S. 421 at 3,862 ft. From Sandy Gap the trail curves northward, then heads northwest about a mile to FR 234; continuing along the crest of the Iron Mountains, it gradually descends to 3,500 ft. at Morfield Ridge. The trail continues northeast at about 3,500 ft. A spur trail curves right, and drops down Butt Mountain to the vicinity of Laurel Creek and TN 91 in the center of Camp A-Hi-S-Ta-Di, a Methodist Church camp north of Laurel Bloomery and near the Virginia line. The main trail continues to the left past Butt Mountain into Virginia. Since this trail follows the crest of the mountain, it may be necessary to drop down the mountainside to find water. Parking at the FR 53 trailhead is limited and on private land, but good parking is available at Sandy Gap and Camp A-Hi-S-Ta-Di.

Unaka Ranger District

The ranger station is located at Unicoi Drive, Unicoi, TN 37692. We have chosen what appear to be the three best foot trails. All are on the Unicoi USGS quad, 199NE.

Patty Ridge Trail. Number 113. Length, 2.6 mi.; rating, difficult in the upper reaches. Follow TN 81 south from Jonesboro and turn right onto FR 136 past Embreeville to the confluence of Patty's Creek and the Nolichucky River. No parking is provided at the trailhead. This trail is a favorite of hunters in season. It goes up Patty Creek to about 1,800 ft. elevation and veers left, climbing to 2,200 ft. in 0.5 mi. It ascends a gentle slope across a ridge, 2,300 ft. maximum elevation, then drops off to Broad Shoal Creek at about 1,900 ft. The Patty's Ridge wildlife food plot is at milepost 2.6. The

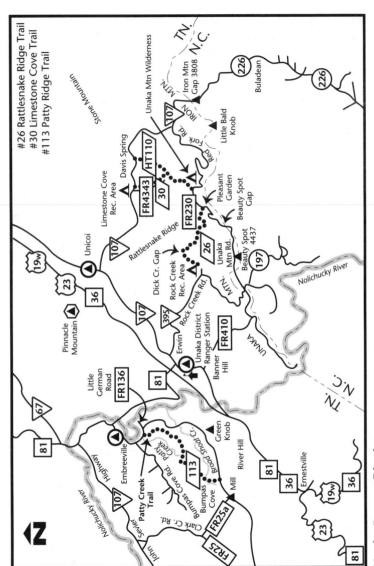

#26 Rattlesnake Ridge Trail
#30 Limestone Cove Trail
#113 Patty Ridge Trail

Unaka Ranger District

trail turns right along the ridge and ends at the Rich Mountain hunter access road. This trail provides a good spring flower walk, with the added pleasure of mountain streams.

Limestone Cove Trail. Number 30. Length, 3.2 mi.; rating, difficult. This is one of two foot trails in the Unaka Mountain Wilderness and has two trailheads. The lower trailhead is 4 mi. east of Unicoi off TN 107 at the Limestone Cove Recreation Area. Park at the recreation area, elevation 2,100 ft., and follow FR 4343 to Rocky Branch, 2,600 ft. It becomes steeper briefly, then levels off slightly on an easier climb to 2,800 ft. It follows an old logging road to the top of Stamping Ground Ridge, crosses the head of a branch at 4,300 ft., and curves left at 4,500 ft. There is an easy slope for 0.5 mi., on which this trail coincides with trail number 110, which is a horseback-riding trail. The Limestone Cove Trail ends at Unaka Mountain Road, FR 230, which provides an easy southwest climb to the Unaka Mountain Overlook and Pleasant Garden, elevation 4,800 ft. The second of the Unaka Mountain Wilderness foot trails begins on the west side of the overlook parking lot.

Rattlesnake Ridge Trail. Number 26. Length, 3.59 mi.; rating, difficult. From Unaka district office go 3 mi. to Rock Creek Recreation Area by TN 395; or continue another 2 mi. to Indian Grave Gap (North Carolina-Tennessee state line) on TN 395, turn left on FR 230, and go approximately 6 mi. to Unaka Mountain Overlook. The trail drops from elevation 4,840 ft. at Unaka Overlook to 2,100 ft. at Rock Creek Recreation Area. It provides views of Beauty Spot in the upper portion and passes through several forest types (cove hardwoods, upland hardwoods, table mountain pine, and white pine-hemlock). It follows Rattlesnake Ridge to Dick Creek Gap, then Rattlesnake Creek to Rock Creek.

Nolichucky Ranger District

The office is located at 124 Austin Street, Suite 3, Greeneville, TN 37745. We find twenty-six trails listed on the trail map, sixteen of

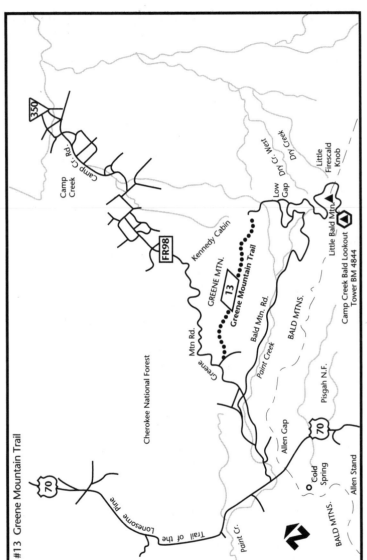

Nolichucky Ranger District, Greene Mountain Trail

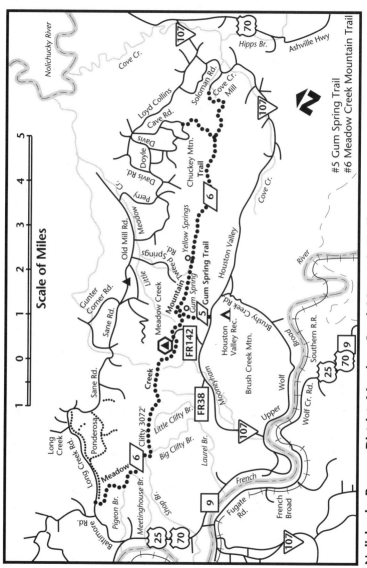

Nolichucky Ranger District, Meadow Creek Mountain Trail

which are designated as hiking trails. Two of the horseback trails are of such scenic value that we also recommend them to hikers. Hikers are asked to step well back from the trail when a rider passes, to keep from spooking the horse. The Squibb Creek Trail, number 23, the link between the Horse Creek Recreation Area and the Appalachian Trail, ends at the Forest Service boundary. We have not described any of the AT because of the numerous other guidebooks covering it. We describe three trails in the district.

Greene Mountain Trail. Number 13. Length, 3.6 mi.; rating, moderate. USGS quad sheets Greystone, 190SW, and Lake Davy Crockett, 181SE. This trail has been designated for horseback and hiking use. To get there take Greene Mountain Road, FR 98, either from the Camp Creek community south of Greeneville, or north from U.S. 70 near Allen Gap on the Tennessee-North Carolina line. The trail starts from FR 98 at a wide curve on the crest of Greene Mountain, where an abandoned timber road leads off to the west. It starts up the ridge on a sharp slope, turns right at 2,500 ft. elevation after about 200 yds., and climbs to 3,700 ft. There is an easy slope for 0.5 mi. to 3,800 ft., then a mile along the crest of the mountain at an average elevation of 3,900 ft. Then the trail doubles back and runs south to end at Kennedy Cabin Road, which intersects Bald Mountain Road about 1.5 mi. down the south side of the mountain. There are views of the Bald Mountains to the south, the high peaks of the Smokies to the southeast, and the Nolichucky River Valley to the north.

Meadow Creek Mountain Trail. Number 6. Length about 14 mi.; rating, moderate. USGS quad sheets Lake Davy Crockett, 181SE, and Paint Rock, 182 NW. Access to this trail is available at four locations: from U.S. 25-70 via Baltimore Road and Long Creek Road, about 10 mi. east of Newport; via FR 142, Meadow Creek Lookout Tower Road, off TN 107, about 4 mi. northeast of U.S. 25-70; via Gum Spring Trail, number 5, from Houston Valley Recreation Area on TN 107; or from TN 107-70 at Cove Creek, 10 mi. south of Greeneville.

Starting from the east end, at the Cove Creek crossing, elevation 1,380 ft., the trail follows the creek upstream 0.5 mi. to 1,600 ft., curves left, and climbs the ridge to 2,000 ft. It curves sharply left and angles up the mountainside to the crest of Chuckey Mountain, elevation 2,300 ft., switches back, and climbs to the top of the ridge over a low peak at 2,650 ft. The trail follows the crest of the mountain southwest, up and down, to arrive at a saddle and the junction with Gum Springs Trail at 2,500 ft. An old telephone pole with an insulator and scrap of wire marks this intersection. There is water a short distance down Gum Springs Trail to the left. The trail crosses the saddle onto Meadow Creek Mountain and climbs to 2,700 ft., continuing along the crest to Meadow Creek Tower Road. Crossing the road, the trail runs west 0.5 mi. to a microwave tower and the Meadow Creek lookout tower at 2,875 ft. From the tower the trail follows the mountain southwest about 2 mi., then begins the climb to Clifty, elevation 3,072 ft. It curves west and drops to 2,400 ft. in 0.5 mi. Following the contour briefly, it drops sharply 200 ft., then slopes easily down to 2,000 ft. Here the trail descends the side of the ridge to 1,600 ft., crosses a low ridge, and drops down to Long Creek at 1,300 ft. U.S. 25-70 is 1.5 mi. down the creek.

Gum Springs Trail. Number 5. Length, 1.3 mi.; rating, easy. Paint Rock USGS quad, 182 NW. This trail provides access to the Meadow Creek Mountain Trail, number 6, from the Houston Valley Recreation Area on TN 107, about 5 mi. northeast of U.S. 25-70. The trailhead is directly across the highway from the entrance to the Houston Valley Recreation Area, which has good running water and a campground. The trails starts at about 1,800 ft. elevation and switches back onto an abandoned road at about 200 yds.; 100 yds. farther another road follows the hillside up a gentle slope. At 0.3 mi. it crosses the toe of the hill and follows downslope along a steep hillside on the right, crosses a ravine, and arrives at another abandoned road. It turns up the road to the right, crossing and recrossing the spring branch for about 1 mi. to the junction with the Meadow Creek Mountain Trail at 2,500 ft. elevation.

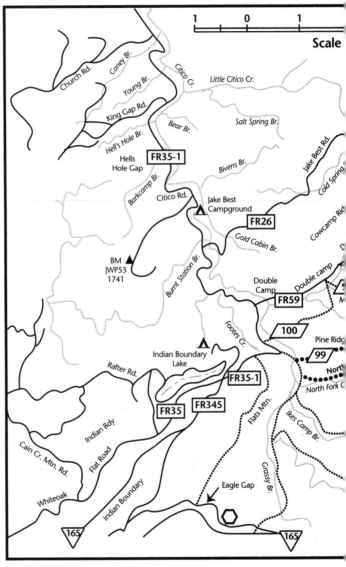

Tellico Ranger District, North Section

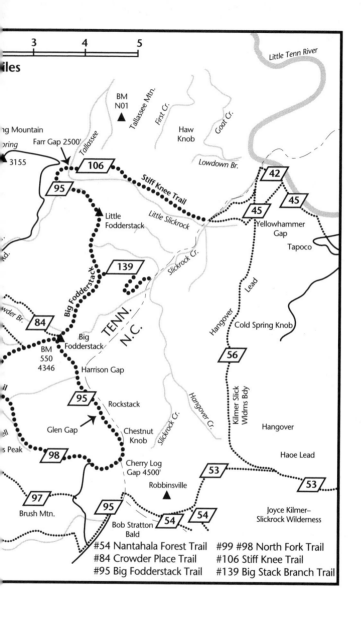

3 4 5

iles

Little Tenn River

BM
N01
Tallassee Mtn.
First Cr.
Goat Cr.
Haw
Knob

ng Mountain
oring
Farr Gap 2500'
Tallassee
Lowdown Br.
3155

106

95

Stiff Knee Trail

42

Little
Fodderstack

Little Slickrock

45

45

139

Slickrock Cr.

Yellowhammer
Gap

Tapoco

Big Fodderstack

wder Br.

84

TENN.
N.C.

Hangover Lead

Cold Spring Knob

BM
550
4346

Big
Fodderstack

Harrison Gap

56

il

95

Rockstack

Hangover Cr.

Glen Gap

Chestnut
Knob

Slickrock Cr.

Kilmer Slick Wldrns Bdy

Hangover

ll

s Peak

98

Haoe Lead

Cherry Log
Gap 4500'

Robbinsville

53

53

97

Brush Mtn.

95

Joyce Kilmer–
Slickrock Wilderness

Bob Stratton
Bald

54

54

#54 Nantahala Forest Trail   #99 #98 North Fork Trail
#84 Crowder Place Trail   #106 Stiff Knee Trail
#95 Big Fodderstack Trail   #139 Big Stack Branch Trail

Tellico Ranger District

The district ranger office is located off Tellico River Road about 4 mi. east of Tellico Plains; the mailing address is Route 3, Tellico Plains, TN 37385. This district has the highest percentage of land in public ownership and the greatest number of hiking trails, thirty-three in all. Most of the trails are well maintained and get a lot of traffic. We describe only a few of the typical trails.

Many backpackers leave their cars at Tapoco, North Carolina, elevation 1,200 ft., on U.S. 129, and take Nantahala National Forest trail number 45 down the Little Tennessee River and up Ike Branch to Hangover Lead on the border of the Joyce Kilmer-Slickrock Wilderness. Going south to Yellowhammer Gap, a total distance of 2 mi. from the trailhead, turn west 0.5 mi. down to Slickrock Creek and the junction with Nantahala trail number 42, elevation 1,320 ft. It is 0.5 mi. up Slickrock Creek to the junction with Cherokee National Forest trail number 106 (Stiff Knee), elevation 1,400 ft., on the Tennessee-North Carolina state line. Stiff Knee Trail, rated moderate, leads up Little Slickrock Creek to Farr Gap and the start of Fodderstack Trail at 2,800 ft., a distance of 3.2 mi. Both trails are in the Citico Creek Wilderness.

Big Fodderstack Trail. Number 95. Length 10.4 mi.; rating, moderate. USGS quad sheet 140NE, Whiteoak Flats. This trail is now listed for horseback and hiking use. To get to the Farr Gap trailhead parking area, take the Double Camp Road, FR 59, from the Indian Boundary Recreation Area, or Jake Best (Cold Spring) Road, FR 26, from Citico Road, FR 35-1. The parking area is at 2,720 ft. elevation. The trail starts on a short climb to the southwest past the junction with Stiff Knee Trail to the toe of a ridge at 3,000 ft., following an old road that has been closed to vehicular traffic. Open fields on the right offer excellent views of the surrounding mountains. The trail curves southward along the wilderness boundary, skirts the peak of Little Fodderstack Mountain, and continues to the junction of Crowder Creek Trail, number 84, 2.65 mi. from Farr Gap, and Big Stack Branch Trail, number 139, at an old farm called the Crowder Place. There are a spring and one of several campsites here, but don't trust the water.

From the Crowder Place the Big Fodderstack Trail follows the crest of the ridge at 3,500 ft to Big Stack Gap, dropping slightly, then climbing back to 4,000 ft. elevation at the junction with trail number 99 on Big Fodderstack Mountain. This trail drops off the mountain to Citico Road. Big Fodderstack Trail turns sharply left and skirts the peak at about 4,200 ft., curves right, and drops to about 3,800 ft. at the state line. Running south by east, the trail climbs to 4,200 ft., skirts Rockstack Peak, passes through Glenn Gap, and crosses the top of Chestnut Knob, following the state line to the junction with the North Fork Trail, number 98, at Cherry Log Gap at about 4,500 ft. Big Fodderstack Trail continues along the state line ridge to an intersection with Nantahala Trail, number 54, near Bob Stratton Bald. From there the trail turns southwest and descends to Cold Springs Gap parking area at an elevation of 4,200 ft. Here the trail terminates. From the Crowder Place to Strawberry Knob, the tread is hand dug.

Trail 98, following the North Fork of Citico Creek, traverses a laurel thicket known as Jeffrey's Hell, named for the ordeal of a hunter who became lost while searching for a lost dog. Hikers may follow the state line from Cherry Log Gap to Bob Bald along trail number 95 and pick up Nantahala Forest trail number 54, Stratton Bald Trail, which leads to the Joyce Kilmer Memorial Forest. From Stratton Bald Trail number 53 leads along the crest between Joyce Kilmer and Slickrock to Haoe Lookout, from which number 56 leads to the Hangover and down Hangover Lead back to Yellowhammer Gap. There are several good trails off North River Road that can be made into day loops. The next trail is in the Bald River Wilderness.

Bald River Trail. Number 88. Length, 5.6 mi.; rating, easy. Bald River Falls USGS quad 140SW. This is a popular trail for day hikes along a roaring mountain stream, but it also has some good streamside campsites. Bald River is a wild trout stream, restricted to fly fishing and requiring a special permit. The trail is easy enough that a hiker can make it both ways in a day; a car shuttle can be

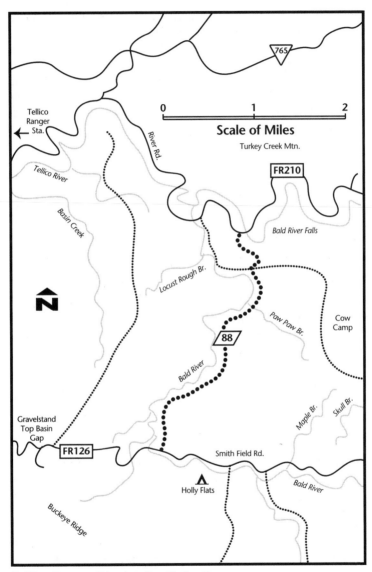

Tellico Ranger District, South Section

arranged, but it requires a 15-mi. trip across a mountain. The trail starts at the parking area on Tellico River Road, FR 210, at Bald River Falls. There is a 200-ft. climb on a paved switchback path to the picnic area above the falls. From the picnic area there is another steep climb to the top of a narrow gorge, a left turn on a rock outcropping, then a steep descent to a trail sloping down along the side of a cliff to a series of waterfalls. From here on the traffic diminishes.

As the trail levels out briefly, there is a rock house on the left, and overhanging rock that provides shelter from foul weather. This is the first trailside campsite. The trail follows an old logging railroad bed awhile, then rises to a narrow path along the side of the gorge, crosses a narrow ridge, and comes back to the railroad bed. This area was logged in the early part of the twentieth century before it became part of the national forest, and the logging company ran Sunday excursions from Tellico Plains to Bald River Falls. At about the halfway point there is another campsite at Pawpaw Branch. From here on the trail becomes easier, with vertical curves that break up the long slopes. The trail alternately follows the riverbank and rises away from the stream as the gorge narrows. The final campsite is at the turnaround for the old logging railroad. Bits of coal in the path mark this spot. At the final rise, laurel and rhododendron grow profusely along the path. A final 100-yd. descent ends under a huge rhododendron at Bald River Road. To the left is Holly Flats Recreation Area. The net elevation change is less than 500 ft. in 5 mi.

Hiwassee Ranger District

This district has two distinguishing features—the Hiwassee State Scenic River and the Gee Creek Wilderness, one of eleven in Cherokee National Forest that are part of the National Wilderness System. The district ranger office is located at 274 Highway 310, Etowah, TN 37331. There has been no trail development in Gee

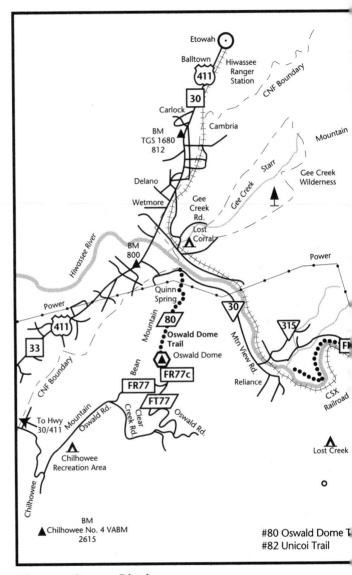

Hiwassee Ranger District

Etowah

Balltown
411
Hiwassee
Ranger
Station

CNF Boundary

30

Carlock

Cambria

BM
TGS 1680
812

Mountain

Starr

Gee Creek

Gee Creek
Wilderness

Delano

Wetmore

Gee
Creek
Rd.

Lost
Corral

Hiwassee River

BM
800

Power

Power

Quinn
Spring

80

**Oswald Dome
Trail**

Mountain

30

315

Oswald Dome

Bean

FR77c

Mtn View Rd.

FR77

FT77

Clear Creek Rd.

Oswald Rd.

Reliance

CSX
Railroad

To Hwy
30/411

33

CNF Boundary

Mountain

Oswald Rd.

411

Chilhowee
Recreation Area

Lost Creek

o

Chilhowee

BM
Chilhowee No. 4 VABM
2615

#80 Oswald Dome T
#82 Unicoi Trail

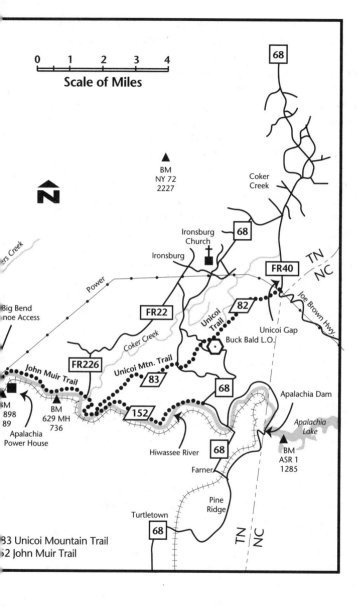

Scale of Miles

0   1   2   3   4

▲
BM
NY 72
2227

Coker
Creek

68

Ironsburg
Church
Ironsburg

68

TN
NC

FR40

Joe Brown Hwy.

Power

82

Big Bend
Canoe Access

FR22

Unicoi
Trail

Unicoi Gap

Coker Creek

Buck Bald L.O.

FR226

John Muir Trail

Unicoi Mtn. Trail

83

BM
629 MH
736

152

68

Apalachia Dam

*Apalachia
Lake*

BM
ASR 1
1285

BM
898
89

Apalachia
Power House

Hiwassee River

68

Farner

Turtletown

Pine
Ridge

68

TN
NC

83 Unicoi Mountain Trail
152 John Muir Trail

Creek Wilderness, but visitors follow old abandoned roads and primitive footpaths. The district has fourteen foot trails, including the John Muir State Scenic Trail. The National Park Service's Bartram Trail Study eliminated the proposal for foot trails extending into the Hiwassee Ranger District.

John Muir Trail. Length, 20 mi.; rating, easy. This trail follows the southeastern end of John Muir's route through Tennessee on his 1,000-mile walk to the Gulf of Mexico (see Chapter 4). It is a National Recreation Trail and is included in the State Scenic Trails System but was built by the U.S. Forest Service with Youth Conservation Corps and Young Adult Conservation Corps labor. To get to the trailhead, turn east off U.S. 411 onto TN 30, left across the bridge at Reliance, and right onto the first road, FR 108, which leads 0.5 mi. to the trailhead at Childers Creek and on to canoe accesses along the river and to the Appalachia Power House. There is also access to the trail at several other points along this road. The trail follows the riverbank, an easy path along a beautiful stream, through lush vegetation with many wildflowers. It crosses the Big Bend parking area 3.0 mi. upriver and parallels FR 108 and the river another 3 mi. to the swinging bridge at the powerhouse. The trail passes under the end of the bridge and continues on upriver to TN 68. Near the end it climbs a rise about 200 ft., then drops back to an old road along the riverbank. Above the powerhouse the river becomes a trickle, as the water flows through a tunnel from Appalachia Dam.

Oswald Dome Trail. Number 80. Length, approximately 4 mi.; rating, moderate. Oswald Dome USGS quad 126NE. The trail starts from Quinn Springs campground, 1.5 mi. east of U.S. 411 on TN 30, elevation 750 ft. There is no water on the trail, so fill your canteen at Quinn Springs. The trail starts uphill in open woods, crosses a power line, and turns uphill to the right; turning left into open woods again, it gradually climbs to 1,040 ft. It switches back to the left at a ravine, curves left across a second ravine, then right around the toe of a hill. There is an easy ascent to the crest at 1,200 ft., where the trail levels out for the first time. It passes through a shallow saddle and up the crest of a hill to 1,400 ft. elevation, then curves left, winding along a rocky hillside on Bean Mountain. There is a continuous upgrade as the trail climbs the left side of the ridge, crossing the end of a hill and switching to the other side of the ridge.

Up the steep side of the ridge to the crest, the trail passes through a thicket into an open space that provides a view of the towns in the valley to the north. It switches back around the point of a ridge, continuing uphill. A pileated woodpecker sounds off nearby. Going southwest up a shallow valley between ridges, the trail arrives at the top of the ridge and switches back right up a moderate slope for 100 yds. It becomes steeper for 0.3 mi., a rocky path along the side of the crest. Topping a rise on Chilhowee Mountain, the trail levels out at about 3,000 ft. elevation in open woods, gently rolling terrain on a broad mountaintop strewn with boulders. A climb of about 0.5 mi. along the crest of a narrow ridge flattens out on top, and the mountain drops off steeply to the west. The trail drops into a saddle, then climbs uphill again to an old logging road. There is a gentle upgrade the last 0.8 mi., flattening out the final 100 yds. to arrive at Oswald Dome fire tower, elevation 3,500 ft. FR 77 leads from Oswald Dome to Chilhowee Recreation Area in the Ocoee Ranger District.

Unicoi Mountain Trail. Number 83. Length 6 mi.; rating, moderate. Farner and McFarland USGS quads, 133 NE and 133 NW. This trail runs from TN 68 to the mouth of Coker Creek at FR 22B. To get to the mouth of Coker Creek, turn west off TN 68 on the road to Ironsburg Church, then left onto FR 22. The trailhead on TN 68 is 6.4 mi. south of the Coker Creek Post Office at a gap in Unicoi Mountain, elevation, 1,700 ft. From there the trail follows an old logging road in a southwesterly direction 0.8 mi. and gradually rises to 2,000 ft. in the first 1.3 mi.; it follows the crest about a mile at this elevation. A ruffed grouse walks into the trail ahead, fluffs it ruff, and bobs its tail nervously, then flies. The trail swings gradually to the west, then curves south and drops off the toe of the ridge to about 1,400 ft. There is a slight rise over a hill before it veers right to follow a long slope back to 1,400 ft. Left down a ridge to 1,200 ft., it crosses another hill and drops to the Hiwassee River at about 950 ft. elevation.

Unicoi Trail. Number 82 Farner USGS quad, 133 NE. Length, 4.5 mi.; rating, moderate. This trail runs from TN 68 south of the Unicoi Mountain Trail to Unicoi Gap on the state line. A gravel road known as the Joe Brown Highway crosses the historic gap 3 mi. from the Coker Creek Post Office and continues through Nantahala National Forest.

This trail is marked as a motorcycle trail from TN 68 to Unicoi Gap. Starting at 1,700 ft. elevation, the trail follows an old roadbed in a steady climb along the side of the mountain about a mile to the junction mentioned above, at 2,200 ft. Buck Bald picnic area and scenic view is above on the right, at 2,348 ft., but heavy timber hides the tower from view on the contour of this hill. The trail follows the crest of Unicoi Mountain at an average elevation of 2,000 ft., rises over a peak near the end, and drops off to cross a power line, then heads downhill to Unicoi Gap. Most of the trail runs through open woods inhabited by deer, squirrels, ruffed grouse, wild turkeys, and a host of songbirds.

Ocoee Ranger District

The office is 3 mi. east of Parksville on U.S. 64. The mailing address is Route 1 Parksville, Benton, TN 37307. The Ocoee Ranger District of Cherokee National Forest lies entirely within Polk County in the southeastern corner of Tennessee. U.S. 64 provides easy access from Chattanooga and Cleveland. The recreation pressure along this corridor exceeds that of the Tellico District. Parksville Lake at the western entrance and the Ocoee River above this impoundment attract many boaters, fishermen, and white-water enthusiasts. A number of outfitters provide raft trips on the most exciting white-water streams in the nation, site of the 1996 Olympic canoe and kayak events and numerous international competitions. A 40-

mile network of hiking and biking trails is gradually being developed near the Ocoee Whitewater Center, site of the Olympic slalom course. In spite of the heavy traffic along the Ocoee River and the popularity of recreation areas north of U.S. 64, much of the section south of the river remains remote and wild.

The Cohutta Wilderness spills over from the Chattahoochee into the Ocoee District, and the Big Frog Wilderness adjoins this. The Cherokee National Forest trail map lists twenty-two foot trails, most of which have received maintenance since 1986. Trails may not be well marked, however, and the ruggedness of the terrain makes careful planning essential. This includes checking with the district ranger on the condition of the trails you plan to hike and carrying the relevant USGS quadrangle topos and a compass, flashlight, and foul-weather clothing. Many of the trails are blazed in white, but the USFS is in the process of removing paint blazes in all wildernesses. We describe an outstanding loop bordering Cohutta Wilderness and the Chestnut Mountain Trail, which provides access to the wilderness.

Wolf Ridge, Big Frog, Grassy Gap, Big Creek Trails. Total length 9.5 mi. loop; rating, difficult. USGS Caney Creek and Ducktown quads—126 SE and 133 SW. To get there turn south off of U.S. 64, 0.5 mi. west of the Ocoee River Bridge, onto the Cookson Creek Road. Proceed 2.8 mi. to the sign for Cookson Creek and Church and continue straight ahead on Baker Creek Road, FR 55, 8.4 mi. to site of former Sheeds Creek Checking Station; turn left off FR 221, go 4.1 mi. to FR 221E, turn right, and travel 0.3 mi. to the trailhead. Because of the long grades and rough areas, travel time is included in this description. There is almost continuous upgrade the first 4 mi.

Beginning at Pace Gap, elevation 1,654 ft., Wolf Ridge Trail, number 66, runs generally south about a mile, ascending the ridge to 2,300 ft. It bears right, crosses Bear Pen Hill at 2,640 ft., and drops into Grassy Gap at 2,500 ft. Hiking time so far is thirty-five minutes. Staying to the right at the junction with the Grassy Gap Trail, continue up the crest another twenty minutes to the junction

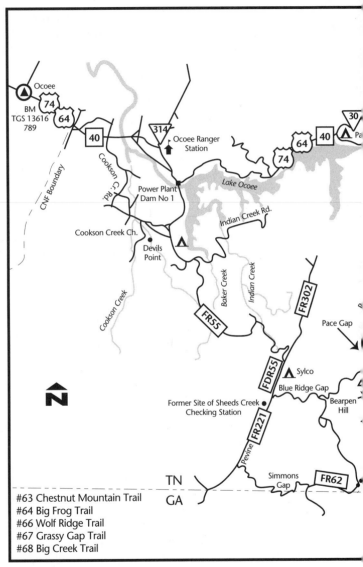

#63 Chestnut Mountain Trail
#64 Big Frog Trail
#66 Wolf Ridge Trail
#67 Grassy Gap Trail
#68 Big Creek Trail

Big Frog Area, Ocoee Ranger District

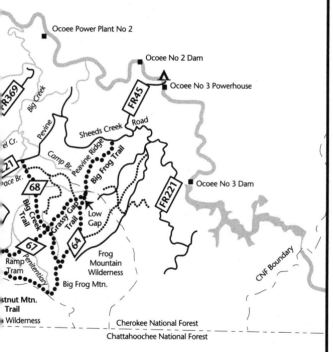

Scale of Miles

Ocoee Power Plant No 2

Ocoee No 2 Dam

Ocoee No 3 Powerhouse

Ocoee No 3 Dam

FR369

Big Creek

Pevine

el Cr.

Camp Br.

Sheeds Creek

Road

Pevine Ridge

Big Frog Trail

FR45

FR221

221

ace Br.

68

Big Creek Trail

Grassy Gap Trail

Low Gap

64

67

Ramp Tram

Penitentiary

Frog Mountain Wilderness

Big Frog Mtn.

CNF Boundary

stnut Mtn. Trail

Wilderness

Cherokee National Forest

Chattahoochee National Forest

with Chestnut Mountain Trail, number 63. Wolf Ridge Trail goes left along Blue Ridge on the Tennessee Valley Divide and fifteen minutes later arrives at the site of the former Polk County Ramp Tramp, at 3,400 ft. elevation. This annual ramp cookout is now held each spring at Camp McCoy on TN 30, 2 mi. north of U.S. 64.

The ramp is a member of the lily family, highly prized by mountain people as a "spring tonic." Another ramp festival is held at Cosby, Tennessee, once called the "Moonshine Capital of America."

From the Ramp Tramp site, the trail continues to the end on Big Frog Mountain and the start of the Big Frog Trail, number 654. Hiking time, sixteen minutes; elevation, 4,000 ft. The total distance from Pace Gap is 4.1 mi., according to a Forest Service engineer.

At left the Big Frog Trail follows a rocky ridge for twenty-nine minutes to the junction with Big Creek Trail, number 68. Turn left here down the Big Creek Trail to descend through a rhododendron "tunnel" fifteen minutes later. Beyond the thicket a few chestnut sprouts still fight the fungus disease that killed the forest giants in the 1920s. A view opens on the right as the trail switches to the left side of the ridge. Gentians bloom in the fall on this ridge. An hour and five minutes from the top of Big Frog Mountain, one might stop beside a branch for a snack. Leaving the branch, switch back northwest around the hill and arrive at a junction of trails beside a stream in a ravine twenty minutes later. A sign indicates the Grassy Gap Trail, and the path to the left leads 3 mi. to Grassy Gap.

The Big Creek Trail, number 68 straight ahead, crosses the toe of a ridge and drops downhill to a branch, then switches back northwest uphill and swings eastward across the ridge. The trail slopes down to another branch, then reverses up to the northwest to a beautiful valley view on the left. Half an hour from the last junction, the trail travels more directly north, ascending another hill for ten minutes to an unmarked trail junction. At the left fork it quickly crosses two branches with water in them and heads downhill at a rapid pace on an old roadbed. There is a short stretch where the trail takes a detour around a fallen tree, swings southwest (a view of the valley is on the left), and heads downhill again on an old road for fifteen minutes. At the entrance to the woods, there is a jeep road, FR 221J, which leads to FR 221, 2.4 mi. from the Big Frog sign. The total hiking time is five hours, twenty-five minutes. To get back to the starting point, turn left onto FR 221 to 221E, another 2 mi., making the total trip 10.3 mi.

Chestnut Mountain Trail. Number 63. Length 1.3 mi.; rating, moderate. USGS Caney Creek quad, 126 SE. The trailhead is located at the parking area for the Cohutta Wilderness, on the left of FR 62, Big Frog Road. Turn right off FR 221, 1.7 mi. east of Forest Development Road FDR 55, and travel 4.1 mi. to the parking area. The trail provides access to the wilderness and to the Wolf Ridge Trail, described above. It leaves the parking area at about 2,500 ft. elevation on a fairly easy grade on an old road, running northeast up the end of Chestnut Mountain to connect with the Wolf Ridge Trail at 3,100 ft. The trail follows an old road that was closed when the Cohutta Wilderness was established.

Benton MacKaye Trail. Benton MacKaye, who first proposed the Appalachian Trail in 1921 (see Chapter 2), originally envisioned it following the western leg of the Blue Ridge south of the Great Smoky Mountains rather than the eastern leg where it actually came to be routed; he also proposed major loops off the AT. In 1980 the Benton MacKaye Trail Association was formed to complete a major loop south of the Smokies by creating the BMT from the southern terminus of the AT Springer Mountain, Georgia, north along MacKaye's original AT route up the western Blue Ridge through Chattahoochee National Forest and along the Tennessee–North Carolina state line through Cherokee and Nantahala national forests back to the AT in Great Smoky Mountains National Park. The Association has, thus far, opened BMT Sections 1-10 in Georgia and Section 11 in Cherokee National Forest from the Tennessee–Georgia state line north to Ocoee River. Together, Sections 10 and 11 offer 13 miles of hiking in the Cohutta and Big Frog Wilderness Areas and 15.7 miles without a road crossing. For information write Benton MacKaye Trail Association, P.O. Box 53271, Atlanta, GA 30355-1271.

Benton MacKaye Trail: Section 11. Length, 11.2 mi.; rating, most difficult. USGS Caney Creek, Ducktown, and Hemptop quads—126 SE, 133 SW, and 127 NE. The northern trailhead is located at Ocoee powerhouse number 3 just across the Ocoee River bridge from the intersection of FR 45 with U.S. 64 (and U.S. 74) 18.6 mi. east of Ocoee. From the parking area at the powerhouse the BMT crosses Little Gassaway Creek and descends along the road through Thunder Rock campground to the end of the road loop, then follows the south bank of the Ocoee downstream. At 0.6 mi. from the trailhead the trail ascends by a series of short switchbacks to the rim of the gorge with a view at the last switchback of Ocoee Lake number 2 below and the rafting put-in downstream. The trail then climbs gradually through a cove densely forested with hemlock, white pine, and rhododendron, with a stream below to the left. At 1 mi. it turns sharply left, climbing through a second cove to a saddle, crosses a high point and into another saddle and, continuing generally south-southwest, skirts the left side of a ridge to reach FR 45 at 1.7 mi.

Crossing FR 45 the BMT descends to the right and follows old FR 45, switching back hard left in a cove to reach a low point at 2.1 mi., then climbs through numerous coves to reach FR 221 at 3.4 mi. and 1,900 ft. elevation. Crossing FR 221 the tail descends along an old road to a saddle then turns right off the old road and continues the descent on graded trail, through dense forest with a stream to the right, to an intersection with West Fork Trail, number 70B, at 4.3 mi.

Turning right onto the West Fort Trail (WFT) the BMT/WFT continues through a remote area heavily forested with hemlock, white pine, and rhododendron to enter Big Frog Wilderness at the culvert crossing West Fork Rough Creek at 5.0 mi. and on to intersect the Rough Creek Trail (RCT), number 70, at 5.6 mi. BMT/RCT continues straight ahead 100 ft., then turns left off an old roadbed to cross the west fork of Rough Creek, crosses another stream to enter a cove, turns left, and ascends along the graded trail. At ridgeline the trail curves right and begins a steeper ascent to intersect Fork Ridge Trail (FRT), number 69, in a saddle at 6.2 mi. and 2,260 ft. elevation. Turning right off the Rough Creek Trail the BMT/FRT ascends along ridgeline for a short distance, then skirts the east side of the ridge and continues a steady climb into a saddle at 7.0 mi. and 2,830 ft. elevation. Following the broad crest of the ridgeline the trail then skirts the west side of the ridge, circles through two coves, and intersects the Big Frog Trail (BFT), number 64, at 8.0 mi.

Continuing straight ahead, the BMT/BFT skirts the east side of the ridge, then crosses the ridge to skirt the west side of Chimneytop where a narrow ridge to the south offers good year-round views to the east and northeast. At 8.7 mi. the Big Creek Trail, number 68 (formerly Bark Legging Trail, number 67) leads off to the right, and good views to the east and northeast are offered from the ridgecrest. BMT/BFT continues straight ahead ascending narrow ridgecrest, then skirts the west side of the ridge and passes through a rhododendron thicket, switches back left and returns to broad ridgecrest, climbing finally to the end of the Big Frog Trail at 9.9 mi. Here, on top of the Tennessee Valley Divide (Tennessee River watershed to the north, Chattahoochee River watershed to the south), the Wolf Ridge Trail, number 66, intersects from the right and the Licklog Trail, number 65, from the left. The Wolf Ridge Trail leads northwest 4.1 mi. to Pace Gap (see above). The summit of Big Frog Mountain, 4,220 ft. elevation, is 100 ft. to the right.

Turning left onto the Licklog Trail (LT) the BMT/LT descends along the ridgeline, which divides the Big Frog Wilderness on the left from the Cohutta Wilderness on the right. At 10.4 mi. the Licklog Trail leads straight ahead and on 5.4 mi to FR 221, while the BMT turns right to follow the Hemp Top Trail (HTT). The BMT/HTT, after a long steep descent, enters Double Spring Gap on the Tennessee-Georgia state line at 11.2 mi. The BMT continues straight ahead into Chattahoochee National Forest 5.4 mi. to Dally Gap, the closest vehicular access to Double Spring Gap.

4. State Scenic Trails

The Tennessee Trails Systems Act, originally sponsored by the Tennessee Trails Association, was signed by Governor Winfield Dunn on April 28, 1971. The act called for the development of three classes of trails, which would be administered by the Department of Conservation. The trail system would include:

"(a) State Scenic Trails, which would be extended trails so located as to provide maximum potential for the appreciation of natural areas and for the conservation and enjoyment of the significant scenic, historic, natural, ecological, geological or cultural qualities of the areas through which such trails may pass." These trails were to be limited exclusively to foot use, except that horses and bicycles could be used on segments approved by the department.

"(b) State Recreation Trails, which will provide a variety of outdoor recreation uses in or reasonably accessible to urban area." These could be foot, horse, or nonmotorized bicycle trails.

"(c) Connecting or side trails, which will provide additional points of public access to State Recreation or State Scenic Trails or which will provide connections between such trails. They shall be of the nature of the trails they serve."

The Tennessee Trails System Act designated seven state scenic trails, including the Appalachian Trail, the first of two national scenic trails designated by the National Trails System Act of 1968. An eighth state scenic trail, the Overmountain Victory Trail, was added to the system in 1976.

Appalachian Trail

This was our first national scenic trail. Its origin in the early 1920s is described in Chapter 2. The trails enters Tennessee near Damascus, Virginia, and follows the crest of the Appalachian Mountains along the Tennessee–North Carolina border; it cuts across a small section of North Carolina and again follows the state line southward through the Great Smoky Mountains National Park, leaving Tennessee at Gregory Bald. Almost all of the AT outside the National Park lies on national forest land, a total of 108 mi. (173 km). For more information write the Appalachian Trail Conference, P.O. Box 807, Harpers Ferry, West Virginia 25425-0807 or call (304) 535–6331.

Overmountain Victory Trail

The newest state scenic trail, located in extreme northeast Tennessee, was added to the system by the state's 90th General Assembly in 1976 during the American Bicentennial celebration. The 60-mile segment in Tennessee is part of the Overmountain Victory National Historic Trail, which was signed into law by President Jimmy Carter in September 1980—almost exactly 200 years after the historic event it commemorates. The trail retraces the route the "Overmountain Men" volunteers followed starting on September 24, 1780, from Abingdon, Virginia, down through northeast Tennessee and western North Carolina and arriving at King's Mountain, South Carolina, on October 7, 1780.

The majority of the Overmountain Victory Trail follows roads for its 225-mi. length. However, there's is a 2-mi. off-road hiking trail segment that starts from the end of Sugar Hollow Road in Roan Mountain and follows the old Yellow Mountain Road up a steep grade (1,300 ft. elevation gain) to intersect the Appalachian Trail at Yellow Mountain Gap. For more information on this 2-mile section, contact Roan Mountain State Park, Route 1, Box 236, Roan Mountain, TN 37687 or call (423) 772–3303.

Each year since 1975 the Overmountain Victory Trail Association has sponsored an annual reenactment of the march to King's

Mountain. It follows the original route and uses the original camp-sites as much as possible. For more information on the Trail or the reenactment, contact Sycamore Shoals State Historic Area, 1651 West Elk Avenue, Elizabethton, TN 37643 or call (423) 543–5808.

—*Contributed by Mike Dahl*

Historical Note: Holston-Watauga Settlements

Early in 1780 Lord Cornwallis had taken Charleston and begun ravaging both the Carolinas and Georgia, and increasing numbers of Carolinians and Georgians sought refuge in the Holston-Watauga settlements in northeast Tennessee. In response to Tory General Patrick Ferguson's threat to burn these settlements and hang their leaders, Colonels John Sevier and Isaac Shelby assembled more than 1,000 Overmountain Men at Sycamore Shoals on the Watauga and on September 25 they set out to check Ferguson's march northward. On October 7 they met and decisively defeated Ferguson's 1,400-man force at King's Mountain, killing or capturing every enemy soldier. Historian Samuel Elliott Morrison noted that the Battle of King's Mountain was "Bunker Hill in reverse . . . giving new life to an apparently lost cause." With his left flank smashed and outrunning his supply line, Cornwallis withdrew to spend the winter in Winnsboro, South Carolina, and early in 1781, he moved north to Yorktown, Virginia, and final defeat at the hands of General Washington and his newly committed French allies. Isaac Shelby became the first governor of Kentucky in 1792 and John Sevier the first governor of Tennessee in 1796.

Trail of the Lonesome Pine

Traveling from east to west, this is the next state scenic trail. As spelled out in the Tennessee Trails System Act, the Trail of the Lonesome Pine "begins near Corryton in Knox County thence running roughly the entire length, northeastward, of Grainger and Hawkins County, following closely the scenic gorges and escarpments of the Clinch Mountain range as the route is determined by the Department." The master plan for the trail was completed early in 1975, just before the Blanton administration in Nashville withdrew funds for the trail system. In 1977 the Department of Conservation managed to get limited funds and, with the help of the Tennessee Trails Association, resumed work on the section from Bean Gap to the Virginia state line. U.S. 25E passes through Bean Gap, which provided an alternate route to the Wilderness Road from the Holston Valley in pioneer days.

The Trail of the Lonesome Pine when completed was to extend along the crest of Clinch Mountain for a distance of 75 mi. The mountain crest, an average of 20 to 30 ft. wide, is characterized by large overhanging rock slabs and huge boulders. Views of the Great Smoky Mountains and the Cumberland Plateau offer the hiker a chance to appreciate the beauty of the Great Valley of Tennessee. The rock-strewn path, steep inclines up and down the gaps, and lack of water add up to make this trail one of the most difficult in the eastern United States. The trail was to start at the southern terminus of Clinch Mountain in Blaine, Tennessee, about 15 mi. northeast of Knoxville, and it was divided into six sections.

Politics killed the project. Some 50 mi. of the trail from the Tennessee-Virginia state line to 5 mi. south of the U.S. 25E crossing were completed in 1980. However, a sudden influx of out-of-state landowners who created pockets of opposition, along with lack of funding for a trail ranger, let the Department of Conservation to cease completion and management of the trail in 1985, after sections 4 and 5 were officially opened. Development of sections 1 and 2 was blocked by a Knox County legislator who notified the commissioner that he would introduce a bill to abolish the Trail of the Lonesome Pine if work started on those sections. By the fall of 1997 all landowner agreements had expired, and hikers are cautioned to get permission before they enter private lands along the trail route.

Cumberland Trail

This is the next state scenic trail to the west and was the pilot project of the Tennessee Trails Association. In 1998 it became Tennessee's newest, and its first "linear," state park (see Chapter 2). It starts from Cumberland Gap National Historic Park, climbs to Tristate Peak, and then follows southwestward the line of high ridges and deep gorges lying along, or near, the eastern escarpment of the Cumberland Plateau and, finally, follows along the rim of the "Grand Canyon of the Tennessee River" to Signal Point National Military Park. Traversing a corridor of rugged beauty, the CT is a footpath across the geological, ecological, and cultural history of the eastern Cumberlands.

The Cumberland Trail route lies close to major fault lines created by the Allegheny orogency 230 million years ago (see Appendix), and it connects many scenic and historically important gaps. Through these gaps in prehistoric time, Native Americans crossed the highlands barrier on hunting, raiding, and trading forays. In the mid-1700s explorers and longhunters first entered Kentucky and Middle Tennessee through these gaps naming them as they passed—Cumberland Gap, Emory Gap, Crab Orchard Gap, and the Narrows of the Tennessee River Gorge. The Narrows of the Tennessee played a role in the French and Indian War and later provided an almost unassailable refuge for the Chickamauga Indians during the Revolution as they harassed pioneer American settlements in Middle Tennessee. In 1775 Daniel Boone cut the Wilderness Road through Cumberland Gap, the first settlers' route to Kentucky and Middle Tennessee. By the early 1800s wagon roads had been cut through all the major gaps in the eastern Cumberland Plateau, and homesteaders streamed westward through them. Some families stopped to settle at the foot of the escarpment, and many of the lesser passes took their names—Bruce Gap, Wheeler's Gap, Winter's Gap, and d'Armand Gap.

The War Between the States saw dramatic movements of troops, both Northern and Southern, through the gaps and up and down the valley. Equally dramatic after the War was the extension of new railway lines along the valley and up through the major gaps, opening the coal-rich Cumberlands to large-scale deep mining. At iron ore deposits along the foot of the escarpment, towns such as Chattanooga, Dayton, Rockwood, Harriman, and LaFollette sprang up around mines, furnaces, and foundries.

New industry attracted new workers, including Welsh miners with a tradition of organized labor. In the late 1800s the "Coal Creek War" erupted over the leasing of state prison convicts to work the mines during periods of labor unrest. Once again armed antagonists, this time mining union members versus company guards and the state militia, surged up and down the valley and through the gaps, often in commandeered railroad trains. The "War" ended in 1896 with repeal of the state convict lease law.

Mining and logging soon polluted area rivers and streams to the point of extinguishing most aquatic life. Later, large-scale strip mining of coal from the steep slopes of the Cumberland Mountains deeply and permanently scarred the face of the land itself. Prosperity turned to depression as the region's resources were depleted or markets dried up, but in the 1930s the Tennessee Valley Authority brought low cost hydro-electric power and economic renaissance to the region. The TVA also promoted natural resource conservation, restored natural beauty and established public parks and outdoor recreation areas along the Powell, Clinch, and Tennessee river valleys at the foot of the Cumberland escarpment.

The Cumberland Trail thus showcases natural and historic values of national significance. With this in mind Stan Murray, then Chairman of the Appalachian Trail Conference, suggested in 1969, at the Tennessee Trails Association's first annual meeting, the Cumberland Trail's inclusion in a spur off the AT down the Allegheny-Cumberland Front from Pennsylvania to Alabama. More recently, Russ Manning, in the *Historic Cumberland Plateau—An Explorer's Guide,* envisioned the Cumberland Trail as part of a regional footpath that would allow you "to walk virtually the entire length of the Cumberland Plateau" from northern Kentucky to Gadsden, Alabama.

Cumberland Trail: Cumberland Mountain Segment.
Length 9.9 mi.; rating, difficult; location, northern trailhead on
Tennessee Avenue in LaFollette (going north through LaFollette,
turn left at the seventh traffic light). Trailhead parking is on your
left. The southern trailhead is in a residential neighborhood north
of the park boundary of Cove Lake State Park in Caryville. Trail
maps are available from the Cumberland Trail Conference, Route
1, Box 219A, Pikeville, TN 37367 (E-mail address is cumberlandtrail
@rocketmail.com).

This segment of the CT offers spectacular views of the Powell
River Valley to the south and the Cumberland Mountain range to
the north. It is recommended that this segment be hiked from
north to south as the northern portion is more rocky and rugged.

Tank Springs is a developed spring at the LaFollette trailhead
parking lot. Many local residents avail themselves of this delicious
water for home use. The trail starts on a dirt road following the
railroad grade along Big Creek and makes a left turn to pass under
the railroad bridge, then follows Ollis Creek for a short distance before turning left and switchbacking up to the crest. The first mile
of the climb offers beautiful, fragrant rhododendron in mid-to-late
June. Once on the crest, the trail follows the ridgeline. At mi. 1.8
there is a rock outcropping with a magnificent view. It appears the
trail comes to an end but it actually continues down through a
crevice in the rock. A spring is located at mi. 1.9 and a primitive
campsite at mi. 2.1. After leaving the campsite the trail follows a
wet-weather stream with a vertical rock wall on the right. Be on
the lookout for Window Rock, an opening in this sheer rock wall
on your right. Returning to the ridgeline, the trail often lies on the
exposed ends of vertical rock strata that form the southwest lip of
the Cumberland Block and the spine of Cumberland Mountain. At
mi. 6 the trail comes out onto Old Kentucky Road, or Eagle Bluff
Road as the locals call it. Turn right onto Eagle Bluff Road and walk
0.3 mi. to a side trail on the left going up to Eagle Bluff Overlook.
The trail turns left off the road a short distance after the Eagle Bluff
Overlook spur trail and returns to the woods. Pay attention to the

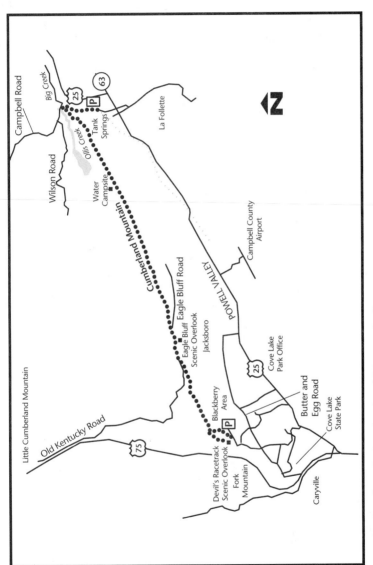

Cumberland Trail: Cumberland Mountain Segment

blazes for the first .5 mi. as there are many four-wheel paths in this fairly level area. This is the site of an old village that was located along the road in the 1800s. The trail continues on the crest for another 2 mi. to a junction. The main trail turns left and descends into Cove Lake State Park. This portion has earned the name "Suck Air" if you happen to be traveling it in the uphill direction! A spur trail out to the Devil's Racetrack is a ten-minute walk straight ahead to the southern end of Cumberland Mountain, where its spine outcrops spectacularly as several parallel upended rock strata towering above Interstate 75 far below in Bruce Gap, with Fork Mountain, Wheeler's Gap, and Cross Mountain lying beyond and perpendicular to Cumberland Mountain. If you hike this trail in late July, you will be rewarded with blackberries on the Suck Air descent. The trail comes out in a subdivision north of Cove Lake State Park. Follow the gravel road down the mountain into the park.

—Contributed by Arlene Barnett

Historical Note: The Cumberland Mountain Segment

The northern trailhead of the Cumberland Mountain Segment lies in Big Creek Gap, the only water gap that breaks the entire 125-mi. length of Cumberland Mountain. Here Big Creek passes through the mountain to flow southeast into Powell Valley in the Tennessee River watershed. At every other gap on the mountain, including Cumberland Gap, the ridge is not broken, and streams arise near the top on either side, flowing from the northwest side into the Cumberland River watershed, and from the southeast side into the Tennessee River watershed.

The cove at Cove Lake, the southern trailhead of this segment, is a beautiful and scenic spot at any season and was a favorite stop for Native Americans on the trail from Emory Gap to Cumberland Gap. At the time of Henderson's "Transylvania Purchase" in 1775, about 3,000 Cherokee lived there, and their patches of corn, beans, and pumpkins were all around the cove. Longhunters named it

Walnut Cove for the prolific walnuts it provided the Indians, as well as hickory nuts, wild cherries, and plums. A temple mound there and a burial mound still below Eagle Bluff indicate occupation during the Mississippian and Woodland periods. Micajah Cross was the first white to move his family into the Cove, in 1798, and, in 1799, an overshot mill was built on Bruce Creek in the gap. Thomas Wheeler moved into the Cove in 1806 with two brothers, and his family settled at "a bold spring" at the foot of Fork Mountain. Wheeler was a prominent farmer and leader, and Walnut Cove soon became Wheeler's Gap.

In 1799 a trail was cut from the earliest settled part of Richard Henderson's grant (awarded by North Carolina in 1783; see Chapter 1) around Cumberland Gap, down Powell Valley to Big Creek Gap, and on to Walnut Cove. In 1805 the Tennessee General Assembly authorized a road to be built from Walnut Cove over Cumberland Mountain to the Kentucky line where it would intersect one being built south from Danville.

In 1806, Campbell County was created by the State General Assembly and named for Colonel Arthur Campbell. Campbell, who had long been a pioneer leader in the Holston settlements, was born in Virginia in 1742 and captured by Indians in 1757 while serving with militia on the western frontier. Held captive for three years, he escaped from French Fort Detroit and trekked 200 miles before joining a British detachment for which he served as guide on its campaign against the western tribes. He came to the Holston in the 1780s.

The first county court session of the new county was held near Big Creek Gap at Richard Linville's inn (Linville's father, Captain William Linville, and his older brother were killed by northern Indians in 1766 below a beautiful waterfall in Linville Falls, North Carolina). In 1808, a county seat was laid out near Walnut Cove beneath Eagle Bluff. It was named Jacksborough in honor of Judge John Finley Jack, whose father, Captain Patrick Jack, was one of the few whites to escape the Cherokees' massacre of the British soldiers retreating after their surrender at Fort Loudon in 1760. Judge

Jack was named for Captain Jack's close friend, John Finley, who guided Daniel Boone on his first trip through Cumberland Gap into Kentucky in 1769.

According to Campbell County historian, Edwin A. Carr, Jr., the Jacksborough Road (later, the Kentucky Road) was probably built by the new county around 1808 and maintained by landowners who from 1810 to 1830 were required to work two days a month on roads near their lands. The road was used mainly by drovers herding cattle and hogs from Powell Valley to market at Richmond in central Kentucky. In 1861 Confederate engineers building defensive works at Cumberland Gap found the Jacksboro Road to be "the best wagon road west of Cumberland Gap" but "blockaded with trees and masses of rocks." Control of Cumberland Mountain changed hands several times, but in 1864 a train of over 600 wagons was moved by the Union Army over this road from central Kentucky to Knoxville in ninety-three days. After the war it continued to be used to drive livestock to Kentucky until the railroads came in the late 1800s.

In 1893, Harvey M. LaFollette, a wealthy Indianan and cousin of Senator Robert M. "Bob" LaFollette, became interested in industrial prospects for the area. He acquired thousands of acres in and around Big Creek Gap, and in 1894 a large mining camp was established; at that time the Big Creek Gap post office changed its name to LaFollette. In 1897 a Southern Railway line was extended from Caryville to LaFollette, and the LaFollette Coal and Iron Company built one of the largest iron furnaces in the South and many coke ovens nearby. Then began the "Great Railroad War" between the Louisville and Nashville Railroad, pushing a line south into the Cumberland Block from Jellico, and the Southern System pushing a route north up Big Creek with each racing to be the first across the Block. A shooting war soon erupted between rival grading crews backed by hired armed mercenaries. The matter was finally settled in the courts before there were actual casualties, the line was built, and coal mines sprang up along the railway and its spurs throughout the Block.

Source: Much of this historical material was taken from *The Land of the Lake* by Dr. G.L. Ridenour, Jacksboro, TN: Action Printing, Ltd.

Cumberland Trail: Obed Wild and Scenic River Segment (WSR). Length, 6.4 mi.; rating, difficult. Reminding us of the age when all our rivers ran free, the Obed River has worn a wild and crooked channel through the Cumberland Plateau. Its gorge is cut deep with green waters that delight the eye and offer solitude to those daring enough to explore. Lying within Obed WSR National Recreational Park and Tennessee's Catoosa Wildlife Management Area, this segment will eventually stretch over 17 miles. Currently, two portions of the "trail of a thousand steps" are complete. Trail maps are available from the Cumberland Trail Conference, Route 1, Box 219A, Pikeville, TN 37367 or through E-mail at cumberlandtrail@rocketmail.com

Nemo Bridge Trail: This portion of the Obed WSR Segment, within the Obed and Emory River gorges, incorporates the Obed's 2.5-mi. Nemo Trail and an additional 1.5-mi. segment built by the Cumberland Trail Conference, Tennessee Trails Association, and Breakaway Volunteers, giving a total one-way distance of 4.0 mi. The initial 2.5 mi. is rated moderate, and the final 1.5 mi. strenuous. From the Nemo Trailhead the hiker gradually climbs along the foot of bluffs to the left with glimpses of the Emory and Obed rivers to the right. As you rise to the top of the gorge amidst a drier forest of oak and hickory, you will soon walk on the tailings of an old strip mine. Notice the pools of water trapped by these old tailing piles—what aquatic creatures have benefited from these pools? At 2.5 mi. the trail crosses old Alley Ford Road and continues 1.5 mi. into and out of the Obed Gorge to the rewarding Breakaway Bluff, a dramatic overlook of the Obed Gorge. On your way to the bluff notice and give thanks to the trail builders' talent, particularly when you reach "the door," a 40-ft. drop from the bluff into the gorge below.

To reach the Nemo Trailhead, take I–40 to exit 347 and go north on U.S. 27 to Wartburg. Follow the signs in downtown Wartburg to the Nemo/Catoosa Road and travel 7 mi. to the Nemo Bridge crossing Emory River. Cross the bridge and take the first right down into the Rock Creek Camp Area and the Nemo Trailhead.

Devils Breakfast Table Trail: This portion of the Obed WSR Segment, built by Morgan County Regional Correctional Facility, covers 2.4 mi. one-way and currently terminates deep inside Catoosa WMA at the Rain House. From the Devils Breakfast Table Trailhead, the trail winds on the right side of the road for 0.2 mi. before crossing the road and dipping down below the bluff. You now find yourself in Daddys Creek gorge, rich with rhododendron, and for the next mile you will walk under sheer bluffs and on rock steps laid down by the trail builders. Once again, the significance of "a trail of a thousand steps" becomes apparent here. At 1.2 mi. you will rise out of the canyon through a cove of hardwood forest overlooking a 90-ft. sheer bluff cut by a cascading stream. Cross the stream and proceed a short distance to the aptly name Blueberry Bluff side trail, with views of Daddys Gorge. Return to the main trail and continue north 0.75 mi. to a side trail to Morgan's Overlook, offering views of Daddys to the north. Rejoin the main trail and travel 0.4 mi. to the Rain House, a sandstone overhang so named for the shelter it offered the builders of this trail on many a day. Here the trail ends, with trail work underway down in the gorge of Daddys Creek as it winds its way steadily north to join the Obed River and connect with the Nemo Bridge Trail.

To reach this trailhead take I–40 to exit 320 Peavine Road and head north 1.8 mi. to a left onto Firetower Road. Take Firetower Road 14.7 mi. to Daddys Creek and the Devils Breakfast Table parking area across the bridge on the right. Park and walk northeast 40 yds. on the road to the trailhead.

—Contributed by Rob Weber

Cumberland Trail: Grassy Cove Segment. Length, 11.3 mi.; rating, moderate. This segment traverses Black and Brady mountains, remnants of the Crab Orchard Mountains, an anticlinal

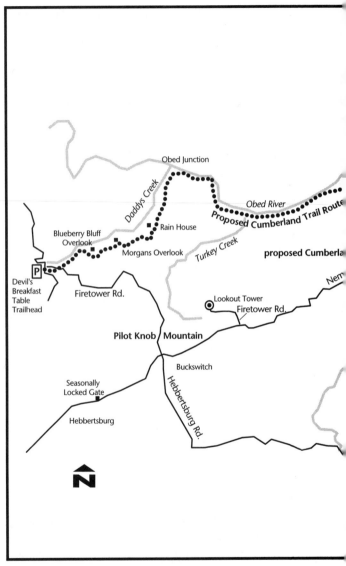

Cumberland Trail: Obed Wild and Scenic River Segment

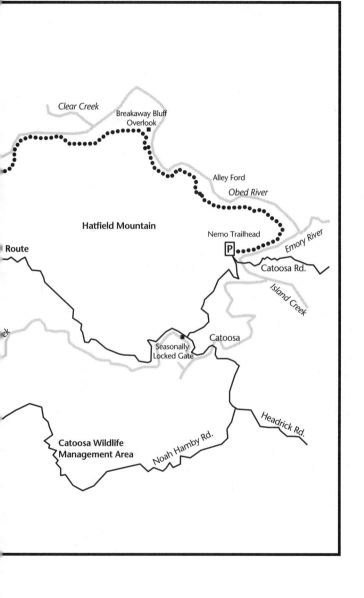

Clear Creek

Breakaway Bluff
Overlook

Alley Ford

Obed River

Hatfield Mountain

Nemo Trailhead

Route

P

Emory River

Catoosa Rd.

Island Creek

Seasonally
Locked Gate

Catoosa

ek

**Catoosa Wildlife
Management Area**

Noah Hamby Rd.

Headrick Rd.

ridge the southern end of which is being continuously undermined as the Sequatchie River cuts headward through a progression of limestone sinks along the anticline. It offers unspoiled views of Grassy Cove, a huge (5 mi. by 2 mi.) karst sink, the southernmost of four coves transitional between the Crab Orchard Mountains to the north and the Sequatchie Valley to the south. Along the crests of Black and Brady the hiker strolls through upland hardwood forest of chestnut oak, black oak, pignut hickory, sourwood, red maple, sassafras, and black gum with mostly Virginia pine and mountain laurel near the rocky bluffs. Mementos of Tennessee's historically most valuable nut tree, infertile sprouts of the now blighted American chestnut, are also scattered along the trail.

This segment lies entirely on privately-owned land, and open fires are not permitted. Occasionally, hikers will encounter all-terrain vehicles on the trail, or hunters in spring or fall, so exercise caution. The landowners are tolerant of most recreational users, but please report any destructive or defacing actions observed to the CTC (see below).

While this segment can be done as a long day hike, most challenge the mountains on separate day hikes, and descriptions are written with this in mind. Trail maps are available from the Cumberland Trail Conference, Route 1, Box 2194, Pikeville, TN 37367 or via e-mail at cumberlandtrail@rocketmail.com.

Brady Mountain Trail. Length, 7.0 mi.; rating, moderate. This trail extends along the spine of Brady Mountain, a narrow ridge forming the western escarpment of the Grassy Cove uvula designated by the National Park Service a National Natural Landmark. From the Jewett Road trailhead, ascend 0.5 mi. to Key Reed Gap, crossed by a jeep road between Brady's southern end, Dorton Knob, to the west and by Bear Den Mountain to the east. Cross the road and join the trail leading off through woods to the left to soon rejoin a jeep road that follows a contour north, then northwest, around Dorton Knob, then climbs steeply west to a shallow gap on Brady's Crest just north of Dorton Knob. Turning north, the trail follows the crest over a rise and across a swag. At the end of the swag, a spur trail (yellow blazes) climbs ahead and to the right past a house-size boulder and leads 100 yds. to an overlook, a *narrow* vertical rock stratum. Here you'll find spectacular views of the south end of Grassy Cove, Bear Den to the east, and Dorton Knob, at 2980 ft. the tallest point on Brady, to the south.

You are 1.6 mi. from the Jewett Road trailhead. Rejoin the main trail, which continues north along the crest alternating between broad forested flats and narrower ridge tops and, finally, climbs over Brady's second highest point at 2,920 ft. A long descent from this peak brings you to another spur trail, 1.8 mi. from the first spur trail. This side trail (yellow blazes) to the right is easily missed; it lies about 100 yds. past the entrance of a jeep road into the main trail from the left. Look for a small stack of stones on the right marking the spur trail. The spur leads 50 yds. to a broad-topped rock bluff overlooking Grassy Cove below, Black Mountain to the north, Loden Mountain to the east-northeast and, beyond–Walden's Ridge, the Valley and Ridge, and, on a clear day, the Blue Ridge outlined from Gregory Bald south to Big Frog Mountain.

Back on the main trail, cross the narrowest part of Brady, a rough rocky swag extending about 0.5 mi., then gradually climb over a broadening forested hump of the mountain that soon descends gently and begins to narrow. At 1.8 mi. from the last spur trail you pass interesting stacked rock formations and a large whaleback rock paralleling the trail to the right. At the north end of these rocks lies an "arch" offering dry shelter for the hiker.

Soon, after crossing another broad forested part of Brady, through a big patch of lady ferns midway, the trail begins a steep descent off the north end, stairstepping around the left side of three successive rocky promontories where witch hazel blooms in winter and maple-leaved viburnum and lily of the valley, in late spring. About 1 mi. from the rock "arch" the trail joins a logging road in a deep (low) gap. Follow the road north 1 mi. to the Hwy 68 trailhead.

If you wish to continue hiking the entire Grassy Cove segment,

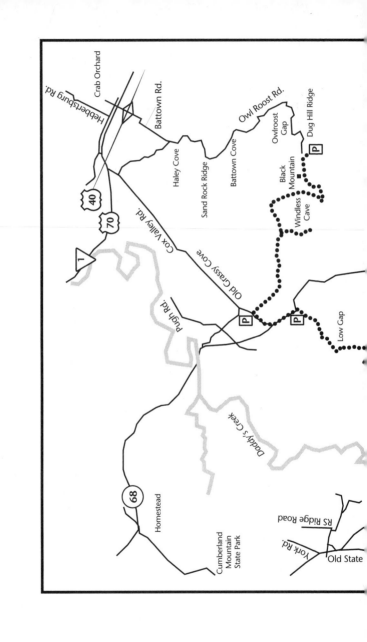

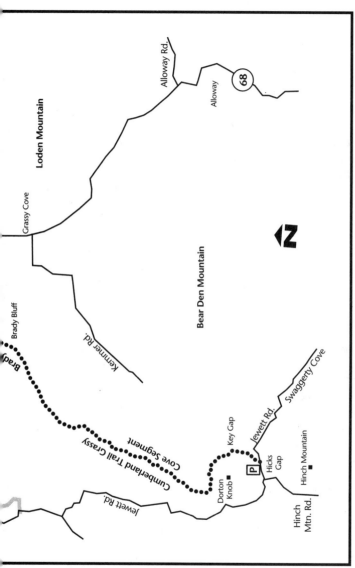

Cumberland Trail: Grassy Cove Segment

you can reach the Black Mountain trailhead by following the powerlines along TN 68 west 0.4 mi. to a right onto Cox Valley Road and north 0.4 mi. to the trailhead on the right.

To reach the Brady Mountain trailhead, take TN 68 4.6 miles from the TN 68/U.S. 127 junction 3 mi. southeast of Crossville. The trailhead is on the right, with ample parking space at a highway pull-off where the trail starts steeply up the mountain as a logging road. Shuttle to the south end trailhead by continuing east on TN 68 through Grassy Cove east 0.4 mi. to Jewett Road, entering TN 68 from the right. Take Jewett Road 6.6 mi. to the south trailhead on the right, with parking for several cars on the roadside. (*Note:* The last couple of miles of Jewett Road are rough, and vehicles with high ground clearance are recommended for the shuttle.)

Black Mountain Trail. Length, 3.5 mi.; rating, moderate. This trail crosses the board, almost flat, top of Black Mountain, part of a 530-acre tract owned by the Tennessee Annual Conference of the United Methodist Church. It is a Registered State Natural Area, but sadly, its extensive bluffs and vistas to the south and east have led to overuse and defacement of some of the rock formations. Please tread carefully and help preserve Black Mountain RNA. Report any misuse observed to the CTC.

A designated campsite lies 75 yds. west-southwest of the trailhead at an old stone springhouse. To the right of the springhouse the trail gently ascends and then crosses the top of the mountain 0.3 mi. to timber steps that descend through a cleft in the bluffs. In winter watch for ice here. At the bottom of the stairway you'll find narrow passageways among rising bluffs and house-size boulders. While there are a number of old campsites here, these are not designated sites, and open fires are not allowed on the Cumberland Trail.

Exit the bluffs and continue 0.3 mi. southwest through an old field and down the nose of a spur of Black Mountain. Watch for a double blaze marking a right-hand turn onto a switchback down the western slope of the mountain. The trail joins an old logging road that continues north-northeast along a contour before turning north-northwest to descent into a gap crossed by a jeep road at 1.5 mi. from the trailhead. Across the jeep road the trail ascends steeply through blueberries and bracken fern to a ridgetop with views back toward Black Mountain to the east. Follow the crest of the ridge 0.5 mi. west-southwest through the dry ridge forest of chestnut oak, post oak, and Virginia and shortleaf pine, with blueberry and greenbrier along the trail to the junction of four jeep roads and an ATV trail in a gap. An interesting side trip can be taken at this point by following the most southerly road fifteen minutes to Windless ("Windlass" on Grassy Cove quad) Cave, where the stream paralleling the road below on the left goes underground to reappear in Grassy Cove. Returning to the four-way road junction in the gap, follow the westernmost road about 500 yds. to a right turn (watch carefully for the blazes), down an old roadbed leading across Clear Branch. The trail follows Clear Branch 0.4 mi. through a small stand of umbrella magnolia, recrosses clear branch amid brilliant prolific cardinal flowers that bloom mid-summer to early fall, and rejoins the jeep road to follow it 1.1 mi. to the Cox Valley Road trailhead.

To reach the trailhead at the foot of Black Mountain, travel 4.2 mi. on TN 68 from the TN 68.U.S. 127 junction 3 mi. east of Crossville to a left turn onto Cox Valley Road, then 0.4 mi. north to the trailhead on the right. Parking for two to three cars is available on a gravel pull-off, by courtesy of the owner, just beyond his residence across the road 100 yds. back toward Hwy. 68 from the trailhead. From here shuttle to the top of Black Mountain by continuing north 3 mi. on Cox Valley Road to a right turn onto Haley Cove Road, then 1 mi. to a right turn onto Battown Cove Road, then 0.9 mi. to a four-way road junction. Take the road immediately to the left and proceed carefully past several sharp turns 3 mi. up Black Mountain, just past a cellular phone tower on the right, and turn left onto a gravel side road proceeding to the CT diamond sign. Parking space for several cars is available on the roadsides, and the trailhead is 50 yds. south of the road next to an old stone springhouse.

The trailhead at the summit of Black Mountain can be reached from Interstate 40 at Crab Orchard by following Battown Cove Road south from I–40 1 mi. to the junction with Haley Cove Road and proceeding as described above.

—Contributed by Rob Weber

Historical Note: Crab Orchard Cove

Crab Orchard Cove is the northernmost of the four transitional coves along the Sequatchie anticline, and it provides the easiest route to Middle Tennessee across the remaining heights of the anticlinal ridge, namely, Crab Orchard, Haley, Black, Brady, and Hinch mountains and the entire eastern escarpment of Sequatchie Valley. From prehistoric times it has also been a favorite stopping place for both game animal herds and people traveling across the Cumberland Plateau. Like Haley, Battown, and Grassy coves to the south, Crab Orchard Cove was, in the 1700s and early 1800s, full of tall grass (probably big bluestem and Indian grass) and crabapple trees, and it also featured a large cave with a spring gushing cold clear water. It and the other coves were probably burned regularly by Amerindians to keep the prairies open and attractive to buffalo, elk, and deer. (Deer still abound here, and, periodically, a wandering black bear appears, while bobcat and, more recently, coyote are not uncommon.) To the south of Grassy Cove many mounds and burial and town sites from the "Head-of-Sequatchie" to its mouth at the lower end of the Tennessee River Gorge evidence extensive habitation throughout the valley by Woodland and Mississippian peoples.

Longhunters coming into the area in the mid 1700s followed the Cherokee Path (later called the Cumberland Trace), which led from the mouth of Clinch River through the Crab Orchard and on to French Lick in Middle Tennessee. They also found an old Indian trail leading south from the Crab Orchard down Cox Valley (where a branch went to Grassy Cove) and along the western foot of Brady Mountain to Devilstep Hollow and the Sequatchie Valley. (Grassy Cove was immortalized in Louis L'Amour's *Jubal Sackett* when the hero came upon this "quiet, secluded, lovely place" in the early 1600s and chose it as the future home of the Sacketts.)

By the 1790s, the more daring travelers to and from Nashville were using the Cumberland Trace instead of the safer, but longer Emory Road to the north. This southerly route was still closed to the United States by the Cherokee, and travelers were frequently ambushed at the Crab Orchard, particularly by the hostile Chickamaugas and Creeks. Here in 1794 Thomas Sharpe Spencer, a Virginia "cavalier" and renowned longhunter, was killed by Doublehead, a Chickamauga chief. Spencer had settled at Castallian Springs north of French Lick in 1776 and was leading a party of settlers on his return from a trip back to his home state. Spencer Rock, where he was ambushed, can still be seen on the north side of Interstate 40 on Spencer Mountain, just east of Crab Orchard.

In the late 1790s, or thereabouts, John Ford, a veteran of the Revolution, and his family were in a wagon train from Virginia headed for Middle Tennessee when their wagon was broken up while descending Spencer Mountain on frozen ground. While his family camped at the Crab Orchard, Ford scouted for a place nearby to settle, and, viewing Grassy Cove from atop Black Mountain, he chose that site. Five other families, including those of three other Revolutionary soldiers, joined the Fords in building log cabins, and in 1803 they raised a little log church, perhaps the first on the plateau, on land donated by Ford. The beautiful little white-steepled brick Methodist Church there today is its direct descendant. Meanwhile, Greenberry Wilson, another war veteran from North Carolina, had brought his family down the Sequatchie Trail from Crab Orchard into the "head-of-the-valley" and built a log house on Wilson Branch. He was soon followed by others.

Before long the settlers had put up sawmills and gristmills—Tollett's Mill, Parham Mill, and Hinch's Mill—on the streams and mills at Mill Cave and Head of Sequatchie Spring the entry and exit points, respectively, of the underground drainage system that conducts all the waters from Grassy Cove beneath Brady Mountain and Devilstep Hollow to the head of Sequatchie Valley. Soon, also, the pioneers were making gunpowder at Salpeter Cave in Grassy Cove. Most of the local landmarks take their names from these early settlers, and their descendants live in Grassy Cove and the head of Sequatchi today, still good stewards of their lands.

In 1799, under an agreement with the Cherokee, a new federal road was marked out across the plateau along the old Cumberland Trace and opened in 1802 as the Cumberland Turnpike, more commonly known as the Walton Road for William Walton, its chief builder. In 1800 Sidnor's Stand, a rough hostelry, opened in Crab Orchard, to be succeeded in 1827 by the two-story brick Crab Orchard Inn. By 1834 the Walton Road was part of a great post road "carrying much of the traffic from the Carolinas, Virginia and Pennsylvania westward," states H.B. and J.M. Krechniak in *Cumberland County's First Hundred Years*, Centennial Committee, Crossville, TN 1956 (the source for most of the history in this note).

Cumberland Trail, Tennessee River Gorge Segment.

Length, 13 mi.; rating, difficult, location, Signal and Suck Creek mountains near the southern tip of the Cumberland range. Follow U.S. 127 to the town of Signal Mountain and follow the directional signs to Signal Point National Park parking area. The trail starts about halfway between the parking area and the Tennessee River Gorge Overlook. The trail follows bluff tops and ridges 1,800 and 2,000 ft. above sea level, drops into ravines lush with hemlocks towering over tangled growths of laurel and rhododendron, and crosses Middle, Julia, and Suck creeks. The view from Edwards Point covers a long stretch of the "Grand Canyon of the Tennessee," with historic Williams Island below on the left and the city of Chattanooga in the background. The full length of Raccoon Mountain rises across the river from Edwards Point.

Two primitive campsites are located on the first 11 mi. of the trail, and camping is permitted only at these sites. Parking areas at each end make it possible for backpackers to enjoy a one-way trip, stopping overnight at one of the campsites. It is difficult, if not impossible, to hike the 11 mi. in one day because the trail crosses several rock fields. Day hikes of interest are from Signal Point National Park to Middle Creek with a side trip to Rainbow Falls, a mighty rumbler in wet weather. This jaunt takes about three hours; six to eight hours are required to hike round-trip from Signal Point to Edwards Point or from Signal Point one way via Edwards Point to TN 27. Between Edward's Point and TN 27, the trail follows the top of the bluffs some 2.5 mi. with beautiful views of the Suck Creek gorge, then drops down to a campsite on North Suck Creek. At this point the trail continues across a 225-ft. swinging bridge over North Suck Creek to TN 27.

Starting on the Suck Creek Mountain side, look for the Prentice Cooper State Forest sign on TN 27 and travel to the parking lot near the fire tower. This section attracts many backpackers. It takes three to four hours to hike down to the roadside park on Suck Creek Road (TN 27). Treats include vistas from high places, the Poplar Spring campsite (the water is potable), and abundant vegetation in interesting rock formations. Large jack-in-the-pulpits grow under the bluffs, and the purple rhododendron (*Rhododendron catawbiense)* blooms here a full month earlier than the same species on Roan Mountain.

An interesting side hike is available on a leg of the Cumberland Trail across TN 27, starting at the firetower parking lot. This leg consists of approximately 30 mi. of two loops in Prentice Cooper State Forest. Pot Point Loop Trail overlooks the Tennessee River canyon at many points, and Mullins Cove Loop includes spectacular views of Mullins Cove in the canyon.

—Contributed by Emilie E. Powell

Historical Note: Tennessee River Gorge

The Tennessee River Gorge, and the entire setting of the Chattanooga area, is one of the most dramatically scenic and historic spots in eastern North America. Here, Signal Mountain to the north

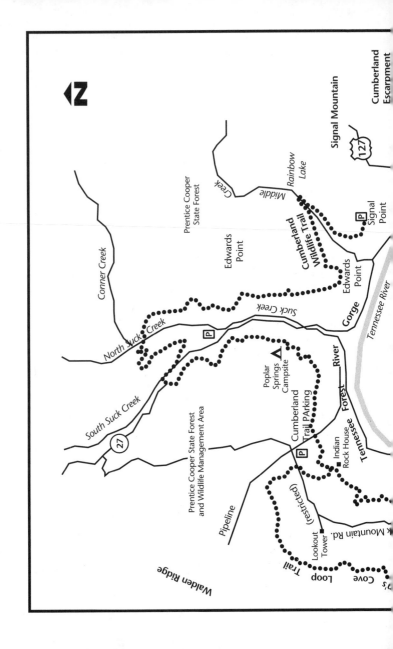

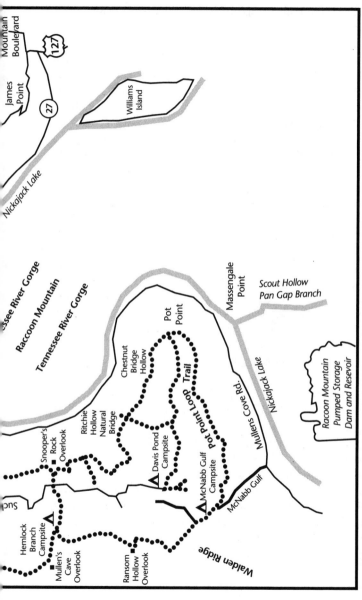

Cumberland Trail: Tennessee River Gorge Segment

and Lookout Mountain to the south face each other across Moss-casin Bend and Williams Island just upstream from the entrance to the Gorge. Where the river enters the Gorge, Suck Creek gorge enters from the north, forming a sharp angle in the escarpment above, Lusk Point, over which Sulfer Branch tumbles in a 600-ft. cascade. Here, between Lusk Point and the north end of Raccoon Mountain begins the Narrows of the Tennessee where a huge boulder jutted into the river just below the mouth of Suck Creek, constricting the river to half its width upstream and diverting the rushing water to bounce off the south bank and form a swirl or "suck." It had forever been a formidable hazard to canoes and, later, flatboats, and steamboats. Just downstream from the Suck was Deadman's Eddy and treacherous rapids such as the Boiling Pot, the Skillet, and Tumbling Shoals. (The boulder was removed by the Corps of Engineers in the mid-1800s, and the Narrows ceased to be a hazard when Hale's Bar Dam was built in 1913.)

The Chattanooga area was for centuries a populous center of Native American habitation. Williams Island State Archeological Area is the site of both Woodland and Mississippian settlements, and there are many such sites on Moccasin Bend and along Chattanooga, South Chickamauga, and North Chickamauga creeks. In historic times the Creek Confederacy controlled the area until their defeat by the Cherokee allied with the British during the Yamassee War in 1716. At the onset of the French and Indian War the British built Fort Loudon on the Little Tennessee to protect the towns of the Overhill Cherokee while their warriors were campaigning against northern tribes allied with the French. Mistreatment by English settlers in the Carolinas, and subversion by French agents, for a while turned the Cherokee against the British. The Indians besieged and took Fort Loudon and invited in the French. Boats loaded with French supplies were sent upriver from New Orleans, but in the Narrows of the Tennessee the Frenchmen found the Suck to be impassable, and they soon returned home. By 1763 the Cherokee had returned to the English trading system, and later in the decade John McDonald, a young Scottish trader, set up a trading post at the mouth of South Chickamauga Creek.

After Richard Henderson's "Transylvania Purchase" (see Chapter 1) in 1775, Chief Dragging Canoe led about 1,000 Cherokee from the Overhill towns to settle in new towns around McDonald's trading post in 1777. From their Chickamauga towns, these bitter opponents of concessions to the white settlers began relentless raids on the farms and settlements in the upper Tennessee Valley, the Carolinas, western Virginia, and Kentucky. Cries for relief from the exposed frontiersmen led Virginia's Governor Patrick Henry to send a 300-man force of militia under Colonel Evan Shelby to destroy the Chickamauga towns in early 1779. Riding the spring flood down the Holston and Tennessee rivers in dugout canoes and pirogues, Shelby's men in two weeks destroyed eleven towns in the Chattanooga area and captured corn, horses, and British supplies. Part of the force continued downriver to join George Rogers Clark's campaign in the old Northwest, and the rest returned to the Watauga via the Great Lakes Trail, stopping briefly at Sale Creek (just south of present Dayton) to divide up the captured booty by auction.

In October 1779 Captain James Robertson set out from the Holston-Watauga settlements along Boone's Trace through Cumberland Gap with a party herding cattle and goats bound for French Lick. In December, Colonel John Donelson, a surveyor-land speculator from Virginia, started down the Holston with all the Robertson and Donelson women, children, and slaves and several other families in a small flotilla of flatboats. After a slow start and some mishaps they reached the mouth of the Clinch on March 5, 1780; there the flotilla had grown to around thirty boats. From there the ride down the now swollen Tennessee was swift. After running the gauntlet of the rebuilt Chickamauga towns with the tragic loss of one boat and family and near loss of another at the Suck, the flotilla ran the Tennessee Canyon as fast as possible, then Muscle Shoals, reached the Ohio on March 24, and finally poled and warped up the Cumberland to rejoin the Robertson party at Fort Nashborough (French Lick) on April 24.

Attacks led by John (Nolichucky Jack) Sevier against the Over-hill towns in 1780–81 and the upper Chickamauga towns in 1782 forced Dragging Canoe and his followers to move into lower towns at the western foot of Lookout Mountain and downstream from the mouth of the Tennessee River Gorge. In 1785 the lower Chickamaugas captured a boatload of trade goods bound for the Chickasaw Nation, and at John McDonald's request, the traders' lives were spared. One of them, Daniel Ross, a young Scot, remained to open a trading post, marry the daughter of McDonald and his Cherokee wife, and sire John Ross, who was to become in 1828 the first elected principal chief of the Cherokee Nation. In 1788 a young Shawnee, Tecumseh, came with his older brother to alongside the Chickamauga, and, after his brother was killed, remained for two years with them raiding the frontier settlements.

In 1790 North Carolina's counties west of the Blue Ridge, which were ceded to the United States, became the Southwest Territory, with its capital at White's Fort (Knoxville) and William Blount its governor. Under the Treaty of Holston in 1791, the Cherokee gave up more land for a $1,000 annual payment by the United States and its promise to protect their remaining land from encroachment, to guarantee the Cherokee's right to self-government, and to provide tools, seed, and aid to help the Cherokee become self-sufficient farmers. Dragging Canoe died in 1792 and was succeeded by John Watts with whom Blount tried to negotiate peace, but undiminished intrusions by whites on Cherokee lands, and incitement and provisioning by the Spanish now controlling the lower Mississippi, kept the Chickamauga, and the Creeks, at war with the settlers. Finally, in 1794, the settlers in middle Tennessee and southern Kentucky, responding to General James Robertson's call for retaliation, gathered 550 volunteers in early September and set out down the Nickajack Trace under Major James Ore. On September 13 they completely destroyed Nickajack and Running Water, the largest of the lower Chickamauga towns, bringing to an end almost two decades of depredations by this small faction of the Cherokee.

In 1805 the Cherokee agreed to the opening of a federal road from Augusta, Georgia, to the heart of the Cherokee Nation near present Dalton, Georgia. From there, one branch continued northward to the Overhill towns and another, the Georgia Road, northwestward across Lookout Mountain to Nickajack Town, then generally along the Nickajack Trace to Nashville. The roads opened markets to progressive Cherokee, and along them the Cherokee prospered.

Daniel Ross was soon operating a tannery and new trading stand where the Georgia Road crossed Chattanooga Creek east of Lookout Mountain. His son John, after attending an academy in Kingston and working in a mercantile store there, served as adjutant of the Cherokee Regiment in Andrew Jackson's campaign against the Creeks. Then he opened a store at Hiwassee Old Town and, around 1815, established a warehouse and ferry at Ross's Landing (at the end of Market Street in present Chattanooga).

In 1828 the first steamboat, the *Atlas*, came up the Tennessee through Muscle Shoals and into the Narrows negotiating the Boiling Pot in fourteen minutes and the Suck in eleven. In 1831 the 100-ft.-long *Knoxville*, built in Cincinnati, came through the gorge bound for its home port. Rock removal through the Pot and the Suck under state contract in 1831 and 1832 improved the channel, but the Narrows remained impassable during low-water periods. Shallow draft boats were necessary even after installation around 1849 of a pier with horse-powered windlass to warp vessels around the Suck. In 1838 the Ross's Landing Post Office changed its name to Chattanooga.

In 1853 the Nashville and Chattanooga Railroad completed a line from Nashville through Stevenson, Alabama, to Bridgeport, and steamboats carried the freight and passengers from there through the Gorge to Chattanooga. In 1854 the railroad was completed across the river from Bridgeport, up Falling Water Creek, down Lookout Creek, and around the foot of the mountain into Chattanooga. By 1857 the Memphis and Charleston line joined the N. & C. at Stevenson to enter Chattanooga along the N.& C. tracks.

When Tennessee in 1861 voted by referendum 2-to-1 for secession, the Sequatchie Valley counties and those east of Walden's Ridge voted pro-Union, and, despite the threat of arrest and execution, individuals and groups from those areas began fleeing north to join the Union Army. Many of them were guided by the "Red Fox," Richard Flynn, mostly by night along his "underground railway" up Sequatchie Valley and across the Plateau to Kentucky with stops at "stations"—first on Walden's Ridge, next in Sequatchie Valley, and finally at Fox's cabin on Big Laurel Creek in present Cumberland County. Later in the war, eight of Andrews' Raiders who had stolen the Confederate locomotive, *The General*, and had been captured at Ringgold, Georgia, after a thrilling railroad chase, escaped prison in Atlanta and were passed along the route through "Red Fox Station" to Kentucky.

General Ulysses S. Grant took Fort Henry and Fort Donelson in February 1862 and, with them, control of the lower Tennessee and Cumberland rivers, and sent his gunboats and bargeloads of troops steaming up both rivers, to Pittsburg Landing on the Tennessee and to Nashville on the Cumberland. The Confederate military abandoned Middle Tennessee, sending trainloads of sick and wounded troops, supplies, and fleeing civilians down the N. & C. railway to Chattanooga. By mid-March the Confederate forces were gathering at Corinth, Mississippi, and on April 6 they attacked the Federals at Pittsburg Landing, but on the following day the Confederates withdrew to Corinth after bloody fighting around Shiloh Church. The Union forces took most of northern Alabama by early June including the Memphis and Charleston Railroad as far east as Bridgeport. From there a cavalry unit under General James S. Negley crossed Battle Creek and Sequatchie Valley to Anderson's Cross Roads. Here he climbed Walden's Ridge along an old farm road improved in the 1850s to become the Anderson Turnpike, still just a rough wagon road zigzagging up the steep slope. Negley descended the east side of the Ridge on the equally bad "W" Road, and on June 7 began shelling the Confederates in Chattanooga from the north side of the river. He soon withdrew by the same route back across the Sequatchie, and the still weak Union force fortified the west side of Battle Creek from the Tennessee River to the brow of the mountain, content to watch the Anderson Pike and skirmish with Confederate cavalry probes from Chattanooga.

By mid-July, Confederate General Braxton Bragg had concentrated his army at Chattanooga, determined to protect this vital railroad junction, to secure the upper Tennessee Valley "breadbasket," and to campaign into Kentucky to rally southern sympathizers and cross the Ohio or retake Nashville. In late August his 27,000-man force marched up the "W" Road, down Anderson Pike, and up Sequatchie Valley to Pikeville and then to Sparta and on into Kentucky. By early November Bragg's army was back in Chattanooga having failed in its mission because of the general's vacillations. The Union Army, having paralleled his movement northward, was now in Nashville, and Bragg moved his Army of Tennessee up the N. & C. railroad to Murfreesboro. There, after the bloody battle of Stones River, he withdrew on January 3, 1863, to occupy a defensive line along Duck River until he was outflanked and forced to withdraw to Chattanooga in July.

The Federal army, now under General William S. Rosecrans, pursued cautiously but in early September crossed the Tennessee around Bridgeport and advanced in three widely separated columns across Lookout Mountain. Bragg withdrew from Chattanooga southward into Georgia and turned on the Federal columns piecemeal as they emerged from the gaps on the east side of Lookout. On September 19 and 20 Rosecrans's army was driven from the battlefield along south Chickamauga Creek northward into Chattanooga and pushed back to the river within a tight perimeter. With Confederate artillery along the heights of Missionary Ridge to the east and Lookout and Raccoon mountains to the south and west, all river traffic, railroads, and roads entering Rosecran's position were controlled by the Confederates except one road leading north to Walden's Ridge from a pontoon bridge across the river behind.

The Union Army's supply base at the end of the N. & C. railway line at Bridgeport became vital to holding Chattanooga, and the only supply line open from there was via trains of mule-drawn wagons moving across Battle Creek and Sequatchie Valley up the Anderson Pike and down the "W" Road. The roads on both sides of Walden's Ridge were steep, narrow, one-way, zigzag, rocky, in places miry, in other places rickety log corduroy supported on the downslope side by pilings. Each side sometimes took five or six hours to climb or descend by wagon.

So as not to interrupt the inflow of essential supplies, the wagons returning to Bridgeport used the old Haley Road (said to be part of the same stagecoach route of the 1830s that appears as the McMinnville Stage Road in the South Cumberland State Park; see Chapter 6) until Confederate fire from Raccoon Mountain shut it off and forced the opening of a new return route up Shoal Creek about where U.S. 127 climbs Signal Mountain today. With the telegraph line to Bridgeport cut, a line of wigwag and fireflash signal stations was set up from Cameron Hill in Chattanooga, to Signal Point, to the western edge of Walden's Ridge, and then to Jasper and Bridgeport.

This whole lifeline was vulnerable to Confederate cavalry raids. One of the most devastating began early on the morning of October 2 when CSA General Joseph Wheeler, leading a 1,500-man cavalry force down Sequatchie Valley, came upon a Union wagon train at Anderson's Cross Roads stretched out of sight down the Valley from the top of Walden's Ridge. Driving off the escorting cavalry, Wheeler's men began systematically burning the wagons and killing the mules except for those they could use themselves. Those in Chattanooga could hear the distant sound of exploding ammunition wagons and could soon see clouds of smoke billowing beyond the crest of Walden's Ridge. Arrival of a division of Federal cavalry late in the afternoon forced Wheeler to retreat toward McMinnville, but the raid seemed a disaster for the troops in Chattanooga. They were already on quarter rations and, with cold weather coming on, ill-clothed, ill-shod, and increasingly bereft of firewood.

Providentially, on October 6 advance units of a 20,000-man relief force from Virginia under Union General Joseph Hooker arrived by rail at Bridgeport. By October 26 General Grant, now supreme commander of the Division of the Mississippi, had taken over in Chattanooga and quickly secured a bridgehead on the south bank of the Tennessee at Brown's Ferry just downstream from Lookout Mountain. Next day Hooker's men came down Lookout Creek just west of the mountain to cut off the Confederates on Raccoon Mountain and open up the road from Kelly's Ferry midway in the Tennessee River Gorge to Brown's Ferry where a pontoon bridge now crossed to Moccasin Bend. On October 30 a newly built steamer, the *Chattanooga,* reached Kelly's Ferry towing bargeloads of supplies from Bridgeport, and by mid-November enough had been transported over this "Cracker Line" into Chattanooga to allow Grant to launch an assault on the encircling Confederate lines. Indeed, on November 24, Hooker drove the Confederates off Lookout Mountain (see Chapter 7), and on November 25 the combined forces of Generals Hooker, George H. Thomas, and William Tecumseh Sherman drove Bragg's Army of Tennessee from Missionary Ridge to break the siege of Chattanooga.

U.S. Army Engineers soon cleared again the channels through the rapids in the Narrows and installed a windlass warping steamboats around the Suck. They continued to keep the Gorge open to river traffic, when water depth permitted, until construction of Hales Bar Lock and Dam by the Chattanooga and Tennessee River Power Company in 1913 submerged forever the hazards of the Narrows. The Anderson Pike continued to be used by people in the lower Sequatchie until U.S. 127 was built in 1930. A record flood in 1867 washed away the wooden bridge built by the Army in Chattanooga to replace the pontoon bridge used during the siege, and many smaller bridges, a viaduct, and many miles of N. & C. track were washed away below Chattanooga. Nevertheless, a spur line from Bridgeport to Jasper was completed that month, and by 1891 the N.C. and St. L. (formerly the N. & C.) had extended the line up Sequatchie Valley to Pikeville.

Today, the Tennessee River Gorge segment of the Cumberland Trail, together with 30-odd miles of loop trail around Mullens Cove, affords the hiker superb views, from the canyon's northern rim, of the Suck, the Pot, the Skillet, and the other now-flooded hazards of the Narrows. It crosses the old Haley Road at the head of Mullens Cove, and when the CT is extended up North Suck Creek it will intersect the old Anderson Pike (a possible future connector to a proposed rails-to-trails project along the old Sequatchie Valley Railroad) near the lookout tower on U.S. 127. At its Signal Point terminus the CT looks down on the routes of the old Shoal Creek Road and the "W" Road.

Source: Most of the above history was taken from *Sequatchie: A Story of the Southern Cumberlands* by J. Leonard Raulston and James W. Livergood, The University of Tennessee Press.

Trail of Tears

This trail, as designated in the Trails System Act, is not feasible as a hiking trail. The act was amended in the 1978 session of the General Assembly to make it a scenic route, with historic sites, scenic loops, and recreation trails pinpointed along the corridor.

In 1987 the Trail of Tears National Historic Trail was designated by Congress to be developed as an auto route connecting relevant historic sites. A National Park Service management and use plan for the TOTNHT shows four different historic land routes and a water route, the Tennessee River from Ross's Landing (Chattanooga) to the Ohio and the Mississippi. It indicates the northernmost land route as the most heavily traveled by the migrating Cherokee. With small divergence's the TOT State Scenic Trail follows this northern land route.

While funds are scarce, cooperative development of sites and signage by NPS and the State Department of Environment and Conservation for the Trail of Tears seems assured. Meanwhile, the

City of Savannah in west Tennessee has built a paved 700-ft. river-bank trail, the Savannah Historic Trail, along the water route of the Trail of Tears as a demonstration project that can be emulated by other communities along the Tennessee River. Savannah's trail is designed for use by pedestrians, bicyclists, and the disabled and was built to NPS standards as an official interpretive component of the National Historic Trail.

The route of the State Scenic Trail starts from the Red Clay Council Grounds of the Cherokee at Red Clay State Historical Area in southern Bradley County. If follows TN 60 to Dayton; TN 30/284 to Fall Creek Falls State Park; TN 284, 111, and 8 to McMinnville; U.S. 70S to Murfreesboro; U.S. 231 to Lebanon; U.S. 70N to Hermitage; TN 45 to Whites Creek; U.S. 431 to Springfield; U.S. 41 to Adams; TN 76/238 to Port Royal; and TN 238 on to the Kentucky state line near Guthrie.

Hiking opportunities within the corridor include a 2.3-mi. loop trail at Red Clay, the Bowater trails near Dayton, Fall Creek Falls State Park, the Shellsford-Cardwell Mountain Trail near Cumberland Caverns, the Rutherford County Hike-Bike Complex, Cedars of Lebanon State Park, the Corps of Engineers trails around Percy Priest Reservoir, and a 1-mi. loop trail at Port Royal State Historical Area.

Shellsford–Cardwell Mountain Trail. Length, 8 mi.; rating, moderate. The Trail of Tears State Historical Route is a 260-mi. automobile tour that follows as closely as possible the route taken by the Cherokee Indians in the removal of 1838. This hiking trail is one of the several significant features along that route recognized by the Tennessee Department of Environment and Conservation for their interpretive value. The Shellsford Trail allows the hiker to walk in the steps of the Cherokees along an old stage road beside the beautiful Collins River.

The trail begins at the Cumberland Carverns parking area, 6 mi. east of McMinnville, a short distance off TN 8. Interpretive literature and trail information can be obtained at the caverns office. In the first several hundred yards, the trail makes a gradual descent to the Collins River. Here the Cumberland Caverns Nature Trail, which has coincided with the Shellsford Trail to this point, turns back toward the caverns. The Shellsford Trail continues along the bank of the river for 2 mi. to the Shellsford Community. Here may be seen the ruins of the old gristmill where corn was ground for the Cherokees. A bridge across the river leads to the historic Shellsford Church, whose cemetery holds the remains of two Cherokee children, among the many who died of cold and disease on the 1838 trek.

From Shellsford the return to the parking area may be made over Cardwell Mountain, an outlier of the main Cumberland range. The 6-mi. return trail, with a vertical climb from the river of almost 1,000 ft., passes through hardwood forest. The top is notable for sandstone cliffs, and there is a panoramic view in winter when there is no foliage. Except for the area around Shellsford, the entire 8-mi. trail is devoid of pavement, power lines, and other forms of visual pollution.

Historical Note: Cherokee Nation

By 1800, missionaries were bringing both the Gospel and education to the Cherokee, and they proved to be quick and eager learners. Completion in 1807 of a federal road from Augusta through the heart of the Cherokee Nation in north Georgia to the Overhill towns in East Tennessee, and a branch to Nashville, opened markets for Cherokee products. Many of the Cherokee families near those roads established prosperous dynasties as farmers, millers, blacksmiths, ferrymen, and merchants. Around 1817 the nonsectarian American Board of Foreign Missions bought trader John McDonald's land on South Chickamauga Creek and began, with federal aid, what became the Brainerd Mission. For the next two decades the Mission, and its several branches throughout the Nation, taught countless Cherokee students to be "useful citizens, and pious Christians."

Despite such progress by the white man's standards, new

treaties in 1805 and 1817 continued to shrink the Cherokee homeland; the 1817 treaty provided a tract in Arkansas and boats and provisions to carry any Cherokee voluntarily migrating there, as well as remuneration for improvements lost on lands given up. The Treaty of 1819, negotiated by John C. Calhoun, sought to divide the remaining Cherokee homelands into reservations to be granted to those members of their Nation who had made considerable improvements on their land, were capable of managing it productively, and intended to reside on it permanently. President James Monroe favored full citizenship for such Cherokee in the states where they resided, but the states, particularly Georgia, opposed anything but full removal of the Indians from within their borders.

In 1821, an artistic and talented but uneducated Cherokee of mixed-blood, Sequoyah, gave his people a syllabary of eighty-six characters that allowed them to read their spoken native tongue, and literacy quickly swept through the Nation. Soon a New Testament translation was produced, and in 1828 the Brainerd missionaries secured a printing press and cast type in the new syllabary. Set up in New Echota, the Cherokee capital (near present Dalton, Georgia), the press began turning out a bilingual weekly national newspaper, *The Phoenix,* and many religious publications.

Taking the Treaty of Holston's promise of self-government as a solemn obligation, the Cherokee Nation held a constitutional convention in 1826 and in 1827 adopted a document based on that of the United States, forming a democratic republic with the checks and balances of three branches of government. In 1828 John Ross was elected Principal Chief, the constitutional executive.

Also in 1828, gold was discovered at Dahlonega in northeast Georgia on land the Cherokee held under the Treaty of Holston and all the later treaties. Despite the federal guaranty, Georgia quickly enacted legislation confiscating all the Cherokee lands. An opinion of Chief Justice John Marshall of the U.S. Supreme Court in 1832 held that Georgia's legislation was void, but later that year the state sold the Cherokee lands by lottery and began evicting the owners by force in favor of the white lottery winners.

In 1828 Andrew Jackson, whose army had been saved from disaster by his Cherokee Regiment at Horseshoe Bend during the Creek War, campaigned for president supporting removal of all the Indians from east of the Mississippi. With this support, the Georgia congressional delegation introduced an Indian removal bill in 1830. One congressman from Tennessee, David (Davy) Crockett, parted company with his constituents, and most of the South, in bitterly opposing the bill. He was joined by a number of the members from the New England states, Delaware, and Indiana as well as such notables as Henry Clay, Daniel Webster, Ralph Waldo Emerson, and Sam Houston. The Removal Act nevertheless passed, and President Jackson sought a new treaty with the Cherokee for peaceful removal.

Increasingly, atrocities against Cherokees as well as Chickasaw, Choctaw, Creeks, and Seminoles, were occurring. John Ross himself was evicted from his farm and ferry in north Georgia in 1833, and his family moved into a one-room cabin near the new capital at Red Clay council grounds in Southeast Tennessee. Encouraged by John Marshall's opinion of 1832 and confident that the United States would abide by its treaties, Ross urged peaceful resolution, but his people were divided. A tiny faction, over Ross's opposition, signed a Removal Treaty in 1835, and Congress ratified it in 1836 when outbreak of the Seminole War raised fears of a spreading Indian rebellion.

About 2,000 Cherokee migrated voluntarily over the next two years, the first group leaving Ross's Landing on flatboats in early 1837. Most went about their normal lives hoping that Ross's confidence in the United States' integrity would be justified. When General Winfield Scott came into the Nation with 7,000 troops early in 1838 proclaiming a deadline of June for the removal, Ross began seeking the best terms possible for remunerating his people for their losses, for establishing them on their new lands in Oklahoma, and for making their journey as comfortable as possible. Meanwhile, Scott's men began rounding up the heartbroken holdouts and herding them into stockades at Hiwassee Agency, Ross's Landing (Chattanooga), and Gunter's Landing. Most from Georgia went to Ross's Landing, where the first two groups left in June on flatboats towed by steamboat and another group by wagon and foot. The heat of summer resulted in such high mortality among these first migrants that Scott allowed the rest to wait in the stockades for the cooler weather of September and agreed to let Cherokee leaders superintend the resumption of the removal. About 2,000 died during the wait in the stockades.

Some of Scott's troops, despite his orders to treat the Cherokee humanely, were brutal and abusive during the roundup. In the Middle Towns one chief, Tsali, resisted the rough treatment of his family, and a soldier was killed. About 1,000 of Tsali's people fled to the fastnesses of the Great Smoky Mountains, and Scott, realizing the difficulty of finding them, agreed to let them remain if Tsali and his brother and two sons would surrender themselves for certain execution. They agreed, and Tsali's people were left in the mountains where their descendants still live in the Qualla Reservation at Cherokee, North Carolina.

From the end of September to early November, thirteen contingents of 1,000 each departed from Red Clay council grounds along the Nuna-da-ut-sun'y, "The Trail Where They Cried," essentially the route of the old Black Fox Trail down the Hiwassee and across the Tennessee at Jolly's Island (where Sam Houston, "the Raven," had passed youthful years, later to become governor of Tennessee, the victor of San Jacinto, first president of the Republic of Texas, and governor of the state of Texas). They then traveled on to Pikeville, McMinnville, Murfreesboro, Nashville, Port Royal, Hopkinsville, then through southern Illinois, Missouri, Arkansas, and, finally, Oklahoma in March and April. Some 4,000 are believed to have been lost, many from pneumonia particularly after frigid weather began in Illinois. John Ross laid his wife to rest in Arkansas, and continued working for the benefit of his people until his death in 1866. Most of the Brainerd missionaries went west with their flock, and one, too ill to make the journey, remained to care for the mission until it was put up for sale. He bought the mission cemetery himself to prevent its desecration or destruction.

Source: Most of the above history was taken from *The Chattanooga Country, 1540–1976: from Tomahawks to TVA* by Gilbert E. Govan and James W. Livingood; The University of Tennessee Press.

John Muir Trail

This is the fourth state scenic trail designated in the Tennessee Trails System Act, which prescribed that it run roughly from the mouth of Wolf River in Fentress County through Pickett State Park and south along the Big South Fork of the Cumberland River to Frozen Head State Park intersecting the Cumberland Trail, then southeastward to the Hiwassee Scenic River and the North Carolina line.

To date, two widely separated sections of the trail have been built. The northwestern section runs northeastward from Pickett State Park headquarters parallel to Thompson Creek to a junction with Sheltowee Trace near the Kentucky line. It turns south, then west across Divide Road, where there is parking. It follows No Business Creek several miles, angles to the southeast, and follows the Big South Fork of the Cumberland River, crossing the Leatherwood Ford Bridge, to the old O&W Railroad Bridge. (See Chapter 8 for a description of a section of the John Muir Trail at Leatherwood Ford accessible to those with disabilities.) This section of the John Muir Trail is about 48 mi. in length. At 4.5 mi. south-southeast of the O&W Bridge, another section of the John Muir Trail, not yet connected to that just described, starts at Burnt Mill Bridge. It coincides with the counterclockwise leg of the Burnt Mill Bridge Loop Trail for 1.3 mi., where it branches off the Loop Trail to the right and proceeds about 2 mi. downstream paralleling Clear Fork. This section of the JMT is to be eventually extended to the O&W Bridge. A map of the Big South Fork is available from the Big South

Fork National River and Recreation Area, P.O. Box 630, Oneida, TN 37841. The Southeastern section of the John Muir Trail on the Hiwassee River in Cherokee National Forest is described in Chapter 3.

The John Muir Trail has been extended westward from Pickett State Park headquarters 5 mi. to the gravel road on the former western boundary of Pickett State Forest. The recent addition of 5,000 acres to the state forest makes possible a further 3 mi., or more, westward extension of the trail to the new boundary. A further extension of about 4 mi. would bring it to York Mill State Historic Site, the homeplace of Alvin C. York at Pall Mall in the "Three Forks of the Wolf River Country."

Meanwhile, the Cumberland Trail Conference is exploring the possibility of extending the John Muir Trail from Burnt Mill Bridge in the Big South Fork NRRA up Clear Fork to historic Rugby (established in 1877 as an experimental colony by British author Thomas Hughes), and from there southeastward to an intersection with the Cumberland Trail near the Emory River. At this time the JMT is unfeasible as a hiking trail from the eastern edge of the Cumberland Plateau across the Valley and Ridge to Cherokee National Forest, but it has great potential as a scenic and historic auto route.

Historical Note: John Muir Trail

The route of the John Muir Trail approximates the one Muir followed through Tennessee in 1867 on his "thousand mile walk to the gulf." In a book so titled, and edited by William Frederick Badé in 1916 after Muir's death, Muir gave a day-by-day account of his trip. The address inside the cover of his field notebook on the journey, "John Muir, Earth-planet, Universe," suggests his cosmopolitan view of nature.

At twenty-nine years of age, working in a wagon factory, Muir was already accustomed to long walking trips botanizing in the Midwest, the Great Lakes area, and Ontario. Carrying only notebook and plant press, he often slept in the woods covered by the clothes he wore and took meals with friendly farmers or from field and forest—or did without. He had planned this route through Tennessee, his longest trip, earlier, but an accident in March 1867 threatened blindness in his right eye and forced long confinement to a dark room. When recovered enough to emerge from darkness, Muir wrote, "As soon as I got out into Heaven's light, I started on another long excursion,, making haste with all my heart to store my mind with the Lord's beauty, and thus be ready for any fate, light or dark . . . determined to devote the rest of my life to the study of the inventions of God."

Planning "to push on in a general southward direction by the wildest, leafiest, and least trodden way I could find, promising the greatest extent of virgin forest," he left Indianapolis on September 1 and crossed the Ohio to enter Louisville the next day. He covered about 25 miles a day through Kentucky, over Salt River, through the Knobs, across the black oak "Barren," and through Munfordville, where just five years earlier General Braxton Bragg's invasion of Kentucky was turned back less by the enemy than by Bragg's irresolution. On the way to Horse Cave, Muir rode awhile with "an old negro driving an ox team" who gave a first-hand account of the recent fighting between Yankees and Rebs and his earnest wish for "no mo wa, Lo'd no." Muir wrote, "Many of these Kentucky negroes are shrewd and intelligent, and . . . eloquent in no mean degree."

A villager at Horse Cave told him he had never bothered to visit Mammoth Cave, just 10 miles distant, since it was only "a hole in the ground," and Muir wrote, "He was one of the useful practical men—too wise to waste precious time with weeds, caves, fossils, or anything else he could not eat." Later that day, he marveled at the grandeur of the "houserooms and halls" of Mammoth Cave and the good fortune of its being left "unimproved," and found it an "abrupt contrast with paltry artificial gardens" of the "fashionable hotel grounds" nearby.

At Burkesville on September 8, he found "the scenery on approaching the Cumberland River becomes still grander," and concluded, "the Cumberland must be a happy stream," adding, "I think I could enjoy traveling with it in the midst of such beauty all my life." September 9 was "another day in the most favored province of bird and flower" where "the grandest of all Kentucky plants are her noble oaks."

Passing the Tennessee line and through, or near, Pall Mall (later the home place of World War I hero Sergeant Alvin C. York) on September 10, Muir wrote: "After a few miles of level ground in luxuriant tangles of brooding vines, I began the ascent of the Cumberland Mountains, the first real mountains my foot ever touched or eyes beheld . . . by a nearly regular zigzag slope, mostly covered up like a tunnel by overarching oaks" with "a few openings where the glorious forest road of Kentucky was grandly seen, stretching over hill and valley." Later that day he "passed the poor, rickety, thrice-dead village of Jamestown, an incredibly dreary place." Finding lodging and a meal of cornbread and bacon at a blacksmith's house he was warned that "walking across the Cumberland Mountains still was far from safe on account of small bands of guerrillas who were in hiding along the roads." His host, doubting that "picking up blossoms" was work fit for a "strong-minded man," was satisfied by Muir's arguments that Solomon, the world's wisest, not only picked but studied and wrote about plants from the great cedars of Lebanon "even unto the hyssop that springeth out of the wall" and "that Christ told his disciples to 'consider the lilies how they grow,' and compared their beauty with Solomon in all his glory."

Next day he crossed long stretches of level sandstone "dimpled with shallow groove-like valleys and hills" noting predominantly oaks and scattered pines, large areas beneath the trees covered with greenbrier "plant mancatchers" and abundant milkworts, asters, and goldenrods with cinnamon and royal ferns along each brook and laurel and azaleas fringing the larger streams. "Houses were far apart and uninhabited, orchards and fences in ruins—sad marks of war." Becoming aware of ten long-haired men on scrawny horses watching him, and taking them to be a guerrilla band, he boldly walked through them with a friendly "Howdy" and was allowed to pass because, he assumed, his plant press marked him, as a poor herb doctor. . . common. . . in these mountain regions." At dark he found the home of a black family who gave him a meal of cornbread, stringbeans, and buttermilk, and he spent the night under the trees.

On the 12th he "awoke drenched with mountain mist" and soon passed through Montgomery (just west of present Wartburg), a "shabby village at the head of the east slope of the Cumberland Mountains." Crossing Emory River he lingered in "a grand rock-dwelling full of mosses, birds, and flowers" where he found resurrection fern, big leaf magnolia, and towering clumps of beautiful Canada hemlocks. Later, he forded the Clinch, "a beautiful clear stream" and, reaching Kingston before dark, expressed his plant collection home to his brother.

Muir walked all the next day across small parallel valleys that "appear to have been formed by lateral pressure, are fertile, and contain some fine farms, though the seal of war is on all things." On September 14 he passed through Philadelphia in Loudon County, "a very filthy village in a beautiful situation" where black oak and Christmas fern "were most abundant." At Madisonville, "a brisk village," he "came in full view of the Unaka Mountains, a magnificent sight," and spent the night at a farmhouse.

Admiring "most billowy glorious mountain scenery" on September 15, he followed a road "in many places cut into the rock. . . winding about among the knobs and gorges." Stopping for the night at a mountaineer's cabin he went with him the next day to some gold mines, and the following day, to a "remarkably simple" grist mill, observing, "This is the most primitive country I have seen."

On September 18 he went "up the mountain on the state line" where "the scenery is far grander than any I ever before beheld. . . the view extends from the Cumberland Mountain to the north far into Georgia and North Carolina to the south. . . an ocean of wooded, waving, swelling mountain beauty and grandeur." At a mountain cabin that night he was warned to look out for thieves, murderers, and feuding neighbors. "Most of the food in this house was coffee without sugar, cornbread, and sometimes bacon," he observed, adding that "coffee. . . the greatest luxury which these people knew" was obtained "by selling skins or 'sang,' that is ginseng, which found a market in far-off China."

All next day Muir walked "along the leafy banks of the Hiwassee, a most impressive stream. . . its channel very rough, as it crosses the edges of upturned rock strata, some of them standing at right angles, or glancing off obliquely to right or left. . . its forest walls vine-draped and flowery as Eden. . . how fine a song it sings!"

Reaching Murphy, North Carolina, that evening, the next day he "was shown the site of Camp Butler where General Scott had his headquarters when he removed the Cherokee Indians to a new home in the West." Passing through Blairsville, Georgia, on the 21st and crossing the Blue Ridge on the 22nd, "the last summit on my way," he faced the very different prospect of "a vast uniform expanse of dark pine woods, extending to the sea."

Muir continued through Georgia to Savannah, then by boat to Fernandina on the east coast of Florida and across the peninsula to Cedar Keys on the Gulf in late October. After a bout with fever, he took a schooner in January to Cuba where he spent a month before taking another schooner carrying oranges to New York. There he booked steerage passage to Panama, crossed the isthmus by rail, then traveled steerage again to San Francisco, pausing there only a day before setting out for the Yosemite Valley. So ended a remarkable journey by a remarkable man who became the father of our Conservation Movement and the Sierra Club.

Natchez Trace Trail

The Trails System Act described this trail as following closely the Natchez Trace Parkway from the Tennessee state line in Wayne

County to Nashville, but development under the State Trails System Act was given a low priority. The Natchez Trace National Scenic Trail, however, was authorized by Congress in 1983 as a hiking and horseback trail to be built within the Natchez Trace Parkway right-of-way. In 1988 the National Park Service initiated development in three separate prototype sections of about 20 mi. each in Tennessee, Alabama, and Mississippi. The Tennessee section of the Trail was completed in 1992 and is maintained primarily by the National Park Service through its Volunteers in Parks program. It is described in Chapter 7.

The Natchez Trace Parkway, a unit of the National Park Service, was created in 1938 as a motor route to closely follow the course of the original trace.

Historical Note: Natchez Trace Trail

Countless centuries before the white man came, Native Americans used hunters' trails along the series of watershed divides that trend generally northwestward from the lower Mississippi River to the central basin of Tennessee. In 1540 Hernando de Soto's expedition wintered among the Chicasaw towns in northeast Mississippi near an ancient trail along this route. The old trail led from the towns of the Natchez, a people of basically Mississippian tradition in southwest Mississippi, through the Choctaw and Chickasaw nations to a game-rich hunting ground in middle Tennessee.

In the late 1600s French hunter-traders from the Illinois country first paddled up the Cumberland River to a great salt lick at the northern end of the ancient trail. Besides abundant buffalo, deer, elk, and bear, and some tenuous Shawnee settlements nearby, the Frenchmen found long-abandoned townsites and mounds of much earlier occupants.

By 1716 the Chickasaw and their eastern neighbors, the Cherokee, had driven the Shawnee out of middle Tennessee. That year, also, a French colony was planted among the Natchez at the southern end of the old trail. French hunters returned often to the great lick on the Cumberland and floated their pelts down the rivers to French Natchez.

In 1763 Natchez was ceded to England. Six years later a group of longhunters from Virginia came through Cumberland Gap in east Tennessee and over the highlands north of Cumberland River down to "French Lick." After a long and successful season, five of them set out in December down the Cumberland in canoes and buffalo boats loaded with pelts and bear meat. They reached Natchez the following spring. One of them, Kaspar Mansker, returned through Georgia to Virginia, possibly following the old trail northeast from Natchez to the Chickasaw towns, then turning east along the English traders' path to Augusta.

In the winter of 1779 several groups of families from Virginia and east Tennessee crossed Cumberland Gap and followed the longhunters' route to French Lick. They built a number of small forts, or "stations," in the area, including one on a cedar bluff just upstream from the lick. In 1784 the little town of Nashville was laid out on the hill above the cedar bluff as the seat of North Carolina's new Davidson County. These early Nashvillians used the old trail leading to the southwest to communicate with the friendly Chickasaw and thus knew it as the Chickasaw Trace.

By 1785 American settlers along the Ohio and Cumberland rivers had established farms and begun floating crops and products down the rivers to markets in Natchez and New Orleans, then under Spanish control. After selling the cargo, and their flatboats for lumber, the farmer-boatmen would return home by the most direct route, the old trace from Natchez to Nashville. They usually traveled in groups for safety and rode a tough mixed breed of horses called "Opelousas" caught from wild herds in Texas. Their trampings soon turned the old trace into a clearly marked path with frequent wide mud holes.

The American frontier's downriver trade grew rapidly after 1795 when Spain granted free access to the Mississippi and ceded Natchez to the United States. By 1800, the U.S. Postmaster General had contracted for mail to be carried monthly on the Trace between Natchez and Nashville.

One early mail carrier wrote of leaving Nashville on Saturday evening with the monthly mail pouch and riding almost 25 miles to reach the last white man's home by midnight. Climbing Duck River Ridge and riding another 20 miles, he breakfasted and fed his horse at John Gordon's ferry on Duck River. From there another 80-mile ride brought him to George Colbert's ferry on the Tennessee River.

George Colbert, son of a Scottish trader and his Chickasaw wife, was an influential Chickasaw leader. He started his ferry around 1800 and played a prominent role in the 1801 treaties with the Chickasaw and Choctaw that allowed the United States to open a wagon road along the old trace.

Once the treaties were signed, U.S. Army troops immediately began work clearing and widening the Trace on the approaches to Colbert's ferry and north to Duck River. John Gordon, Nashville's first postmaster, began operating his Duck River ferry in 1802 under a profit-sharing arrangement with George Colbert. The soldiers' work suddenly ceased in January 1803, when they were moved south of Natchez in response to Spanish threats.

The Louisiana Purchase in April 1803 gave the United States control of the Mississippi River and provided new impetus to traffic down the rivers and up and down the old Trace. Later that year, however, a detachment of Tennessee militia marching down to Natchez, and back to Nashville in early 1804, still found it to be "an excessively bad road." In May 1804, President Jefferson sent his young secretary, Meriwether Lewis, and William Clark, both Army officers, to explore the Purchase and, perhaps, to find a water route to the Pacific.

In 1805 the Choctaw and Chickasaw agreed to allow inns, or "stands," to be established along the Trace. The early stands were mostly crude one-room structures offering little more than a roof and shelter, a hard floor to sleep on, and simple meals such as milk, cornmeal mush, and fried bacon. They provided travelers a welcome respite, however, from bad weather, sickness, injury, or ambush by notorious bands of thieves and cutthroats such as those of John Murrell, Samuel Mason, John Hare, and the Harpe brothers.

In 1806 Congress appropriated $6,000 for building the Natchez Trace Road, and another $3,000 in 1809, but with such meager funding it never became a real road except near Natchez and Nashville. After the tramping of soldiers and volunteers down the Trace for many months before the Battle of New Orleans in January 1815, Andrew Jackson and his wife Rachel were able to ride in a carriage from Natchez to Nashville behind his victorious army as it marched northward that spring. The Natchez Trace, however, was always rough on wheeled vehicles and best traveled by horseback.

In 1811 the appearance of the first steamboat on the Mississippi heralded the end of the Natchez Trace as a national road. Within a decade flatboatmen were increasingly returning north from Natchez by this safer and faster mode. Tom Lincoln and his son Abe, for example, were both employed to take cargoes of goods by flatboat to Natchez, the father in 1806 and the son in 1828. Lincoln senior made his way as best he could over the Trace back to Kentucky. Abe had his return fare on a steamboat paid by his employer.

From the 1700s to the 1820s the Natchez Trace was the most significant highway of the old Southwest. During this brief period, five new states linked by the Trace—Kentucky, Tennessee, Louisiana, Mississippi, and Alabama—were admitted to the Union. Even in 1823 the U.S. Post Office considered it to be the safest and best, though circuitous, route from Washington to New Orleans.

During its heyday, many notable figures traveled on the Trace. James Robertson, founder of Nashville, rode it countless times from the 1780s to the 1800s, negotiating and sustaining the Americans' friendly relations with the Chickasaw Nation. Botanist François A. Michaux, seeing the Army working on the Trace in 1802, predicted, mistakenly, that it would be one of the finest roads in the United States.

Thomas Jefferson's vice president during his first term, Aaron Burr, was dropped by the Republican party from Jefferson's re-election ticket in 1804. In 1805 Burr traveled downriver to New Orleans and returned on the Natchez Trace, allegedly gathering support in a complex conspiracy to conquer Mexico and separate Louisiana and much of the old southwest from the Union to form a new republic. On a second trip to the Natchez district he was arrested on Jefferson's order and returned to Richmond for trial on a charge of treason. With Chief Justice John Marshall presiding, Burr was tried in mid-1807 and acquitted on account of conflicting evidence. Burr's leading accuser, General James Wilkinson, governor of the Louisiana Territory, was suspected, and later proved, to be in the pay of Spain, and barely escaped indictment himself.

Meriwether Lewis, just back from his exploration of the West, attended Burr's trial at Jefferson's request. With confidence in Wilkinson gone, Jefferson appointed his trusted former secretary as the general's successor. Shortly after his arrival in St. Louis in March 1808, Lewis found his assistant, who had been acting governor in Wilkinson's absence, to be devious and resentful. Early in 1809, with his mentor, Jefferson, no longer president, Lewis' expense drafts on the War Department were being denied and his financial management being questioned. Determined to defend his honor Lewis left St. Louis by flatboat in September bound for New Orleans and by sea to Washington, accompanied only by two servants. At Fort Pickering (now Memphis), where he had been commander a decade earlier, he learned of threats of war with Britain, and decided to proceed overland to avoid loss of his records if captured at sea. Proceeding east through the Chickasaw Nation with his two servants and Major James Neely, the Indian agent, and crossing the Tennessee River about October 8 he started north along the Natchez Trace. Thunderstorms on the 10th spooked two of the horses carrying Lewis' papers, and Neely remained to capture them while Lewis and the servants pressed on to reach Grinder's Stand (at the present Meriwether Lewis National Monument) just across the Chickasaw boundary in Tennessee. Late that night Lewis was shot, either by his own hand or by an assassin, and he died the next day, as told by the few witnesses present. Thomas Jefferson and other credible friends of Lewis concluded it was suicide as claimed by the witnesses, but others, including Lewis' sister and William Clark, his companion in the West, felt he was murdered; the mystery is debated to this day.

Alexander Wilson, the "Father of American Ornithology," traveled from Philadelphia through Kentucky and down the Trace by horseback and alone to Natchez in 1810. Leaving Nashvile he forded Harpeth River and probably climbed the ridge at the present Garrison Creek trailhead of the Natchez Trace National Scenic Trail, noting "cane growing, which increased until the whole woods were full of it," and "The road. . . winded along the high ridges of mountains that divide the waters of the Cumberland from those of the Tennessee" (Duck River Ridge). He stopped in early May at Grinder's Stand "where our poor friend Lewis perished" and heard Mrs. Grinder's apparently convincing account of the suicide.

In August 1811, Shawnee chief Tecumseh, accompanied by his younger brother, The Prophet, and twenty-four braves, came by canoe from the Wabash downriver on the Ohio and Mississippi to Fort Pickering then by trail to the Tennessee River and the Natchez Trace. Having united the northern tribes into a confederacy to stop the whites' advance into the Northwest, Tecumseh now came south to win the southern tribes to his cause. Failing to persuade George Colbert and the Chickasaws he continued down the Trace to the Choctaw and was again rebuffed. Only the Creeks agreed to war against the whites. In his oratory Tecumseh predicted that fire would cross the sky and the earth would shake as a sign of his coming victory, and, sure enough, a comet appeared in September brightening into October, and in December a series of tremors began along the New Madrid fault that lasted until March 1812 and caused the Mississippi to reverse flow and fill the sinking land to form Reelfoot Lake in extreme northwest Tennessee.

Tecumseh's confederacy met defeat that year at the battle of Tippecanoe, and he was killed in August 1813, soon after the

107

Creeks had massacred the garrison and all the settlers taking refuge at Forth Mims at the juncture of the Alabama and Tombigbee rivers. In March 1814, Andrew Jackson, Major General of U.S. Volunteers, met and defeated the Creeks at Horseshoe Bend on the Tallapoosa River in Alabama. In his army were 200 Chickasaw under George Colbert as well as the Cherokee Regiment. Two years earlier Jackson had received the name "Old Hickory" while marching his Tennessee volunteers up the Trace, and he had already ridden its length often over two decades and was to do so over another decade or so on both personal and official business.

A last poignant chapter of Natchez Trace history was written during Jackson's presidency when, in 1830, the Choctaw, and, in 1832, the Chickasaw ceded the last of their tribal lands east of the Mississippi to the United States and began their migration, some down the Trace, to resettlement in Oklahoma. By the end of the 1830s most of the Natchez Trace had reverted to a quiet forest lane of only local significance.

Source: The history above was mostly taken from *The Devil's Backbone: the Story of the Natchez Trace* by Jonathan Daniels; McGraw-Hill Book Company, New York, 1962.

Chickasaw Bluffs Trail

This trail, the seventh designated in the Trails System Act, is to run roughly from T.O. Fuller State Park south of Memphis to Fort Pillow State Park in Lauderdale County and, continuing northward, will terminate at Reelfoot Lake State Park. Implementation of this trail was halted in 1975 because of problems with the landowners, but short sections were laid out in Meeman-Shelby Forest State Park and Fort Pillow State Park. Descriptions of these sections are found in Chapter 5.

While the Chickasaw Bluffs State Scenic Trail has never materialized as the long hiking trail envisioned by the Tennessee Trails

System Act, a 177-mi. long bicycle back-country road route, the Mississippi River Trail, has been marked with roadside MRT logo signs from Memphis to Reelfoot Lake. From the I–40 Welcome Center in Memphis, the bike trail extends northward across Wolf River through Meeman-Shelby Forest State Park and along the Chickasaw Bluffs, across Hatchie River to Fort Pillow Sate Historic Park, then down onto the Mississippi River floodplain along ox-bow lakes past Plum Point and back onto the bluffs, across the Forked Deer River, and finally along the levee on the Great River Road to the Reelfoot Lake Visitors' Center. For a descriptive brochure detailing directions and mileage points or for detailed information regarding food, lodging, camping, bicycle service, points of interest, and other specifics contact: Mississippi River Trail, 7777 Walnut Grove Road, Box 27, Memphis, TN 38120, (901) 753–1400; http:/www.magibox.net/~lmddc/.

There are plans to extend this bicycle route along the Mississippi south to New Orleans and north to Lake Itaska, Minnesota.

Historical Note: Chickasaw Bluffs Trail

The Tennessee Trails System Act specifies that the Chickasaw Bluffs Trail follow "the scenic flood plains and bluffs of the Mississippi River." As described in the Appendix to this book, during the Ice Age dust created by the scouring action of the advancing glaciers was deposited as loess over West Tennessee, and then huge volumes of debris-choked melt water released by the retreating ice sheets cut the broad Mississippi Alluvial Plain from those deposits. Left along the eastern side of the Valley was an escarpment of slump-prone loess bluffs up to 100 feet high.

The productivity of this river system, the Alluvial Plain, and the Loess Plain east of the bluff—in terms of plants, fish, shellfish, game animals, and waterfowl—is legendary. From prehistoric times Native Americans cherished this rich and fertile land. In historic times the Chickasaw fought fiercely for their homeland here against the Spanish, the French and their Choctaw allies, and against the Shawnee and Creeks. The British respected Chickasaw lands and won their steadfast friendship as did, later, the Americans.

The first record of Europeans in the area is that of de Soto's crossing of the Mississippi at the fourth (southernmost in Tennessee) Chickasaw Bluff in 1541. In 1673, missionary Father Jacques Marquette and fur trader Louis Joliet came downriver by canoe or pirogue stopping briefly at an Indian town there. In 1682 Robert Cavalier de la Salle's party of French and northern Indians came downriver and camped a night at Plum Point about 2 miles upstream from today's Fort Pillow State Historic Park. The next day they stopped at the first Chickasaw Bluff, which they named *Fort Prudhomme* when their armorer Paul Prudhomme was lost for a time hunting, and a fort was built for the party's protection while searching for him. On the return trip, la Salle stopped here forty days to recover from a fever.

All these chroniclers mentioned abundant buffalo along the Mississippi. The journal of a French official, Diron d'Artaguette, who toured the river in 1723, contains numerous entries such as: "About noon we landed to go after a herd of more than a hundred buffaloes, both bulls and cows, of which we killed five and wounded more than twenty. We cut out only the tongues. . . We came to spend the night at the River a Margot (Wolf River) where we killed four buffaloes, of which we took only the tongues." By the mid-1700s large parties of French hunters frequented the river beneath the Chickasaw Bluffs killing staggering numbers of buffalo to meet commercial demand for tallow. Little wonder that by the late 1700s the buffalo was essentially extinct east of the Mississippi.

In 1729, in response to French demand for more land for their colony among the Natchez, 235 of the colonists were massacred by the Indians. The French retaliated by wiping out most of the Natchez people and burning four at the stake in New Orleans, leaving a small remnant to flee northward to refuge in the Chickasaw towns. At the end of the French and Indian War in 1763 France ceded New Orleans and Louisiana west of the Mississippi to

Spain, and their holdings on the east bank from Natchez to Illinois were ceded to England, which, in turn, recognized the Chickasaw claim to north Mississippi and West Tennessee.

Glowing reports of the fertility of the Mississippi Valley led to a series of attempts to colonize it, particularly by Virginians who believed western Tennessee and Kentucky lay within their colony's bounds. They were thwarted by England's prohibition of her colonies' expansion beyond the Appalachians into the lands of her Indian allies. However, the first American settlements on the frontier in Kentucky in 1775, and in Tennessee in 1779, were completely dependent upon the Cumberland, Ohio, and Mississippi river trade route giving new impetus to controlling the Mississippi. James Robertson in 1782 established a depot at "Chickasaw Bluff" (Memphis) to distribute supplies to the Chickasaw to keep them loyal to the Americans in the face of British overtures.

Samuel Cole Williams, in his *Beginnings of West Tennessee,* wrote: "The history of West Tennessee during the last decade of the 18th century is largely that of Chickasaw Bluffs. The interior was a closed country to all but the Chickasaw. . . . But the Bluffs were commanding because of their strategic location; and craved as a possession by Americans and Spaniards alike."

In 1795 the Spanish landed troops on the east bank at "Chickasaw Bluff" and started building Fort San Fernandino de las Barrancas. Upriver at New Madrid they stopped American boats bringing supplies to the Chickasaw. A treaty in November, 1795, however, opened the Mississippi and New Orleans to free passage for American goods and ceded Natchez, and all other Spanish claims northward on the east bank of the Mississippi, to the United States.

In 1797 the Americans built Fort Adams at the site of the abandoned Fort San Fernandino and in 1801 erected Fort Pickering 2 miles downstream on higher ground. Meanwhile, Spain had ceded New Orleans and Louisiana back to France. The Louisiana Purchase in 1803 and a treaty with the Chickasaw in 1818 that sold their lands east of the Mississippi to the United States finally gave the U.S. complete control of this artery so vital to the western states.

Settlement of West Tennessee followed rapidly in the 1820s, most of it flowing from North Carolina, which was especially hard hit by the panic of 1819, and by a severe drought in 1826. Some settlers came overland on the Walton Road and Glover's Trace, but many traveled by flatboat down the Tennessee, Cumberland, Ohio, and Mississippi and up the Forked Deer, and Wolf and, particularly up the Hatchie. The interior counties along these tributaries, believed to be healthier and less flood-prone than the Mississippi floodplain, were settled first. By the 1830s, the counties along the Mississippi were growing more rapidly. Randolph, just below the mouth of the Hatchie, was a busy riverport and promised to get busier when, in 1825, the legislature authorized a canal to connect the lower Tennessee River with the upper Hatchie, but this project never materialized. With the accelerated dominance of "King Cotton" in north Mississippi and in Shelby and the adjacent counties of Tennessee, Memphis soon became the major steamboat riverport between St. Louis and New Orleans and the cotton trading center of the region.

The first steamboat to pass the Chickasaw Bluffs, the *New Orleans* built at Pittburg by Nicholas Roosevelt, came down the Mississippi just ahead of the worst shocks of the earthquake along the New Madrid fault in 1811. Until the 1820s travel on the river and its tributaries was by keelboat or lesser craft, but in 1828 a steamboat went up the Hatchie to Brownsville, and in the early 1830s another plied the Forked Deer as far as Jackson, but found the channel blocked in places by keelboats abandoned during low water. Demands upon the state for channel improvements met with so little success, and navigation on the tributaries remained so uncertain, that the rapidly growing interior towns began building bridges and opening their own roads and turnpikes. By 1840, according to Samuel Cole Williams, "there was a network of post and stage roads throughout the District." By 1861 three railway lines spanned West Tennessee, including the Mobile and Ohio from Columbus, Kentucky through Jackson, Tennessee to Corinth, Mississippi and Mobile.

In May 1861 Tennessee mobilized troops under the command of Gideon J. Pillow, a West Point graduate and Mexican War veteran. Pillow moved quickly to close the Mississippi as an inviting invasion route for Union forces already controlling the Ohio, the Mississippi upstream from Cairo, Illinois, and most of neutral Kentucky. He began fortifying Memphis, Randolph, and, especially, the First Chickasaw Bluff.

After Tennessee's secession in June, Confederate General Leonidas Polk took command of its troops and continued building Fort Pillow at the First Chickasaw Bluff. In September, Polk occupied Columbus, Kentucky, barely ahead of General U. S. Grant coming down from Cairo, and he began making it a major strongpoint with Island No. 10 and New Madrid, Missouri, as back-up defenses downstream. Grant countered by occupying Paducah on the Ohio just downstream from the mouths of the Cumberland and the Tennessee.

By January 1862 it became apparent that invasion via the Mississippi was not the immediate threat as Grant assembled troops, gunboats, and supplies for a thrust just across the Tennessee line up the Tennessee at poorly located Fort Henry and up the Cumberland at still unfinished Fort Donelson. With the fall of both forts in February, Federal gunboats steamed quickly up the Tennessee to Pittsburg Landing and up the Cumberland to Nashville. The Confederate forces soon withdrew from Middle Tennessee and by early April were concentrated at Corinth ready to cross into Tennessee and strike the Federals at Pittsburg Landing. Polk, outflanked and vulnerable, withdrew from Columbus to Corinth leaving garrisons at Island No. 10 and New Madrid.

On April 7, while Grant was repelling the attack on Pittsburg Landing in bitter fighting around Shiloh Church, Island No. 10 and New Madrid fell to a combined Federal ground and naval attack. On the 14th the flotilla of gunboats and 20,000 troops on transports began bombarding Fort Pillow. On the 17th all but 1,500 of the Federal troops left to join in besieging the Confederate army in Corinth, and the siege of Fort Pillow became a naval bombardment punctuated by sharp engagements between Federal and Confederate gunboats. On June 4, a few days after the Federals captured Corinth, the Confederates evacuated Fort Pillow, and it was occupied by the Federals until General Nathan Bedford Forrest recaptured and destroyed it in April 1864 (see Chapter 7).

Meanwhile, the Confederates had fallen back to Tupelo and Vicksburg in Mississippi and their attempt to retake Corinth in October 1862 failed. Except for Forrest's slashing calvary attacks in West Tennessee along the Mobile and Ohio, the action had moved south and centered along the Chickasaw Bluffs at Vicksburg. When Grant took that stronghold in July 1863, almost simultaneously with Lee's defeat at Gettysburg, the tide clearly turned against the Southern cause. Bragg was retreating from Middle Tennessee, and, though victorious at Chickamauga in September, he was beaten by Grant at Chattanooga in November, and the Army of Tennessee began its strategic retreat to Atlanta.

An equally compelling drama probably more profound and lasting in its effects than the Civil War, has played out along the Chickasaw Bluffs since the mid 1800s. Drainage of wetlands, incredibly rich biologically and essential as nature's flood control and soil conservation mechanism, and their conversion to cotton and, more recently, soybean fields, was unrelenting—first by private landowners, then by quasi-governmental drainage districts and the U.S. Army Corps of Engineers.

The first serious resistance to wholesale drainage occurred at Reelfoot Lake, the 25,000-acre wetland of shallow open water and cypress swamps created in extreme northwest Tennessee by the great quake of 1811–12. In 1899 a landowner, James C. Harris had finally amassed titles to all the parcels underlying the lake and announced his intention to drain it and plant cotton. Many residents on the eastern shore whose livelihoods depended on harvesting its game and bountiful fish joined together to legally contest Harris's title, but the courts ruled in his favor. Harris died before effecting his plan, but his son, in concert with the West Tennessee Land Company, monopolized the marketing of the fish taken from "his" lake, drastically reducing the incomes of the resident fishermen. Again unable to get relief from the courts, many of the fishermen banded together in a secret clan of Night Riders to get justice through intimidation. Though silently supported by many local citizens initially, the clan degenerated into a vehicle for settling private animosities and, sometimes, for racial harassment. Brutal beatings soon lessened local support, and the murder of an attorney associated with the Harris heir brought arrest and trial of the clan leaders and, ultimately, dismissal of the indictments against them because of technical legal errors and long delays. The most important result of the affair was the Tennessee Supreme Court's ruling in 1913 that the lake was navigable and, therefore, the land beneath the lake could not be privately controlled. By 1914 the lake was a protected state preserve and is comprised today of a National Wildlife Refuge, a State Wildlife Management Area, and a small State Park.

In 1940, Edward J. Meeman, editor of *The Memphis Press-Scimitar*, and friends had a vision called the Forest of Discovery extending along the Chickasaw Bluffs. Congress authorized a purchase unit for the land, and 7,000 attended its dedication near Randolph; some of the dignitaries arriving by steamboat. With the onset of World War II in 1941, however, the funds were dedicated to the war effort, and the project died. While the vision never materialized exactly as Meeman saw it, some of it has come to pass through preserves established by the U.S. Fish and Wildlife Service, the Tennessee Wildlife Resources Agency, and the Tennessee Department of Environment and Conservation. These include four National Wildlife Refuges, three State Wildlife Management Areas, and three State Parks.

In the 1960s four individual Nashville citizens who were avid duck hunters and conservationists—Clark Akers, Bill Dillon, Amon Evans, and Sam Harwell—became deeply concerned over the destruction of waterfowl habitat caused by the U.S. Army Corps of Engineers' dredging and straightening of the Obion and Forked Deer river channels and they obtained a court injunction on those activities. These four were successful in awakening the interest of the Corps and the general public in arresting the destruction, and beginning the restoration, of wildlife habitat along the Mississippi River corridor, one of the four major migratory bird flyways in North America and, even at this late date, possessing a significant remnant of its historic endemic bottomland hardwood forest. In recent years many private conservation organizations have actively joined this effort including Ducks Unlimited, The Nature Conservancy, The Tennessee Conservation League, and The Wolf River Conservancy

The Chickasaw Bluffs Trail, like the Cumberland Trail, when completed will traverse the state north to south along an escarpment that forms the boundary of a regional physiographic province. It is replete with geologic, ecological, and cultural significance.

Sources: Beginnings of West Tennessee by Samuel Cole Williams; *Confederate Victories at Fort Pillow* by Edward F. Williams III (Historical Hiking Trails, Inc.); *Night Riders of Reelfoot Lake* by Paul J. Vanderwood (*Tennessee Historical Quarterly*, vol. XXVIII).

5. Trails in State Parks

In 1977 there were 117 trails in Tennessee state parks, and trail development was going forward at a rapid pace. From 1977 to 1987 at least ten new parks were added to the system. Among these newer parks, Roan Mountain, famous for purple rhododendron (*Rhododendron catawbiense*), has an excellent system, including ski trails, connecting with the Appalachian Trail and adjacent national forests in Tennessee and North Carolina. State forests, many of which are adjacent to, or surround, state parks, also contain extensive mileage of trails. Today, Tennessee's State Parks and Forests contain 298 trails totaling more than 850 mi. in length. We describe some of the best of these trails in areas with the greatest public interest, because of special geographic location, scenic values, or vacation opportunities.

Big Ridge State Park

Located on the southern part of Norris Lake, the park is accessible via either TN 61 east from I-75 at the Norris Clinton Exit or west from TN 33 north of Knoxville. The latter approach is not recommended for trailer traffic.

Big Ridge State Park is located within the Ridge and Valley geologic region of Tennessee. There are three large ridges—Chestnut, Pinnacle, and Big Ridge—that bisect the park and run parallel to each other in a northeast-southwest direction. Norris Lake almost completely surrounds Pinnacle Ridge and Big Ridge to form a large peninsula, and the only access to this area is by hiking trails. The park is also home to Big Ridge Lake, a fifty-acre body of water created by the TVA and CCC when they built a small dam across one of the coves of Norris Lake. The level of Norris Lake fluctuates

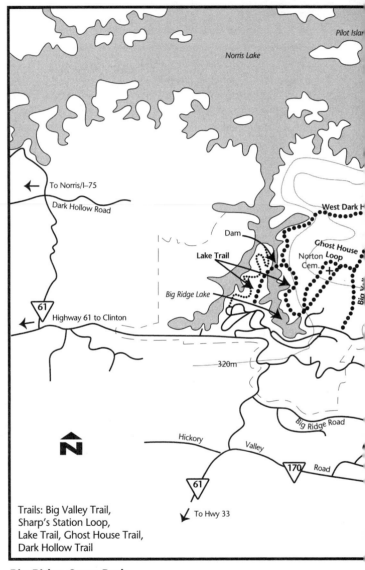

Big Ridge State Park

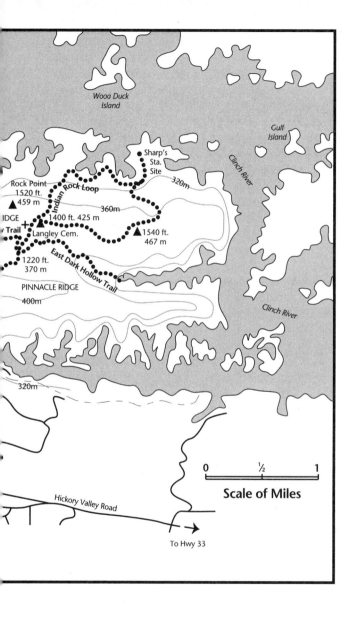

Wooa Duck
Island

Gulf
Island

Sharp's
Sta.
Site

Clinch River

320m

Rock Point
1520 ft.
▲ 459 m

Indian Rock Loop

360m

IDGE
Trail

1400 ft. 425 m

Langley Cem.

▲ 1540 ft.
467 m

1220 ft.
370 m

East Dark Hollow Trail

PINNACLE RIDGE

400m

Clinch River

320m

0   ½   1

Scale of Miles

Hickory Valley Road

To Hwy 33

greatly between summer and winter, so the purpose of creating Big Ridge Lake was to provide a constant water level for the cabins, group camp, boat dock, and swimming beach. Paddle boats, fishing boats, and canoes are available for rent, but motorized boats are not allowed on this lake.

Back-country camping is available at Big Ridge State Park. Campsite information, maps, and a required permit can be obtained from rangers at the park office. The trails are all marked with colors that correspond to the colored lettering on each trail's signs.

Big Valley Trail. Length, 1.3 mi.; rating, moderate, blazes, orange. The trail starts from a park road 100 yds. east of the park manager's residence and the parking area for the grist mill (elevation 1,050 ft). It begins in open pine woods, climbs a gentle rise, and descends through a thicket to cross a shaded glen. Next, it ascends a long slope with a deep ravine on the right. The trail then crosses a low saddle and descends into a little valley through lush ferns before crossing another glen with a footbridge over a tiny stream. The trail climbs a sharp rise for a few yards followed by a long, easy slope on a broad hillside through open woods. The pines begin to give way to young hardwoods such as dogwood, tulip poplar, maple, and elm as the Ghost House Trail intersects the path about 0.6 mi. from the trailhead. Big Valley Trail then becomes steeper for 100 yds. and moves into a mixed pine and hardwood forest as it ascends the toe of Pinnacle Ridge. At the summit, near 1,400 ft. elevation, the trail follows the side of the ridge overlooking a deep valley on the right and begins a gradual descent to a narrow saddle. Yellow star grass blooms along the trail, which passes through a patch of crested dwarf iris as it drops sharply to a low dome, then to another saddle and ends at the intersection with Dark Hollow Trail at 1,220 ft.

Indian Rock Loop Trail. Length 3.0-mi. loop; rating, moderate; blazes, red. This trail begins where the Big Valley Trail ends, at the intersection of the Dark Hollow Trail. It begins with a steep ascent up Big Ridge. The trail passes the old Langley Cemetery, where the only modern gravestone marks the resting place of young Edward Loy who died in 1932 at the age of six. All the other graves are marked with fieldstones at the head and foot and contain no inscriptions. The trail becomes steeper before it levels out on top of Big Ridge at about 1,400 ft. elevation At 0.4 mi. the trail splits to form a loop where the trail to the right continues east, following the crest of Big Ridge and the trail to the left runs north down the ridge toward Norris Lake. The right-fork trail rises gradually to 1,460 ft. then drops through a saddle before climbing back to 1,470 ft. Along the trail are many stone walls and natural rock outcroppings. One of the largest is Indian Rock, which features a plaque marking the spot where Indians ambushed and scalped one of the first pioneers, Peter Graves, in 1794. The highest point in the park, 1,550 ft., is farther along the ridge to the northeast. The trail continues only a short distance past Indian Rock, where it turns north down Big Ridge to meet the other end of the trail loop. The trail plunges straight down the ridge and caution should be taken, because there are no switchbacks in this section. The trail begins to level out in an area filled with many large white oak trees. It then drops down to a trail junction where a short 0.2 mi. side trail to the right leads to Sharp's Station, one of the first frontier stations (forts) in the East Tennessee area. It was built at approximately the same time as James White's Fort, which later became Knoxville. At the end of the side trail, near the shoreline of Norris Lake, is a monument with a plaque marking the site of the station. Returning to the trail junction, the loop continues westward along the lakeshore through cedar glades and then turns back southward into the hardwood forest before climbing to the top of Big Ridge, ending the loop.

Dark Hollow Trail. Length, 3.0 mi.; rating, moderate; blazes, white. This trail begins at the eastern end of the dam from the Lake Trail at Big Ridge Lake. It runs north along the shoreline of Norris Lake then rises sharply past mountain laurel and winds around a steep hillside. After crossing a deep ravine and skirting the end of Pinnacle Ridge, the trail crosses a stream running into a cove of Norris Lake. The trail turns right and runs east up Dark Hollow, which splits Big Ridge and Pinnacle Ridge. This section of trail was at one time Dark Hollow Road. Both ends of the road were closed by the impoundment of Norris Lake in 1937. Along the trail, old rock foundations from cabins and other outbuildings can still be detected, evidence of another period in time. The trail crosses the Big Valley Trail in a saddle between the two ridges and continues east down the old road along another small stream to Norris Lake, where the trail dead-ends.

Lake Trail. Length, 1.5 mi.; rating, easy; blazes, green. This trail circles approximately three-fourths of Big Ridge Lake. The park road from the group camp to the park office completes the loop around the lake, for a hike of approximately 2.0 mi. As you start the hike from the trailhead near the park office (elevation 1,020 ft.), the trail begins to climb through a mixed pine and hardwood forest. At 0.1 mi. there is a side trail to the right. This trail is 0.2 mi. long and leads to Meditation Point where there is a small shelter. The Lake Trail continues to climb and then levels off at 1,100 ft. where, on the steep slope to the right, ice storm and blizzard damage is evidenced by the many pine trees that are lying on the ground. The trail begins a gradual descent and at 0.4 mi. there is another side trail to the left. This trail is 0.3 mi. long and leads to Loyston Overlook (elevation 1,200 ft.). In the winter when the tree foliage is down, the overlook offers excellent views of Norris Lake and Loyston Sea. The name "Loyston" comes from the town that was inundated when Norris Lake was created. The Lake Trail continues to descend until it reaches Big Ridge Dam, where there is a wooden bridge above the concrete dam that offers beautiful views of both lakes. After crossing the dam, the Dark Hollow Trail begins to the left and the Lake Trail continues to the right where it follows the shoreline before turning left to cross a small stream at the end of a large cove. After hiking around the cove, the trail once again comes close to the shoreline where, from a park bench located here, hikers can see the park facilities across the lake. Directly behind the bench, on a little knoll, is the Snodderly Cemetery, the largest cemetery in the park. The Lake Trail continues around the lake where it intersects the Ghost House Trail on the left, and after 100 yds. it ends at the park road near the group camp.

Ghost House Loop Trail. Length, 1.2 mi; rating, easy; blazes, yellow. This trail can be accessed from both the Lake and Big Valley trails. Part of the trail was a road at one time and along it remnants of old homesteads can still be seen along with rock foundations and cisterns. Norton Cemetery is on this trail. It is the destination of night-time hikes where ghost stores are told by park naturalists during the summer. Some of the most popular stories are about area resident Maston Hutcheson, born in 1826 and buried in this cemetery in 1910.

—Updated by Alan Wasik

Pickett State Park and Pickett State Forest

Both park and forest are located on TN 154 about 10 mi. northeast of Jamestown off U.S. 127. From U.S. 27, to the east, follow TN 297 (Leatherwood Ford Road) from Oneida across the Big South Fork National River and Recreation Area to TN 154 and turn right.

There are 33 mi. of day-use trails in Pickett State Park. Camping is restricted to park campgrounds. In addition, the Sheltowee Trace National Recreation Trail, formerly the Great Meadow Trail, and the John Muir State Scenic Trail have been extended to park head-quarters. There are fourteen trails to choose from, all interconnected, making it possible to begin at one end and hike all the trails in sequence. There is a great diversity along the way in both vegetation and landscape. Several places on the trails offer a true feeling of wilderness. Most trails are connected to the main park area at some point, and many of them have rest shelters along the way. These shelters were originally built by the CCC in the early 1930s and are mainly constructed of logs from the American chestnut.

There is a vast territory of wild land surrounding Pickett State Park and Forest. Hundreds of miles of jeep roads and foot trails tra-

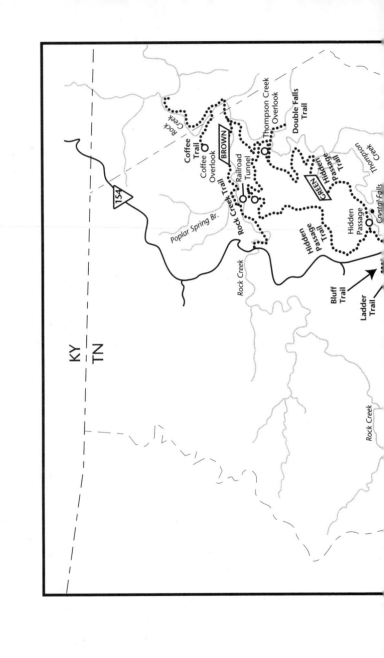

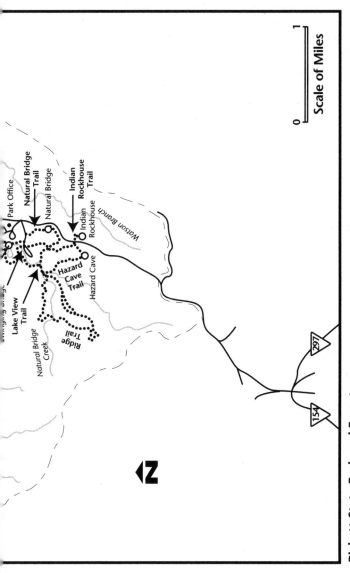

Pickett State Park and Forest

Scale of Miles
0 — 1

Park Office

Natural Bridge Trail

Natural Bridge

Indian Rockhouse Trail

Indian Rockhouse

Watson Branch

Hazard Cave Trail

Hazard Cave

Lake View Trail

Ridge Trail

Natural Bridge Creek

N

297

154

verse the area. The Sheltowee Trace National Recreation Trail connects Pickett's trails with those of the Daniel Boone National Forest in Kentucky. Pickett adjoins the Big South Fork Area, developed by the U.S. Army Corps of Engineers and managed by the National Park Service. There are more than 170 mi. of hiking trails in the Big South Fork. U.S.G.S. topographic quadrangle maps that cover this area are Bell Farm, KY; Barthell SW, TN; Sharp Place, TN; and Pall Mall, TN. These are recommended for planning trips into this area and may be obtained by writing to the Tennessee Division of Geology, L&C Tower 401 Church Street, Nashville, TN 37243, and to the Kentucky Geological Survey, Lexington, JY 40506, for the Kentucky map.

The recent addition of 5,000 acres to the state forest along its western boundary substantially increases the possibility of expanding the already outstanding hiking trail system in this wild and beautiful preserve. Most notably, the thirty-year-old plan to extend the John Muir State Scenic Trail westward about 8 mi. to the Sgt. Alvin C. York State Historic Site should soon be achievable (see Chapter 4).

Only two trails from Pickett State Park are described in this guide. All other trails, except the Sheltowee Trace National Recreation Trail, are color-coded for easier identification, as listed below.

Natural Bridge Trail, brown, 1.5-mi. loop, easy; Indian Rockhouse Trail, orange, 0.5 mi. one way, easy; Hazard Cave Trail, white, 2.5-mi. loop, moderate; Ridge Trail, green, 3-mi. loop, moderate; Lake View Trail, gray, 0.8-mi. loop, easy; Bluff Trail, yellow, 1 mi. one way, easy; Ladder Trail, brown, 1-mi. loop, moderate to difficult; Island Trail, blue, 1-mi. loop, easy; Double Falls Trail, white, 1 mi. one way, moderate to difficult; Tunnel Trail, no blazes, 1 mi. one way, moderate to difficult; Coffee Trail, orange, 2 mi. one way, moderate to difficult.

Hidden Passage Trail. Length, 8 mi.; rating, easy; blazes, green; a trail for all seasons, this loop follows the 1,500-ft. contour above Thompson Creek, a clear stream of spring water that oozes continually from a 300-ft.-thick sandstone filter, the Cumberland

Plateau. Sometimes the sounds of a mighty rushing torrent may be heard from the trail, but at other times a hiker must peer over the edge of the bluff to be sure there is still water in the stream. The trail reverses on the ridge above the confluence of Thompson and Rock creeks. Rock Creek is another clear mountain stream rushing northward into Kentucky to the Cumberland River. For several miles the trail winds along the 1,600-ft. countour above Rock Creek and then returns across a flat ridge to its origin. The Hidden Passage Trail is so named because of a natural sandstone tunnel through a bluff.

There are two spur trails off the main trail. One is the Double Waterfalls, and exciting, one-way, 1-mi. walk from a dry forest setting to the rhododendron-and viburnum-covered banks of Thompson Creek. During early spring this trail boasts many wildflowers with such species as pinxter flower, mayapple, bloodroot, *Trillium flexipes*, and at least five species of violets, to name a few. The other spur is the Tunnel Trail, a winding 1-mi. path through the shade of eastern hemlock, big-leafed magnolia, and tulip poplar to an old railroad tunnel on Rock Creek. The tunnel is unsafe for entry, but it is interesting to stand outside and imagine the labors of the rugged men who built this tunnel in the last century.

The Hidden Passage Trail is a trail for all seasons because of its rugged beauty and interesting variety of botanical species visible all through the year. During the early winter while the deciduous forest is clothed in somber brown, there are still enough greens to suggest the freshness of spring. Then, as winter storms begin, the white cover of snow gives the landscape a cheerful, welcoming appeal. On the ridges, generally above 1,500 ft. elevation, there are shortleaf and Virginia pine. Down in the valleys are the eastern hemlock and white pine. There are many other evergreen plants that add to the winter beauty along the trail. The ground is covered with trailing arbutus, boxwood, huckleberry, and partridgeberry. Interlacing clumps of teaberry, two species of lycopodium, and a fair sprinkling of lichens and mosses add to the allure. Between the trees and ground cover, there is much mountain laurel, rhododendron, and American holly.

There are wild hog tracks and signs of deer scrounging for acorns beneath the snow. In the early morning hours, it is common to see one of the many barred owls that live in Pickett Forest. The pileated woodpecker and the red-cockaded woodpecker have also been spotted there.

Like clockwork each March, as the vernal equinox arrives so do the white blossoms of the trailing arbutus and the pale blue of the bluets, which are followed in continuous succession by an array of wildflowers throughout the summer and into the fall. Some of the rarest of these gems are the grass of parnassus and the roundleaved catchfly, both of which can be seen near the trail. These are only a few of the highlights of the Hidden Passage Trail.

—*Contributed by George Minnigh*

Rock Creek Trail. Length, about 5 mi.; rating moderate, blazes, brown. This one-way trail runs from Thompson Creek Overlook on the Hidden Passage Trail to TN 154, 3.5 mi. north of park headquarters, Sharp Place USGS quad, 335 SE. Actually, the Rock Creek Trail starts about 0.3 mi. from the overlook, but that point makes a natural starting place for this hike. Down the side of a ridge the trail crosses a branch on a slippery log and follows a switchback path up to the junction. The Rock Creek Trail goes to the right, a fairly level path on a broad ridge for 0.3-0.5 mi., drops down the toe of the ridge 200 yds., follows a shelf along a bluff another 200 yds., and then slopes down to Thompson Creek and the confluence with Rock Creek.

Turning left up Rock Creek, the trail crosses to the junction with the Coffee Trail in the shade of yellow and sweet birches and cucumber magnolia trees. The trail goes left from the junction, follows a rocky bluff, and crosses a stream with a tiny waterfall on the right. It climbs high on the bluff a short distance, then follows the Poplar Spring Branch. After crossing the branch it drops back to Rock Creek. A stream flows through a pipe from the right, having traveled underground from a point 0.3 mi. upstream. The trail drops back to Rock Creek and crosses it, then follows an old railroad bed. After crossing the creek two more times, the trail reaches a white pine grove on the left, then ends at a forest road a short distance from TN 154.

During a summer hike it is possible to cross Rock Creek and only wet the soles of your hiking boots. But the water is knee-deep during wet seasons. Also, there are icy spots on the trail in winter.

Fall Creek Falls State Park

This is a combination resort park and natural area, located on the western edge of the Cumberland Plateau between Spencer and Pikeville. It may be reached from TN 30 (north entrance) or from TN 111 (south entrance). The park, which straddles the Van Buren-Bledsoe county line, consists of 19,300 acres—15,800 purchased by the National Park Service in 1935 and 3,500 added in 1995-96 through the State and Local Parks Partnership Fund (to protect the habitat of endangered species and the viewshed from Milliken's Overlook). Some development occurred during the Depression with the help of young men in the Civilian Conservation Corps (CCC) and others working under the Works Projects Administration (WPA). The land was deeded to the state of Tennessee for a park in 1944. The farms that were purchased by the National Park Service have reforested, mainly by natural succession, into almost pure stands of Virginia pine. The rest of the upland areas of the park are second growth oak-hickory forest, while the gorges are filled with stands of hemlock, basswood, yellow poplar, and yellow birch.

The major scenic attractions of the park are the gorges and their waterfalls. Fall Creek Falls, 256 ft. high, is 63 ft. higher than Niagara Falls. Views of the falls at the head of each gorge, as well as a broad overview of Cane Creek Gorge, are easily accessible by trail or by automobile. There are four short trails and two long

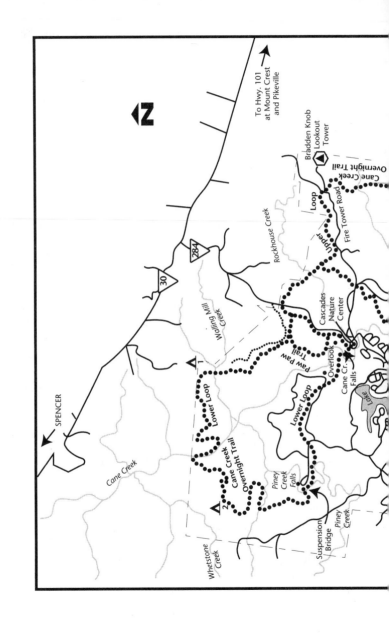

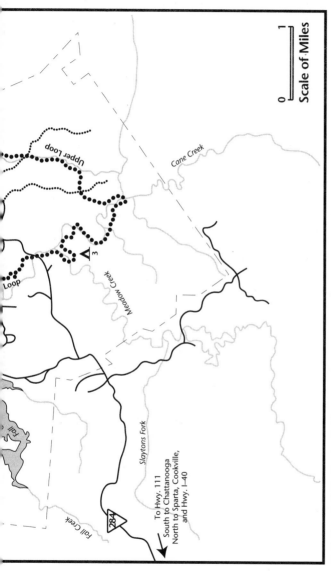

Fall Creek Falls State Park

Scale of Miles

0   1

Upper Loop

Cane Creek

Loop

3

Meadow Creek

Fall

Slaytons Fork

To Hwy. 111
South to Chattanooga
North to Sparta, Cookville,
and Hwy. I-40

284

Fall Creek

overnight loops in the park. A trail map of the park is available for the asking from the Tennessee Department of Environment and Conservation, 7th Floor, L&C Tower, 401 Church Street, Nashville, TN 37243-0446. The map is a composite of appropriate topographic maps of the U.S. Geological Survey, reduced in size. The overnight trails and campsites are marked clearly in red and are accurately represented.

The short trails include the trail to the top of Fall Creek Falls, 1 mi. from the nature center to the top of the falls; the trail to the foot of Fall Creek Falls, 0.5 mi.; the Cable Trail to the foot of Cane Creek Falls, 0.2 mi.; and the Pawpaw Trail, a 4-mi. loop.

The Pawpaw Trail. Length, 4 mi.; rating, moderate. The trail, which is in a hardwood forest rich in wildflowers, leaves the parking lot of the nature center and parallels the road to the north entrance for several hundred yards. The Cable Trail to the foot of Cane Creek Falls leads off to the left 0.3 mi. from the nature center and descends abruptly 200 ft. to the bottom of the gorge. A few hundred yards farther along, a side trail exits to an east rim overlook of Cane Creek Falls. Shortly thereafter, the Pawpaw Trail begins a loop. The eastern side parallels the north entrance road to 1,800 ft. elevation. (The nature center is at 1,600 ft.) At the highest point on the loop, the Pawpaw Trail turns west for 0.5 mi., then south, roughly parallel to the eastern rim of the Cane Creek Gorge back to the beginning of the loop. One may return to the nature center by the connecting trail.

Overnight Trails. The two overnight trails are called the **Cane Creek Overnight Trail—Lower Loop** (length, 12 mi.; rating, difficult) and the **Cane Creek Overnight—Upper Loop** (length, 13 mi.; rating, moderate). Presumably, these designations refer to the lower and upper elevations of Cane Creek. The use of either trail requires registration at the nature center. A parking area is provided for users of the trails at the old Maintenance Center, 0.2 mi. south of the north entrance and 0.2 mi. east (left) of the main road. The parking area, on a trail that connects the two loops, is 0.3 mi. from the lower loop and 1 mi. from the upper loop. Each loop will be traversed in a clockwise directions with the center of each loop as a point of reference.

The Lower Loop encircles all of the gorges within the boundaries of the park. The trail dips into and crosses Cane Creek Gorge—an elevation change of 600 ft.—close to the northern boundary of the park. West of the parking area, the connector trail crosses the road from the north entrance and continues 100 yds. or so to the junction with the Pawpaw Trail. Either side of the Pawpaw Loop may be followed to the Nature Center. The Fall Creek Falls Trail is followed to the falls parking area, then the west road is taken for 25 to 50 yds. to a white blaze well up in the trees on the right. The trail leads to Piney Creek Falls (2 mi.) through rather open forest and glades where blueberries and wildflowers are abundant in the summertime. An alternate route to Piney Creek Falls for those who like scenic overlooks (and don't mind sharing the road with automobiles) follows the Gorge Scenic Drive Motor Nature Trail (4 mi.). For this alternative, take the road north from the Fall Creek Falls parking area.

At Piney Creek there are rock ledges that serve as most satisfactory vantage points for observing the beauty of the falls and the upper end of Piney Creek Gorge. A suspension bridge crosses Piney Creek, and the next 2 miles are again on a gently rolling forest trail ending at campsite 2, as numbered by the Parks Division. The site is in a well-forested area, has three camping "nodes" that are placed to assure the privacy of each occupant, a privy, and a pump that produces clear, cold water. Be forewarned, however, that during dry periods of the year (normally summer and early fall) this well often goes dry. One-third of a mile past the campsite, the trail begins to descend into the gorge. For the most part the trail down is in good condition. However, some of the wooden footbridges may be slick in wet weather, and it is wise to be careful. In addition, there is a stretch of loose rocks where the footing may be insecure. Down in the gorge the vegetation becomes thicker, and at the edge of Cane Creek the trees and moss are thick and lush. From late fall to early spring, Cane Creek is a full, busy, and noisy stream. During all but the periods of highest flow, there are places to rock-hop across. By contrast, Cane Creek may become bone dry in summer. A bridge has been built at this point, providing a safer, more comfortable crossing when the creek is up.

Although water flows over the falls, it quickly disappears and flows underground. At the trail crossing one can usually find a pool within 200 to 300 yds. downstream, nestling in a desert of boulders. With luck, the water will be deep enough to submerge in and share a natural cooling system with timid minnows, crayfish, mayfly nymphs, and maybe even a very shy salamander. The trail out of the gorge follows a zigzag course up to the eastern rim. The 600 ft. of elevation that was lost in descending now has to be regained. Even if it is cool at the bottom, a hiker is warm or even steaming by the time the top is reached. Fortunately, there are some outcrops on the way up that are rich in fossils, giving an excuse for a breather. On the rim the trail again goes through gently rolling upland forest about 1 mi. to campsite 1. It is similar to campsite 2, but the water from the pump, while potable, is unusually rich in minerals. This well, like that at campsite 2, often goes dry during arid periods of the year. There is a creek 75 yds. on down the trail, but this water must be treated before drinking. Two miles past campsite 1 the trail returns to the maintenance center parking area via the north side of the Pawpaw Trail and the connector trail.

The Upper Loop is in the southern portion of the park and is entirely on the gently rolling upland plateau, average elevation 1,800 ft. The maximum variation in elevation along the trail is 200 ft. The southernmost tip of the loop comes within 0.7 mi. of the southern boundary of the park. The outstanding feature of this loop is the vegetation, with extensive fern beds sometimes covering several acres. Reforestation has been successful, and there is abundant animal life. Following the connector trail south, one comes to the beginning of the Upper Loop Trail within a short mile. Following the fork to the east (left), the trail reaches and crosses a gravel road after 1.5 mi. The road leads to the lookout tower on top of

Bradden Knob, about 0.3 mi. off the trail. Bradden Knob is the highest point in the park, slightly more than 2,000 ft.

The trail goes almost due south for the next 3 mi. After a long mile the trail picks up Flatrock Branch and follows it to its confluence with Cane Creek, which it crosses on a suspension bridge. If it is a warm day, this is a good spot to take a swim—or a splash. Even when the creek below the falls is dry, this part usually has water flowing.

The eastern side of this loop has extensive fern beds and patches of blueberries. This part is hardly used, and ferns and other plants have grown in the trail. A wide variety of birds can be observed. On a July day a ruffed grouse and deer tracks may be seen in several areas. A mile past the suspension bridge, down Cane Creek, the trail reaches campsite 3. There are four camping nodes and a privy. The water supply comes from Cane Creek, which is no more than 30 yds. from any of the nodes. The water must be treated before drinking. Past campsite 3 the trail snakes along the Cane Creek bottoms for the next 1.5 mi., crossing Meadow Creek along the way; it crosses Cane Creek on an automobile bridge on one of the roads leading to the south entrance. Beyond the bridge and across the road, the trail enters woods again and ascends 100 ft. or so. After 3 mi. of forest and glades and one more road crossing, the trail reaches the connector trail to the maintenance center parking area.

The abundance of ferns and blueberries along the Upper Loop Trail suggests that an apt name might be the Fern-Blueberry Trail. The Lower Loop might be better named the Gorge Trail.

—Contributed by Jack Neff (updated by Stuart Carroll)

Standing Stone State Park

The park is located about 10 mi. southeast of Dale Hollow Dam on TN 52. It is accessible from I–40, either via TN 42 and 52 from

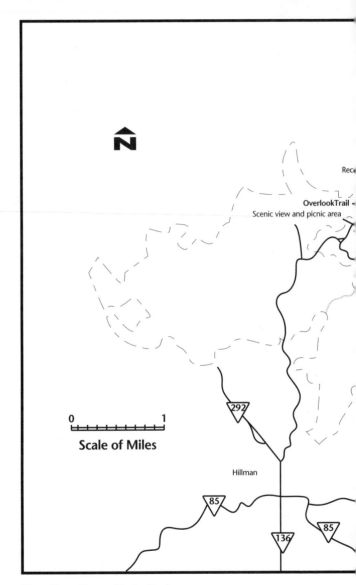

Rec

OverlookTrail
Scenic view and picnic area

292

Hillman

85

85

136

0 ———————— 1
Scale of Miles

Standing Stone State Park

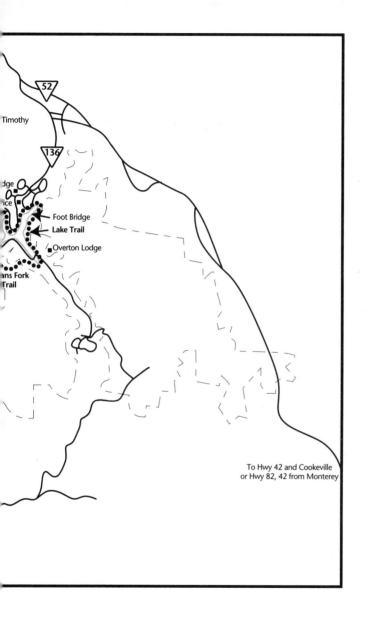

52

Timothy

136

dge
ice

Foot Bridge

Lake Trail

■Overton Lodge

ns Fork
Trail

To Hwy 42 and Cookeville
or Hwy 82, 42 from Monterey

Cookeville or via TN 84, 42, and 52 from Monterey. The park is named for a famous landmark on the old Cumberland Trace, an upright 8 ft.-tall pink sandstone boulder, that stood on a sandstone ledge just west of present Monterey. It was known by the early settlers to be especially esteemed by the Indians. Apparently, by the opening of the Walton Road along the old Trace in 1802, the stone had fallen, and travelers began chipping off as pieces as souvenirs. At some point the remnant of the standing stone was rescued and placed upon a monument in Monterey, where it rests today. There are about 13 mi. of trails in the park and Standing Stone State Forest, but we like the diversity of the day loop described here.

Overlook, Bryan's Fork, Lake Trail Loop. Length, 5 mi.; rating, moderate. The loop may start and end at the swinging bridge below the dam, or an alternate loop may start from the park office parking area and end across the road from the recreation lodge. There are steep grades at both ends of the alternate route.

A steep switchback trail with guardrails leads down the bluff from the office area to the road along the lake. Turn right to a swinging bridge below the stone dam and cross to a trail junction. To the right, the trail goes over the hill to a picnic area and overlook. The left trail follows the lakeshore. The Overlook Trail, a steep switchback path to the top of the bluff, views the X-shaped lake. The trail veers to the left along the top of a narrow ridge, passing through a cedar glade at about 200 yds. from the top of the bluff, then follows an easy slope along the side of a ridge past a deformed tree on the right. The trail becomes steeper for 100 yds., rises briefly, and levels out again, veering back to the edge of the cliff in second-growth hardwoods. It now follows the top of a hill, crosses the head of a ravine, and goes through a stand of big beech trees to arrive at a road and a picnic area.

Crossing the road, the trail leaves the picnic area on a sharp right turn, following a hillside on a fairly level path. It crosses the head of a small ravine, and 100 yds. farther a bigger ravine, then curves left up an easy grade in open woods to the point of the bluff. Passing through an open area with heavy undergrowth, it starts downhill around the head of a ravine, then levels out briefly, following the contour. Descending, it follows the side of a steep hill, curves right, then sharply left across a steep ravine. Still downhill, the trail crosses one more ravine, near the bottom this time, and arrives at a creek and a paved road.

As one turns left across a wooden bridge, Bryan's Fork Trail is on the right. The trail crosses a thicket about 50 yds. wide and turns left along a hillside parallel to the road. It passes under a fallen beech tree at 100 yds., then crosses several fallen trees in open woods to a stand of big beech trees. Following an easy grade along the side of the hill for 0.2-0.5 mi., the trail curves right across the brow of a hill in upland hardwoods—hickory, oak, elm, and beech. The lake is now visible through the trees on the left. The trail curves right around the hill, slopes downward for 200 yds., then curves left around the head of a ravine and passes through a patch of crested dwarf iris. A series of switchbacks provides an easy grade to the bottom of the ravine, and the trial arrives at a road along the lakeshore (end of Bryan's Fork Trail).

Follow the road to the right to a bridge, cross it, and turn left to pick up the Lake Trail behind the Overton Lodge. The trail follows a long slope along the side of a bluff, with rock outcroppings on the right and the lake below on the left. Be very careful, as there is treacherous footing crossing a ravine. Downhill briefly, the trail levels out again. A big rock is wedged between the small trees on the left. The trail now follows a ledge above the lakeshore and passes through a thicket at a ravine crossing, again with treacherous footing. It follows the bluff again, then swings right around the point of the next hill. At a footbridge there are two options: to follow the trail around the end of the lake or to cross and pick it up on the other side. If crossing the bridge, turn right a short distance to pick up the switchback trail up the side of the ravine to arrive at the Recreation Lodge. The other alternative continues around the lakeshore another 0.5 mi. to return to the swinging bridge below the dam.

Cedars of Lebanon State Park

This state park is east of Nashville and south of Lebanon, about 7 mi. south of I–40 on U.S. 231. It is one of the recreational areas along the Trail of Tears State Scenic Route, and it has unique features. A dominant forest type of the inner Central Basin, where horizontally-bedded Ordovician limestone outcrops everywhere, is that of the limestone-loving eastern red cedar. This park and adjacent forest were named for the biblical Cedars of Lebanon, though our "cedar" is a juniper, a different species and genus than that of King Solomon's land. These eastern red cedars were so valuable for making pencils, crossties, and cedar oil that the cedar forests were mostly cut out of the area by 1900. They were replaced by the CCC in the 1930s.

The park is unique in the extensive acreage of cedar glades protected within its boundaries. Unfortunately, these trees are rapidly being lost in the area. Cedar glades are found only in the Central Basin of Tennessee and a few locations in Missouri, Kentucky, northern Alabama, and northwestern Georgia. They provide habitat for more than one-fourth of all Tennessee's endangered plants. Once deemed worthless, because of their inability to support cash crops or hardwood forests, cedar glades are now appreciated for their uniqueness and scientific value.*

* This recognition is the direct result of the 1949 doctoral dissertion on cedar glade ecology by now retired Vanderbilt University biology professor Elsie Quarterman. Her lifetime educating students, the public, and public and private officials led to preservation of some of the best remaining examples of these special ecosystems, and others, now protected in State Natural Areas and Nature Conservancy preserves.

Cedar glade communities are striking biological occurrences. Existing on limestone, or in very thin soil, plants occurring here survive extremes of cold and saturation in winter only to be baked by sun and deprived of moisture in the summer. The Tennessee milk vetch is one example. The milk vetch would grow most ideally in the full sun of an open glade, but open glades do not provide enough moisture. The shade of cedar trees would provide enough moisture but not enough sun, and so the milk vetch grows only on edges of shady areas—a forced compromise of both light and moisture needed to survive.

Increasing threats to cedar glades come in the form of disturbances caused primarily by mankind's encroachment. Development and some agricultural practices such as grazing contribute incalculable damage. The disturbance of native plants often times will open these natural areas to unsightly non-native invasive intruders such as thistles and ragweed. As exotics spread, they take the few remaining spaces suitable for rare plants such as the Tennessee coneflower.

Hikers can greatly increase their enjoyment of these trails by stopping at the Park Headquarters for information or even better, a chat with the park naturalist, about the unique topography of the area, its forests, and the rare plants currently in bloom or fruit.

Hidden Springs Trail. Length, 4.5 mi., rating, easy. The left fork at a Y-intersection just beyond the park office leads to the parking area and the trailhead near the swimming pool. The 0.5-mi. Limestone Sinks Trail is also in this area. The trailhead of the 2-mi. Cedar Forest Trail is at the Y-intersection. All are loop trails. Hidden Springs Trail is a day-use trail, with no camping allowed. Elevation changes are not great. Hours of operation are 8:00 A.M. to 10:00 P.M. in summer; 8:00 A.M. to 8:00 P.M. in winter.

The Hidden Springs Trail is a loop trail that meanders through cedar forests and glades past a broad array of unusual wildflowers and other native plants and trees. The limestone substrate underlying this area is known as karst topography, found also in the Karst

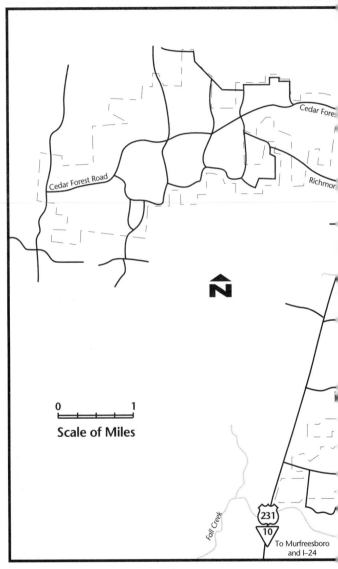

Cedars of Lebanon State Park

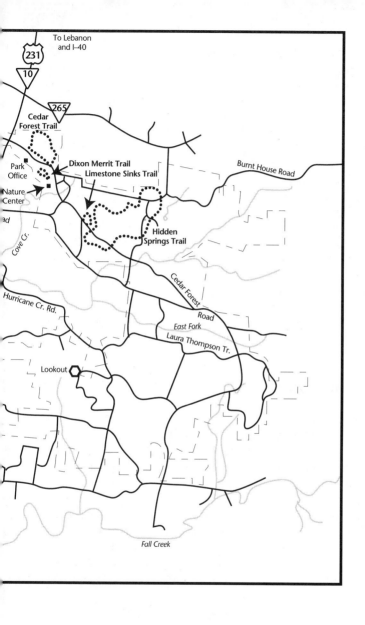

Mountains of Slovenia and Croatia. The trail area is home for nineteen rare species of plants that grow only in middle-Tennessee cedar glades. There is the pink Tennessee coneflower that blooms early in summer. There are small annual herbs in the mustard family, such as the three species of glade cress with white or yellow flowers, and spring and early-blooming perennials such as the pale blue glade phlox on rocky outcrops. There are Tennessee milk vetch with pale yellow flowers; purple glade violets; Gattinger's lobelia; the limestone fame flower; glade savory, a fragrant small mint; and the white-flowered sandwort.

Trees along the trail are shagbark hickory, eastern red cedar, fragrant sumac, honey locust, hackberry, and post oak. Near Hidden Spring on the right is a large limestone outcrop with an abundance of fossils. Hidden Spring Cave was once the location of a moonshine still, making use of the pure spring water and also the concealment of the cave.

Two old millstones are built into the stone wall behind the counter in the park office. There are no running streams in the park, but when the mill was running years ago the water to run it came from a large pond.

Long Hunter State Park

The park is located on TN 171, 6 mi. south of the Mt. Juliet exit from Interstate 40 (7 mi. east of Nashville) and lies along the southeast shore of J. Percy Priest Lake, formed in 1968 by a U.S. Army Corps of Engineers' impoundment of Stones River. The Stones River Basin was a favored hunting ground of the Creek, Chickasaw, Cherokee, and Shawnee Indians and, in the 1760s and 1770s, of the "long hunters." These were skilled woodsmen and marksmen who came across the Appalachian Mountains, mostly from Virginia and North Carolina, in small groups on horseback and spent many months at a time, sometimes more than a year, exploring and hunting. Finding an area they liked, they set up a station camp and hunted until the game became scarce or until enough animal hides and pelts had been collected to make the return from their "long hunt" profitable. Stones River was named for Uriah Stone, one of a party of long hunters who discovered it in 1766. With its rich bottomlands and hardwood forest, the river fostered the settlement and growth of the area, and upstream, at Murfeesboro, it was the site of the historic Battle of Stones River during the Civil War.

Like Cedars of Lebanon State Park, Long Hunter includes increasingly rare cedar barrens and glades under strict protection. One such area, Couchville Cedar Barrens, comprised of seventy-two acres, supports a particularly broad diversity of plant species specially adapted to the harsh and widely variable conditions of these limestone outcrops, including Tennessee coneflower, Tennessee milk-vetch, fameflower, and at least four other federally listed endangered or threatened plants. It was acquired by the state with the aid of The Nature Conservancy.

Park headquarters, featuring exhibits relating to the history and ecology of the area and offering trail maps and information, is located about 1 mi. southeast of the park entrance on TN 171 (Hobson Pike). Couchville Lake, where the trailhead for the Lake Trail and the Bryant Grove Trail is located, lies less than a mile northeast of park headquarters. The trailhead for the Day Loop Trail and the Volunteer Trail is located just west of Hobson Pike, about 1 mi. north of the park entrance.

Bryant Grove Trail. Length, 4 mi.; rating, easy. Hikers may begin either at the Couchville Lake area or at Bryant Grove. From Couchville the trail follows an old roadbed for the first 0.75 mi. The roadbed runs along the Priest Lake shoreline through red cedars, cottonwoods, sycamores, and willows. Watch for herons and waterfowl, and in the afternoon look for sunfish and bass among the underwater roots of the trees. For the next 0.75 mi. the trail winds inland through second growth oak-hickory forest. Many spring and summer wildflowers line the trail. Watch for the crossroads that leads into the cedar glades, a unique habitat harboring a large population of the Tennessee coneflower, recently moved from the federal endangered species list to threatened status. Other unique glade plants include Nashville breadroot, Gattinger's prairie clover, false aloe, prickly pear cactus, and prairie mimosa, which are more commonly associated with arid environments but which thrive in the harsh conditions of the glades. Back on the main trail, over a small rise and back down near the waters edge, the trail skirts the coves of Priest Lake, meandering through more cedar glade habitat. A wooden footbridge passes over Bryant Creek. The last section of the trail winds through cedar forest with limestone rock formations, reaching Bryant Grove, where rest rooms and soft-drink machines await.

Day Loop Trail. Length, 4 mi.; rating, easy. This trail runs through rolling hills covered with second growth hardwood forest. About halfway around the loop a limestone bluff looks west to a scenic vista of Percy Priest Lake.

Volunteer Trail. Length, 6 mi. (12 mi. round-trip); rating, easy. This trail, named for the Tennessee Trails Association volunteers who built (and still help maintain) it, coincides with the first mile, or two, of the Day Loop Trail (depending on which leg is taken) and then continues north through woods and across blufftops always close to the eastern shore of Percy Priest Lake. A primitive camping area is found at the end of the trail, to which there is no road access.

—*Contributed by Nathan Sonderman, Park Naturalist*

☂ **Lake Trail.** Length, 2 mi.; accessible; smooth; foot. Rest rooms, which are accessible to those with disabilities, are near the paved trailhead parking area. This 8-ft.-wide paved loop trail winds along the shore of 110-acre Couchville Lake through mixed hardwood and cedar glade forest typical of Tennessee's control basin. The northwest end of the loop crosses the lake on a 300-ft. railed boardwalk. Spring wildflowers, fall colors, wading birds, and waterfowl are the most popular features. Dominant trees such as chinquapin oaks and shagbark hickories are labeled, and interpretive plaques explain other trail features such as limestone sinkholes, a plant succession area, pond ecology, glade forests, and a field-to-forest transition zone.

Bicentennial Capitol Mall State Park

This, Tennessee's newest state park, was opened in 1996 in celebration of the two hundredth anniversary of her graduation from territorial status to statehood in 1796. Though located downtown in the state's capital city at the foot of the historic State Capitol building, this nineteen-acre park with its 1-mi. loop trail could well be the best first stop for anyone hiking Tennessee trails for the first time and, is most rewarding for veteran Tennessee hikers as well.

The park extends from James Robertson Parkway to Jefferson Street between 6th Avenue North and 7th Avenue North in Nashville, on the north side of Capitol Hill and is entirely accessible to those with disabilities. There is abundant parking space along both 6th and 7th Avenues as well as a large parking area just off 6th Avenue at the south end of the park. Rangers well versed in Tennessee's historical, natural, and recreational attractions are available to chat with visitors or to conduct group tours or programs. For more information call (615) 741–5280.

A park brochure provides some interesting background on the mall and its environs. Located on the most prominent hill in downtown Nashville, the State Capitol was designed by William Strickland. From the 1850s into the 1950s, it stood out above all else in the Nashville skyline as a monument to Tennessee's history.

However, with the urban building boom in downtown Nashville during the late 1950s and early 60s, the Tennessee State Capitol disappeared from sight on the east, west, and south sides. The northern side of the Capitol was not conducive to the construction of skyscrapers due to the swampy conditions that existed in many areas between the Capitol and the Cumberland River. Ironically, the historic French Lick that attracted wildlife, Indians, trappers, and settlers to what would become Nashville also preserved the remaining view of the Capitol and became the home of the Bicentennial Capitol Mall State Park because of its natural attributes. In order to save the one remaining view of the Capitol and to commemorate Tennessee's two hundredth birthday, the concept of a mall similar to the one in Washington, D.C., took shape during the tenure of Governor Ned McWherter.

From the Capitol grounds, visitors can enjoy the view from an impressive overlook (known as a belvedere) of the entire Bicentennial Mall. Across James Robertson Parkway, a 200-ft. granite map of Tennessee embedded in the concrete plaza shows details of each county, with smaller granite maps depicting other unique characteristics of Tennessee.

From this point, visitors enter the park under the railway trestle, which stands as a reminder of the importance of railroading in Tennessee's history. Under one end of the trestle are rest rooms, and under the other end is a Visitors Center. The trestle is still a working part of the railway system, and trains will continue to use the track to transport products and produce.

Visitors entering the mall from the Visitors Center are welcomed by thirty-one fountains designating major rivers in Tennessee. To the right is a trail to the site of the old Sulphur Dell Ball Park.

⑥ **Greenway Path to Sulphur Spring.** Length, 0.1 mi.; rating, easy. This historic spring is represented by three fountains that flow into a rocky water garden. Sulphur Spring is located at the park's eastern end of the greenway path. Along the pathway are various sculpted forms representing wetland wildlife typical of the area and interpretive signage. The Sulphur Dell Minor League Baseball Park was once located in the area.

This trail will soon connect with a Metropolitan Nashville Greenways trail that will lead 0.5 mi. along Cumberland River past a restoration of historic Fort Nashborough, very near its original location, to Nashville's Riverfront Park. From there one will be able to walk across the river on the Shelby Street Pedestrian Greenway Bridge and along the east side of the river via the Stadium Greenway or continue east along the Shelby Street to Shelby Park and the Shelby Bottoms Greenway trail system (described in Chapter 9).

Ⓖ **Walkway of Counties.** Length, 0.3 mi.; rating, easy. This ninety-five-county historical journey along the east side of the park highlights the topographical features of each area, depicting the flat, mountainous, and rolling hills sections of the state. Native trees, shrubs, ferns, grasses, and wildflowers along the walkway represent the diverse vegetation found across Tennessee. This walkway is also the site of ninety-five county time capsules. They are to be opened during the tricentennial celebration in 2096. From the Court of Three Stars at the north end of the mall there is an impressive view southward of the State Capitol atop what pioneer Nashvillians called the Cedar Knob.

Ⓖ **Pathway of History.** Length, 0.3 mi.; rating, easy. Along the west side of the park, a 1,400-ft. Wall of History is engraved with historic events that have occurred over the past two centuries. Each ten-year period along the wall is marked with a granite pylon. The wall "breaks" at the time of the Civil War to represent the divisive effect of the war on the state. A 1796 monument and fountain represent the founding of Tennessee, while an 1896 monument highlights the Centennial Exposition. The Statehood Memorial is placed in alignment with the 1796 column along the Pathway of History. Engraved text tells of Tennessee's birth into statehood. A fountain, the centerpiece of this memorial, serves as a reminder of Nashville's founding. Trappers settled in the French Lick Creek area, which was created by two springs—McNairy Spring and Sulphur Spring. These two springs and the creek still flow underground below the pathway.

Montgomery Bell State Park

The park is 7 mi. east of Dickson on U.S. 70. It lies in a an area that early settlers found to be rich in iron ore deposits, timber, and limestone, the raw materials required for producing cast iron. In

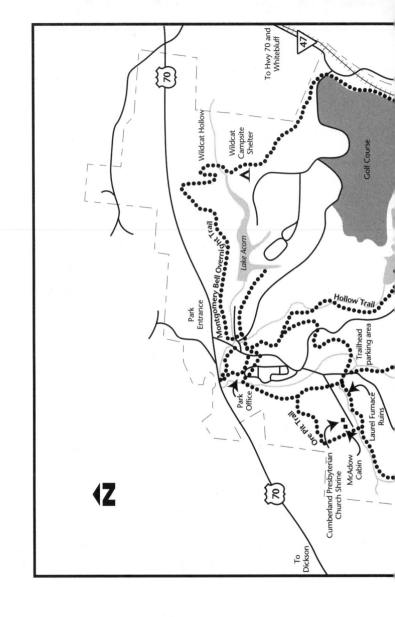

N

To Hwy 70 and
Whitebluff

47

Golf Course

Wildcat Hollow

Wildcat
Campsite
Shelter

Montgomery Bell Overnight Trail

Lake Acorn

Hollow Trail

Park
Entrance

Park
Office

Trailhead
parking area

Ore Pit Trail

Cumberland Presbyterian
Church Shrine

McAdow
Cabin

Laurel Furnace
Ruins

70

70

To
Dickson

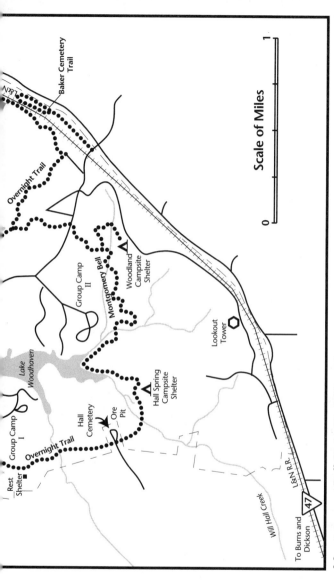

Montgomery Bell State Park/Resort

Scale of Miles

0   1

Baker Cemetery Trail

Overnight Trail

Group Camp II

Montgomery Bell

Woodland Campsite Shelter

Lookout Tower

Hall Spring Campsite Shelter

Lake Woodhaven

Group Camp I

Hall Cemetery

Ore Pit

Overnight Trail

Rest Shelter

Will Hall Creek

L&N R.R.

To Burns and Dickson

47

the late 1700s James Robertson, father of the Watauga settlements and Nashville, founded the Cumberland Iron Works and built Cumberland Furnace (a few miles northwest of the park). In 1804 Robertson sold the company and furnace to Montgomery Bell, a young but already successful entrepreneur, born and raised in the major iron-producing area of Pennsylvania that had supplied cannon, cannonballs, and ironware to the Continental Army. Bell quickly increased production and profits and, under contracts with the War Department, supplied the cannonballs fired by Andrew Jackson's army at the Battle of New Orleans.

By 1830, Bell had bought timberland, ore deposits, and other furnaces throughout the region to become the state's leading iron maker. In 1818 he acquired the site at the Narrows of the Harpeth, where he drilled what is very likely the first tunnel in the United States, 290 ft. long, through a precipitous ridge at the narrow neck of a bend where the river almost doubles back on itself 16 ft. lower at the tunnel exit than at its entrance. With a dam below the input side, enough head was created to power the four huge hammers of the forge Bell completed there in 1832, named Patterson Forge for his oldest brother. The tunnel is on the National Register of Historic Places and is preserved at Narrows of the Harpeth State Historic Area a few miles northeast of Montgomery Bell State Park. Arguably Tennessee's first industrialist, tunnel builder, and ironmaster, Bell freed hundreds of the slaves who formed much of his force of skilled craftsmen, and he endowed a University of Nashville preparatory school that later became Montgomery Bell Academy.

The Montgomery Bell Overnight Trail. Length, 11.7 mi.; rating, moderate; blazes, white. This is a loop trail passing through a very historic and scenic area. From the park office, take the road fork toward the campground. Pass the campground entrance, cross the bridge, take the left road fork past the ranger's residence, and turn left to the parking area at the trailhead. From the trailhead go up the hill, cross the road, and continue on down to a small stream. About 50 yds. downstream are the remains of Laurel Furnace, which was built in 1815 to produce iron. This area contained the necessary ingredients—brown ore, limestone, and timber—for making charcoal. The trail goes uphill across the paved road on a section known as the Ore Pit Trail and soon comes to a small rest shelter. The left fork passes pits where ore was removed, primarily by slave labor. This ore, along with the charcoal and limestone, was removed from the hillside onto a wooden trestle and dumped into the top of the furnace.

The trail continues through this pit area to a point where it makes an abrupt turn to the left (south). A few feet north is one of the largest pits, which usually holds several feet of water. From here proceed down the hill to a log cabin, a replica of Samuel McAdow's home, where the Cumberland Presbyterian Church was organized in 1810. Reverend McAdow, a Presbyterian minister, settled here in 1799 and was active in the Great Revival that swept through most of the western frontier in 1800. When iron ore deposits were found near his home he sold the land to Richard Napier, who became a leading iron manufacturer. The trail goes west on an old road, crosses the stream twice, and bears south uphill to a rest shelter. Continue on to the entrance to Hall Cemetery, cross the entrance road through two gates, and continue south along the old roadbed. About 0.5 mi. south the trail crosses Hall Creek and turns left down a slight hill to the Hall Spring campsite. Hall Spring emerges on the left, and the camping area is situated to the right.

The trail works its way downhill past another mine pit from which much of the sandstone was taken for construction of many of the buildings in the park. The trail then crosses the creek on a rustic bridge and continues through a marsh area to Hall Spring, which emerges from the large area on the right after crossing the next bridge. This is campsite 1, 3 mi. from the start; there is a shelter with eight bunks and a pit toilet. The water should be treated. From here the trail follows the stream, which harbors an active beaver colony. Jewelweed and cardinal flowers grow profusely here, along with several patches of cane.

If this area is approached quietly, there is a good chance of seeing beavers. Ducks and other wildlife also can usually be observed in this area. After the last beaver dam, the stream becomes Lake Woodhaven. There is a good view of the lake, then the trail turns right along the lakeshore for a short distance. Just before reaching a large oak log, the trail turns sharply to the right and continues through a hardwood forest into some nice areas of yellow pine. Shortly after crossing the third stream in this stretch, a spur trail to the right leads to campsite 2, known as Woodland, 4.7 mi. from the start. This campsite, which is 0.3 mi. off the main trail, has an eight-bunk shelter, pit toilet, and a good spring 50 yds. down the path in front of the shelter.

Back on the main trail, turn right uphill into a beautiful open upland forest. After crossing the paved road, the trail runs downhill to the upper end of Creech Hollow Lake, then bears right to a dirt road. Turn left and follow the road slightly more than a mile to the rear entrance to the park, then left on this road about 50 yds. to a sign indicating a right turn back into the forest. The trail follows the park boundary some distance and then descends to a small stream that leads to Wildcat Hollow, campsite 3, at 8.7 mi. The water supply—the stream—must be treated. This site is convenient for fishing, as Acorn Lake backs up to within a few yards.

The trail continues eastward across the creek in front of the shelter and along another stream for a short distance, then turns left across the stream and up the hill. At the crest of the hill, the trail bears left and soon becomes the roadbed that was once the old Nashville-Dickson highway. It is about 1 mi., mostly downhill, to the arts and crafts shop. Cross the bridge behind the shop and walk the paved road a short distance, and the trail picks up again opposite the playground. This section leads through another sandstone pit in which a beautiful grove of pine trees is now growing. There is a steep climb out of this pit, then the trail meanders through a mixed forest, crossing another paved road and off into a hollow. Eventually the trail winds down a stream that is crossed by a bridge just behind the park maintenance building. The trailhead parking area is in front of this building.

—Contributed by Russell Fryer (updated by Sam Reed)

Big Hill Pond State Park

The park, originally developed as Big Hill Pond Environmental Education Area, was designated a state park in 1982, and a new management plan was implemented. It is located southwest of Shiloh National Military Park near the Mississippi state line. Its variety of terrain and ecosystems, from river bottom marshes to dry rocky ridgetops, makes for interesting hiking, birding, and botanizing. It has more than 25 mi. of foot trails with four trail shelters, affording a number of attractive loop options for day hikers or weekend backpackers. It may be reached from U.S. 45, 8 mi. south of Selmer, TN 57 west through Ramer and south at the sign for the park. It is 3.2 mi. to the entrance to park headquarters on the right. The Southern Railroad crosses the area, running northwest to southeast, 0.6 mi. from the entrance. Much of the work was done by Comprehensive Employment Training (CETA) workers and the YCC. U.S.G.S quad sheet Chewalla 4SW includes this area.

Big Hill Pond Trail. Length, 4.8 mi.; rating, moderate. This trail begins on John Howell Road about 0.5 mi. south of the park office. It meanders southward through rolling and steep hills, then swings westward around and down the hillside above the old Big Hill Pond. Turning northward it follows the edge of the marsh and ascends to the head of the hollow above the pond. Climbing out the east side of the hollow and paralleling John Howell Road, it soon meets the Azalea Spring Day Loop, and together the trails cross the road, go north a short distance, and part. The Big Hill Pond Trail first goes east, gradually turning northward, then proceeds along the contour 80 to 100 feet above the east side of Travis McNatt Lake until it crosses a hollow and makes a steep final climb to a trail intersection at the ridgetop. A left turn leads down to a

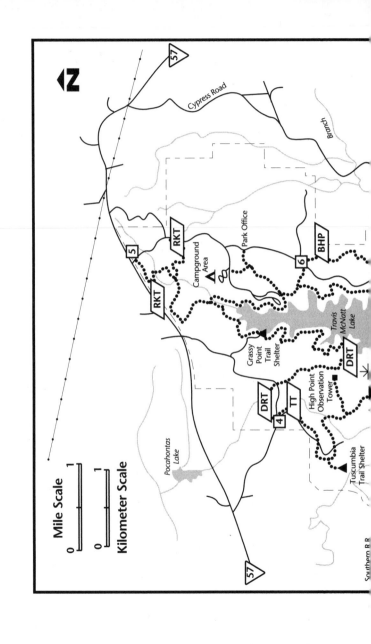

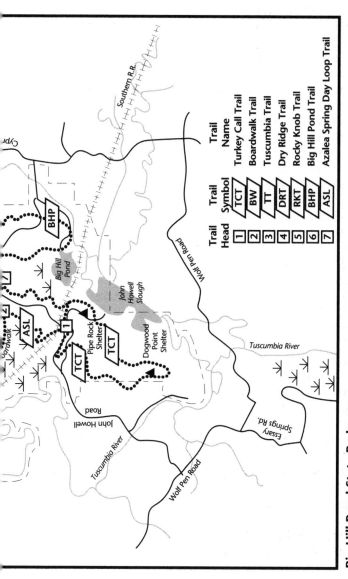

Big Hill Pond State Park

Trail Head	Trail Symbol	Trail Name
1	TCT	Turkey Call Trail
2	BW	Boardwalk Trail
3	TT	Tuscumbia Trail
4	DRT	Dry Ridge Trail
5	RKT	Rocky Knob Trail
6	BHP	Big Hill Pond Trail
7	ASL	Azalea Spring Day Loop Trail

footbridge across an arm of the lake and on to the boat dock or picnic area. A right turn leads 0.3 mi. back to the original trailhead.

Azalea Spring Day Loop. Length, 2.6 mi.; rating, moderate. This trail starts on John Howell Road about 2 mi. south of the park office. Coincident with the Big Hill Pond Trail, it goes north a short distance then leaves the latter and heads northwest to round the point at the south end of Travis McNatt Lake. Rounding the next hollow it descends toward the dam, rounds the point above it, and swings southward to follow the edge of Dismal Swamp (Tennessee has one, too) to the Southern Railroad. It follows the rail line a scant 0.5 mi. before turning north, climbing to the ridgetop, and following it back to the trailhead. Along this trail is a severely burned area with a section demonstrating prime reforestation.

Turkey Call Trail. Length, 3.8 mi.; rating, moderate. This trail begins at the intersection of John Howell Road and the Southern Railroad. It heads east coinciding with the Azalea Spring Day Loop for about 0.2 mi., then south to the Pipe Rock Shelter side trail. Continuing generally southeast along the edge of John Howell Slough, it crosses several small watercourses, then goes south at the foot of a long ridge. Just past an ox-bow in the slough, the trail turns sharply north to climb the steep southern end of the ridge among interesting rock outcroppings approaching Dogwood Point Shelter. It then follows the crest of the ridge between Tuscumbia River and Cypress Creek for almost 2 mi. back to the point of origin.

Boardwalk. Length, 0.8 mi.; rating, easy. This boardwalk connects Azalea Spring Day Loop with the Tuscumbia Trail. It crosses Dismal Swamp, a unique area with abundant wildlife.

Tuscumbia Trail. Length, 1.3 mi.; rating, moderate. This section of trail is probably the most scenic on Big Hill Pond State Park; it offers many vistas along the rim of the Tuscumbia River Bottom. Along the trail is a 75-foot observation tower and Tuscumbia Trail Shelter. It connects the Boardwalk Trail with the Dry Ridge Trail.

Dry Ridge Trail. Length, 7.5 mi.; rating, moderate. From its intersection with the Tuscumbia Trail, this trail circles along the crest of a horseshoe-shaped ridge to the northeast, then east, then south. Rounding a high point above the lower end of Travis Mc-Natt Lake, it follows the west side of the lake northeastward, crossing several small watercourses and passing Grassy Point trail shelter and an old cattle dipping vat (circa 1930). Well upstream of the lake, it crosses Dismal Branch and follows the east side of the valley south to the boat dock and picnic area.

Rocky Knob Trail. Length, 0.6 mi.; rating, moderate. Starting on John Howell Road just inside the park entrance, a short section of the trail climbs to the top of the knob just east of the road. Starting at this trailhead most of the trail winds west of the road through this area, unique for its large boulders and rock outcrops, and returns to the road about 0.3 mi. southeast of the trailhead. Midway along this loop a connector trail, less than 1 mi. in length, branches off to the right, leading first west then south to the northernmost point of the Dry Ridge Trail.

Meeman-Shelby Forest State Park

The park is on the third Chickasaw Bluff, 13 mi. north of Memphis. It was named for Edward J. Meeman, editor of *The Memphis Press-Scimitar*. In 1940 Meeman proposed the creation of a National Forest, to be called the Forest of Discovery, extending along the Mississippi River floodplain and the Chickasaw Bluffs. The project dies aborning with the onset of WWII. The park lies in Shelby County—named for Col. Isaac Shelby, a pioneer leader in East Tennessee in the late 1700s and, with Andrew Jackson, negotiator of the Chickasaw Purchase in 1818. To get there, go north on North Watkins Street from either I-240 or U.S. 51 and watch for the signs. The route is well marked from the end of North Watkins. There are about 11 mi. of hiking trails in the park, plus a 5-mi. bicycle path. The trails have been "adopted" by the Memphis Chapter of the Tennessee Trails Association. The Tennessee Department of Conservation built 6 mi. of the Chickasaw Bluffs State Scenic

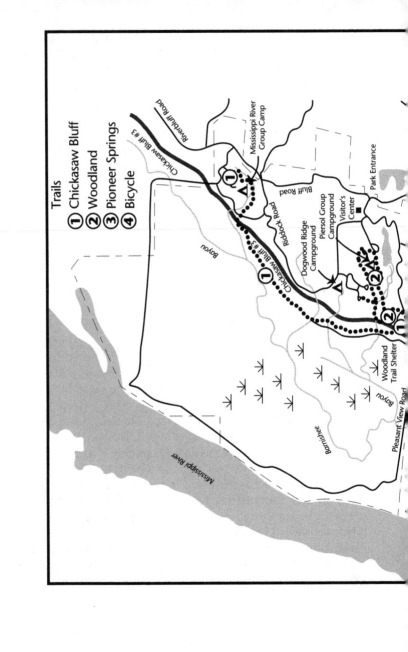

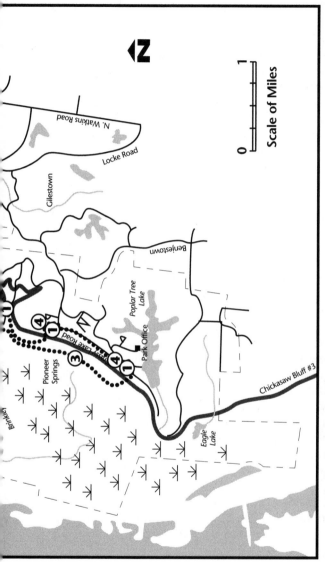

Meeman-Shelby Forest State Park

N

Scale of Miles

0   1

N. Watkins Road

Locke Road

Gilestown

Benjestown

Poplar Tree Lake

Park Office

Pioneer Springs

Brinkley

Poplar Lake Road

Eagle Lake

Chickasaw Bluff #3

Trail in 1976. The terrain is hilly, interlaced with small streams and forested with huge bottomland hardwood trees.

Chickasaw Bluffs Trail. Length, 8 mi.; rating, easy to moderate. The trailhead, with a nearby parking lot, is at the north end of the park, just east of the Mississippi River Group Camp. The trail, blazed in white, begins at the top of a ridge, descends steeply, and follows a horsetail-lined stream, crossing it several times. The group cabins are on a hill to the west; high, erosive bluffs are to the east. In between is thick hardwood forest. Beware of newly fallen trees that may obstruct the trail.

After crossing a road, pick up the trail a short distance to your right. For a long stretch the trail is straight and level, surrounded by beech trees. Continue along the left edge of an open field, with the wildlife management area on your right. Cross the old road bridge, which is closed to vehicles. The trail leaves the roadbed to the left and continues on a slight rise, never more than 100 ft. from the road. It rejoins the road briefly, then reenters the forest to the left and meets the Woodland Trail Juncture (blazed in red). The trail ascends steeply to Woodland Trail Shelter.

After leaving the shelter, cross the end of a paved road and pick up the trail just to the right of the bike path. It now converges with the Pioneer Springs Trail, blazed in blue. After twisting and turning, climbing a ridge and descending, the trail crosses a gravel road and levels off, paralleling the bike trail, which is just a few yards to the left. The trail narrows as it bisects a dense horsetail thicket. A short distance farther, look on your left for the tree growing through the roof of an ancient rusty car. Washed-out bridges over several streams may require some detouring.

The bluffs on the left become higher, while on your right are swampy bottomlands filled with cypress "knees." (Mosquito repellent here is imperative.) The trail passes around the makeshift shelter over Pioneer Springs. Observe—but don't drink—the water as it bubbles up from the sand. The 1.5 mi. of trail from here to Poplar Tree Lake are heavily used. A very steep hill leads up to the terminus at the lake parking lot.

Woodland Trail. Length, 3 mi.; rating, easy to moderate. This is a loop trail, blazed in red, that begins and ends at the park's nature museum. It starts as a straight path along a ridge heading west, then descends to the left down "steps" formed by tree roots. At the bottom of this hill, you have a choice: Go to the right for a short 1.0 mi. loop, or go left, cross the bridge, and climb a steep hill for the full 3 miles. On this route, the trail will pass a precipitous sheer bluff and turn left, meandering through beautiful forestland (look for beds of trillium in April). The trail crosses a stream (with no bridge), climbs another steep hill, and turns right. After leveling off briefly, it descends to the stream, turns left, rises and falls, crosses a bridge, climbs again.

Here you will meet up with another arm of the trail, also blazed in red. Turn left and watch for a trail juncture. From this point, if you go south, you'll emerge on an old road that is now part of the bike path. If you continue west, you'll meet up with the Chickasaw Bluffs Trail (blazed in white) and follow it up to the Woodland Trail Shelter, which has benches for eating lunch but is not designed for camping.

Returning from the shelter to the juncture point, take the western leg of the trail, which, in contrast to the first half, is almost completely level. Go down to the stream and cross it to the left (no bridge). Look for the stands of bamboo, and for the pileated woodpeckers that live in the trees here. About halfway back, there is a trail spur to your left that reaches the Dogwood Ridge campground in 0.8 miles.

Continuing straight, the trail generally follows the stream, eventually crossing it and climbing a hill back to the museum. An interpretive brochure about the plants encountered on this trail is available at the park office (901–876–5215), as is a topo map of all the trails in the park.

—Contributed by Memphis Trail Club
(updated by Debbie Gilbert and Ken Novak)

⎆ **Bicycle Trail.** Length, 1 mi. (2 mi. round-trip); accessible; fairly smooth; multiuse. The trail is a 16-ft.-wide paved park drive, Piersol Road, now closed to motorized traffic. It starts from the paved parking area at picnic shelter no. 2, where there are accessible rest rooms. The trail extends west along the top of a ridge through tall mature hardwood forest and offers a pleasant, shaded walk, among large sweetgums, walnuts, and all the oaks typical of this area. It ends at a paved circle and picnic shelter on the brow of the Chickasaw Bluffs. Scattered along the trail in grass openings are seven picnic tables with benches. This is a particularly nice, level, open but well-shaded trail for wheelchairs and elderly walkers. Cross slopes reach 7 percent to 8 percent for 30 ft., or so, in a couple of gentle curves.

From the paved circle the bicycle trail goes south along the brow of the forested Chickasaw Bluff. Here it is an 8-ft-wide paved path rated challenge level 1 for wheelchair use for the first 0.4 mi. Toward the end of the section, the grade reaches 7 percent for 200 ft., then 8 percent for a shorter distance, before the trail turns sharply left and drops steeply on switchbacks to the bottom of the bluffs. A warning sign and rail fencing on either side of the trail just before the sharp left turn and steep descent clearly mark the end of the section suitable for wheelchair use.

To reach the trailhead go west from the park entrance, take the first road to the left just past the visitor center, and follow it 1 mi. to picnic shelter no. 2.

6. Trails in State Natural and Wildlife Areas

The Tennessee Natural Areas Preservation Act of 1971 provides protection for significant examples of geological features, rare species, and endangered natural communities and ecosystems through acquisition and management of these areas by the Tennessee Department of Environment and Conservation (TDEC) or through cooperative management of the areas with other government or private landowners. Designated State Natural Areas (DSNAs) are regulated by the state under rules of management that prohibit activities within such areas that are "inconsistent" with the purpose of "perpetual preservation" of the natural elements they contain. DSNAs are classified as scenic-recreational (Class I) or natural-scientific (Class II). Both classes are open to the public, and most have foot trails, but Class II natural areas are generally more ecologically sensitive and may contain globally rare elements. DSNAs may lie within state parks or other publicly owned lands or they may be self-contained natural areas. All DSNAs are administered by the Natural Heritage Division (NHD) of the Tennessee Department of Environment and Conservation, but those within state parks or forests or other government lands are managed by those agencies under NHD oversight.

The Tennessee Wildlife Resources Agency has many Wildlife Management Areas (WMAs) across the state, some in association with state parks or forests, and there are many miles of trails within them. As in state forests, WMA hikers in some cases must share trails with equestrians, mountain bikers, or motorized off-road vehicles. TWRA has in recent years increasingly emphasized non-game Watchable Wildlife opportunities in its WMAs and has developed foot trails for this purpose. (Watchable Wildlife is the official title of a TWRA program that marked with logo signs most of the outstanding wildlife observation areas on its own lands and those of other public and private landowners across the state.)

Not to be forgotten, though not described here, is the unparalleled opportunity to walk countless miles within seven large National Wildlife Refuges in West Tennessee, observing waterfowl, shorebirds, eagles and other raptors, songbirds, and other avian species, along with all the myriad forms of animal and plant life that comprise the ecosystems of the Southern Coastal Plain, the Loess Plain, and the Mississippi Alluvial Plain. These are managed by the U.S. Fish and Wildlife Service, and brochures and maps for each of the Refuges are available from that agency.

Described here are some of the best trails within State Natural Areas or Wildlife Management Areas across the state.

House Mountain State Natural Area

House Mountain is located approximately 8 mi. northeast of the Rutledge Pike (U.S. 11W) exit off I–40 in Knoxville. Turn left off Rutledge Pike onto Idumea Road and go 0.5 mile to a left onto Hogskin Road. The trailhead parking area is 0.7 mi. on the right.

Purchased in 1987, House Mountain State Natural Area is one of the newest state parks in Tennessee, but it was a long time coming. In the early 1970s proponents for the park started pushing the Department of Conservation to buy 500 acres on the south side of the mountain from Albert Kern, the largest landowner on the mountain, who wanted to see his land become a park. Opposition existed from locals who thought a park would be bad for the area. Supporters persisted and in 1986 The Trust for Public Land purchased the property and held it until funding permitted the state to buy it in 1987. It was left alone until 1990, when a park manager was assigned to the area and twenty-five more acres were purchased for the development of a picnic area, ranger's residence, visitor's center, and maintenance area. As of early 1998, none of the development has begun, but in 1993 and 1994 nearly 4 miles of hiking trails were built by volunteers. In June of 1993 Knox County built a small trailhead parking area and the park was officially dedicated.

In the late 1700s, as settlers entered what is now Knox County, they observed the mountain, with its appearance of a house top at each end, sitting about 2 miles from the southwestern end of the Clinch Mountain Range. The mountain apparently ended up there after great compressions in the earth's surface over 200 million years ago created the Clinch Mountains; House Mountain perhaps broke away from them in the years that followed.

Massive boulders of sandstone make up the upper third of the mountain, which rises 2,100 ft. above sea level, making it the highest point in Knox County. The trees are second growth due to past logging and fires. Table mountain pine and Virginia pine are numerous on top and chestnut oak is the most prevalent of the oaks in the area. The park is home to raccoons, grouse, and even a few fox squirrels along with gray squirrels, turkeys, and the ever-present turkey vultures that sail on the winds over the high bluffs. Fire pinks, wild geraniums, phlox, Christmas ferns, and many other wildflowers are numerous at the lower levels, while mountain laurel is plentiful near the top of the mountain.

The trails to the top are strenuous, with an elevation gain from the parking area to the top of about 900 ft. There are no facilities available so it is recommended that hikers bring water and a snack and wear sturdy hiking shoes. At a steady pace, a minimum of two hours round-trip to the west overlook should be expected and a minimum of four hours round-trip to the east overlook.

House Mountain is a day-use park. The park gate opens at 8:00 A.M. and closes at dusk Wednesdays through Sundays; the park is closed on Mondays and Tuesdays. No camping is allowed.

—*Contributed by Judy Wasik*

Mountain Trail. Length, 1.2 mi.; rating, moderate; blazes,

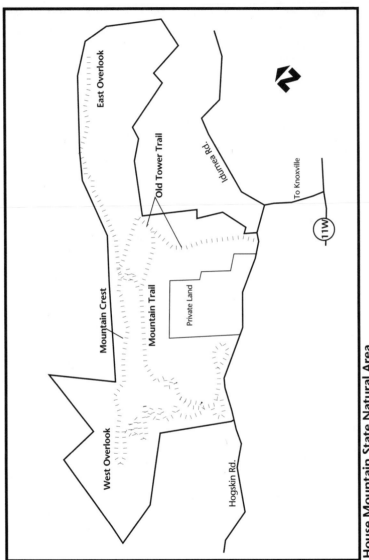

House Mountain State Natural Area

blue. This trail extends from the trailhead parking area to the Turkey Trail. It descends to the Old Tower Trail and is not heavily used here since it does not continue upward until reaching the Old Tower Trail.

Turkey Trail. Length, 0.3 mi.; rating, difficult; blazes, white. This trail was created after the Mountain Trail and it allows hikers to avoid the extremely difficult Old Tower Trail. It provides beautiful views toward the Smoky Mountains.

West Overlook Trail. Length, 0.9 mi.; rating, very difficult; blazes, yellow. This trail extends from the trailhead parking area to the West Overlook. It is the shortest hike to any overlook and to the only overlook that provides a view of both the Smokies and the Cumberland Mountians. Knoxville is also visible to the west. It is recommended to hike up this trail and then along the mountain crest to the Turkey Trail for descent.

Mountain Crest Trails. Length of each, 0.8 mi.; rating, moderate; blazes, red toward west. These trails extend 0.8 mi. each from their intersection at the Turkey Trail to the East and West Overlooks. Because the trail to the east crosses private property at one point, it has been deemed best to allow hikers to follow the existing trail without blazing. The trail follows the crest where barbed-wire fencing still exists, so be cautious. There are also rocks to climb over and around, but staying on the crest will guide hikers to the overlook, which offers views of the Smoky Mountains and eastward toward the Clinch Mountains.

Old Tower Trail. Rating, extremely difficult; blazes, none. This trail is on the House Mountain State Natural Area trail map because it was the only way to the top for years. It is not being maintained because of its rating of extreme difficulty. It is mentioned here to avoid confusion should a hiker choose to hike it.

Sawmill Hill Loops. Length, 0.5 mi. each; rating, easy; blazes, white. The right loop is an interpretive trail.

Frozen Head State Park and Natural Area

The park is located in the eastern part of Morgan County. The access road turns north of TN 62, 4 mi. east of the junction of U.S. 27 and TN 62 at Wartburg. This park, the former Morgan State Forest, is managed jointly as a state park and natural area. It has one of the finest trail systems in Tennessee. Developments include the trail system, picnic areas with rest rooms and running water, a primitive campground limited to tents and folding trailers, an outdoor amphitheater, a visitor's center, and personnel housing. Frozen Head State Natural Area includes several of the highest peaks in the Cumberland Mountains, with their connecting ridges and interlaced valleys. They are the eroded remnants of the Cumberland Mountains, but, because the stratigraphic basin lying immediately beneath them retarded their erosion relative to the rest of the Plateau, they remain much higher than the adjacent area to the south and west. The mountains, of sedimentary origin, are composed of alternate layers of sandstone and shale, with intervening layers of coal.

The massive layers of sandstone provide many of the more attractive features of the park, such as the great cap rocks, the rock houses, and the massive boulders in the narrow valleys. Rock enthusiasts will find small waterfalls, rock houses in the undercut bluff, or fine overlooks at the top of the bluffline, which can be followed for miles with relative ease.

Topo USGS quad sheets covering the park include Camp Austin, 122 SE; Gobey, 122NE; Fork Mountain, 129NW; and Petros, 129SW. Trail maps are available at park headquarters or from the Tennessee Department of Environment and Conservation, 7th Floor, L&C Tower, 401 Church Street, Nashville TN 37243-0446. The trails are color-coded, and the color of the blazes, length, and name of each trail are noted in the legend on the map. Many more interesting features may be found off the trails by those experienced in using topo maps. A permit is required for cross-country hiking or hiking on closed trails. All the developed trails are in the northern end of the park. They have been arranged to form loops and were all refurbished and upgraded between 1985 and 1988. Many miles of trails in the southern portion of the park have not been maintained in recent years. Only experienced hikers with good map-reading skills should try these overgrown trails. This is copperhead and rattlesnake country, but there is little danger of being bitten if ordinary precautions are used. Be careful around rocks, fallen trees, and old logs.

There is a shortage of water here during late summer and fall. Springs are not plentiful, nor as large as those in the Smokies. All trails in Frozen Head are rocky, and some are fairly rough, requiring sturdy shoes for hiking. A turned ankle or a bruised foot can ruin a hike very quickly. Most of the trails start from a common trailhead parking lot near the picnic area on Flat Fork Creek.

Panther Branch Trail. Length, 2 mi.; rating, moderate; blazes, blue. This trail starts at the gate, at the old concrete bridge across the north prong of Flat Fork Creek, slightly more than 0.5 mi. upstream from the picnic area, elevation 1,400 ft. A parking area is provided at the end of the road. The first mile follows an old road along the creek, with many boulders along the road and in the creek. Many people enjoy wading in the stream in spring and summer. One-half mile from the beginning, an overlook has been built at DeBord Falls, with steps leading to the bottom of the falls. In winter many large clumps of evergreen sedges and Christmas ferns can be seen on the north slope across the stream. Just upstream from the junction of Panther Branch and the creek, at 1,800 ft. elevation, the trail drops down a high bank and crosses the north prong of Flat Fork, entering a flat area of about one acre. This was the location of a logging camp more than a half-century ago.

The left trail follows a switchback railroad bed up Emory Gap Branch to a waterfall. Panther Branch Trail swings back right, soon picks up an old railroad bed, and follows it a few hundred yards to the crossing of Panther Branch. Hundreds of people visit this area every weekend in April to view one of the finest spring wildflower shows in the country.

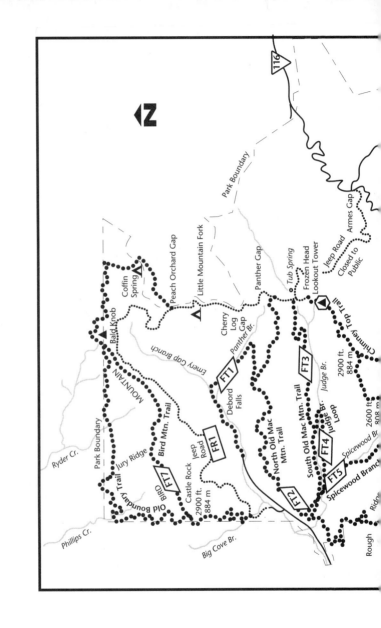

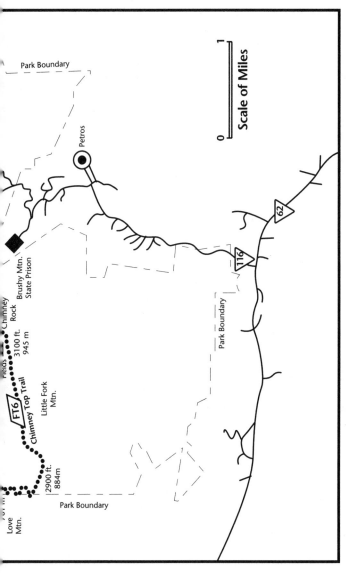

Frozen Head State Park and Natural Area

Scale of Miles
0 — 1

Park Boundary

Petros

Brushy Mtn.
State Prison

Chimney
Rock
3100 ft.
945 m

Fields

FT6

Chimney Top Trail

Little Fork
Mtn.

2900 ft.
884m

Love
Mtn.

Park Boundary

Park Boundary

116

62

The trail begins to climb rather steeply at the Panther Branch crossing and soon is a considerable distance above the stream. The trail then crosses a very thick outcropping of black shale exposed in a cascade in a small stream. The footing is narrow here for a short distance, becoming steep and rocky. Panther Branch is a series of small waterfalls in the upper reaches of its watershed. About 0.3 mi. above the cascade, the trail turns sharply, leaves the stream at 2,200 ft., and passes through a hardwood forest that faces directly north. An abundance of wildflowers bloom on this mountain slope in spring. Approximately 0.5 mi. after leaving Panther Branch, the trail ends at the North Old Mac Mountain Trail at 2,500 ft. To the right, this trail leads back to the trailhead. A high rock overlook is located about 200 yds. to the north of the junction.

North Old Mac Mountain Trail. Length, 3.6 mi.; rating, moderate; blazes, red. This trail starts from the main trailhead parking lot, passing through a nice pine plantation on nearly level ground. About 0.3 mi. after leaving the trailhead, the trail makes a 90-degree turn to the left. The Spicewood Branch Trail continues straight ahead. A few yards farther the trail turns to the left again and starts to climb around the western end of Old Mac Mountain at 1,500 ft. elevation. After rounding the end, the trail follows the north side of the mountain to the northeast, alternately going around small ridges and dropping into large north coves. The trees and other plants on his north slope provide shade, making this an ideal summer trail. During the hotter months this trail is much more comfortable than those on the south side of the mountain.

About 2.2 mi. after leaving the trailhead, this trail reaches the junction with the Panther Branch Trail at 2,500 ft. elevation. Just prior to the junction, there is a designated backpack campsite. A short trail to the left leads to a high rock overlook on the point of a ridge. From the junction the Old Mac Mountain Trail leads almost due east, and the ridges and coves of the lower reaches are nearly absent. The constant north slope makes an ideal habitat for wildflowers, and many fine displays can be found in April all along the trail in these upper reaches. On the north slopes of Old Mac Mountain and in Panther Branch Valley at the foot of the slope, a superior strain of tulip (yellow) poplar has evolved. Several of these trees have been selected by the Department of Forestry at the University of Tennessee as a source of genetic material to be used in establishing seed orchards.

Near the junction with the jeep road, a spur trail leads to Panther Gap Rock House. Three-fourths of a mile above the intersection with the Panther Branch Trail, a prominent line of sandstone bluffs will be seen above the trail. Some interesting fossils can be viewed on the underside of the overhanging rock. It is illegal to remove such articles from the site. Spring wildflowers are abundant around the base of this line of bluffs. A few minutes of walking from the bluffs brings the hiker into Panther Gap. Tub Spring is about 0.3 mi. to the right, and the Frozen Head lookout tower is about 0.3 mi. beyond the intersection of the road near the spring.

Along the approach to the intersection, the road to the left, leading down to TN 116 at Armes Gap, has been closed to the public. The tower on top of Frozen Head Mountain is the highest point in the park, 3,324 ft. elevation. It provides spectacular views of the high country to the east and the Tennessee River Valley to the southwest. On a clear day the Tennessee Valley, Great Smoky Mountains, and Cumberland Plateau are visible in the distance.

South Old Mac Mountain Trail. Length, 2.8 mi.; rating, moderate; blazes, yellow. From the trailhead parking lot, this trail coincides with the North Old Mac Mountain Trail. About 200 yds. beyond the North Old Mac trailhead, just before the bridge across Judge Branch, the trail angles to the left and enters an attractive hemlock grove. Three-fourths of a mile farther up the trail, it connects with the Judge Branch Loop, an extension of the former Wildflower Trail, 1.7 mi. from the Spicewood Branch Trail. From the hemlock grove, it stays in the valley a few hundred yards before beginning to climb the south slope of the mountain. One point of interest along this first section is an old building with thick walls. It was used to store explosives during the construction of trails in the 1930s. From this storehouse to the top of the mountain, the trail has a southern exposure. It is an excellent winter trail when the warm rays of sun are welcome, but this exposure makes it a hot summer trail. However, the southern exposure makes this one of the best trails when looking for early spring wildflowers. Several of the earlier species begin blooming by mid-March.

This trail is the shortest route between park headquarters and the tower on top of the mountain. Many hikers use one of the longer trails to reach the top and descend by the more direct route. The trail comes out at the road intersection near Tub Spring at 3,000 ft. To the right the road leads to the Frozen Head lookout tower.

Spicewood Branch Trail. Length, 2.5 mi.; rating, difficult; blazes, purple. This trail also leaves the parking lot on the same route as the Old Mac Mountain trails. One-tenth of a mile beyond the turnoff from the South Old Mac Mountain Trail, the Judge Branch Loop leads to the left. The former Wildflower Trail has been extended across a bridge on Judge Branch and circles to the left to a junction with the South Old Mac Mountain Trail. This is one of the easiest trails in the park, and its attractions include the great white trillium, huge beech trees, a hemlock grove, and moss-covered fieldstone bridge abutments. Continuing straight ahead from the junction, the Spicewood Branch Trail follows an old road about 0.3 mi., passing some large hemlock trees growing along Spicewood Branch. Just above the last of the hemlocks, the trail leaves the old roadbed near a small branch crossing at 1,700 ft. elevation, then turns at a right angle, proceeding directly up the mountainside. There is a campsite at the foot of the mountain. This section was not a part of the original trail but was put to use as a shortcut between the graded trail and the old road it follows on the lower end. Fortunately, this section is short, and the trail soon gets back on the graded tread. It passes through several north-facing coves as it works its way up the mountain, crossing the headwaters of Spicewood Branch (now little more than a deep cove).

The trail rounds a west-facing point at 2,650 ft. elevation, leaving the Spicewood Branch drainage. A short distance beyond this point, the trail crosses some of the steepest slopes in the park. Three-fourths of a mile from the point, the trail ends at the Chimney Top Trail, on top of the ridge at 2,900 ft. Frozen Head tower is 1 mi. to the left, and Mart Fields Spring and campsite are 0.8 mi. to the right. The Spicewood Branch Trail is a good summer trail, mostly on north slopes which makes for cooler hiking. The woods are more attractive than those found along some of the other trails.

Chimney Top Trail. Length, 6.9 mi.; rating, difficult; blazes, green. The trail leaves the main trailhead and visitor's center parking lot at 1,400 ft., skirts park headquarters, and ascends the north slope of Rough Ridge along the park boundary. It crosses the rocky crest at 2,300 ft., about 1.8 mi. from the trailhead. It then descends into the upper end of Rocky Fork Creek, 1,950 ft. elevation. Near the bottom of this valley, the trail crosses an old logging railroad grade. Exploration of this grade will show the ingenious methods used by the early loggers to get their trains into the mountains, by use of switchbacks in the roadbeds.

From Rocky Fork the trail leads up the north slope of Love Mountain, passing through some nice woods in a deep cove. Near the top of Love Mountain there is a spring just uphill to the right of the trail, marked by a small hemlock growing in moist soil. The water may or may not be potable, depending on how well the spring has been cleaned out. The trail leaves the old constructed trailbed at the top of the ridge at 2,900 ft. and makes a sharp left turn off the ridge, which is fairly level here. A few hundred years after leaving the graded trailbed, the trail climbs directly up the point of the ridge. The last half-mile is a strenuous climb to Chimney Rock, 3,100 ft. elevation. This segment of the trail is listed as only 3.4 mi. in length, but by the time you reach the top of Chimney Rock, it seems twice that far. There is a campsite here, but no water.

Inexperienced climbers have only one way to the top of this

great boulder. Approach the rock, turn left, and follow its base to the northeast corner, watching for a trail that can be used to get to the top by pulling oneself up on trees and shrubs growing out of cracks in the rocks. Be cautious when climbing, as rattlesnakes have been seen around the rocks during the summer months. On a clear, crisp day the view from the top is ample reward for the strenuous effort it takes to get there: To the north are the Cumberlands; to the northwest the Cumberland Plateau extends as far as the eye can see. To the west the Crab Orchard Mountains stand out in bold relief; to the southeast the Tennessee Valley with its TVA lakes is visible; and to the east are the Smokies. Mount LeConte and Clingman's Dome are easily recognizable.

Chimney Rock is the largest of several ancient cap rocks to be found along the crest of Chimney Top Mountain. Exploring some of these remains, particularly in seasons when snakes are not active, can provide an enjoyable experience. From Chimney Rock, the trail passes near several cap rock formations, descending to a narrow gap at 2,750 ft. It passes through the gap and ascends along a broken line of sandstone bluffs to the ridgetop. The terrain flattens in a young forest at the site of an old mountain farm known as Mart Fields. The trail follows the ridge to a campsite with a spring that provides water year-round. From Mart Fields the trail continues along the original CCC trail, following the foot of the bluff along the east side of Mart Knob to the junction with the Spicewood Branch Trail.

From the junction, the trail follows the road along the crest of the mountain at about 3,000 ft. and swings left around the west side of Frozen Head Peak to the intersection with the road to the lookout tower, which is maintained and provides an excellent platform for photographers. Here is some of the most spectacular scenery in Tennessee. To the left the road leads to Tub Spring and a campsite with a stone fireplace built by CETA labor in 1978. An Adirondack shelter was planned here but has never been built. Beyond Tub Spring, the old road down to Armes Gap on TN 116 has been gated and is closed to the public.

Bird Mountain Trail. Length, 4 mi.; rating, difficult; blazes, white. This trail is closed for maintenance on the section that lies on the north slope of Bird Mountain. The Bird Mountain Trail, formerly part of the Boundary Trail, is a circuitous route that offers an opportunity for a two- or three-day backpacking experience. It connects with the Chimney Top Trail at Tub Spring to form a 15-mi. loop. The average hiker should allow two days to complete the circuit, since the first few miles are a series of steep climbs and sharp descents. From the trailhead parking lot at 1,400 ft. to Squire Knob at 3,100 ft., a hiker will climb a total of 4,400 ft. and descend a total of 1,700 ft. in a distance of about 6 mi. There are elevation changes up to 1,200 ft. in relatively short distances.

Leaving the trailhead parking area, cross the bridge to the north and follow the old jeep road for several hundred yards past the campground to the first small stream crossing. The trail leaves the old road and works its way up the side of Bird Mountain through a total of fourteen switchbacks. This trail crosses the park boundary line onto private property part of the time. It arrives at the top of the mountain (2,900 ft. elevation) about 2 mi. from the trailhead. Just to the right at the crest is Castle Rock, the most massive cap rock in the park, nearly 0.5 mi. long. It contains several interesting rock houses and small sandstone "caves." There is an overlook on top of the bluff with an outstanding view of Panther Branch Watershed and Frozen Head Mountain.

From here the trail was rerouted in 1992 to follow the crest of Bird Mountain to Bald Knob. There are spectacular views from the ridgetops along this route, and the trail is less rugged than the original route, on which maintenance has been discontinued. A few hardy hikers, preferring the greater challenge, may continue to use the old trail. A permit is required to use closed trails. Elevations range from 2,800 to 3,000 ft., and the ups and downs are less strenuous. The trail passes around the north side of Bald Knob at about 3,100 ft.

The old Boundary Trail drops off the top of Bird Mountain into a large north cove, the upper end of Phillips Creek Watershed, which is an outstanding area for spring wildflowers. The woods are very beautiful here, but much of them are on private land, and the timber may be cut at any time. The trail continues down Phillips Creek to the corner of the park at about 1,400 ft. elevation, turns east, and almost immediately starts to climb Jury Ridge. After a rugged climb to the top of Jury Ridge (2,300 ft. elevation), the trail continues around the north slope of the mountain and crosses the upper watershed of Rayder Creek. From Rayder Creek it begins the long climb up Bald Knob.

Back on the Bird Mountain Trail, from Bald Knob it descends into a north cove, passes around the point of a ridge, and then descends into the extreme upper reaches of the Emory River Valley. A short distance from the valley, the trail turns onto an old overgrown road that it follows up the mountain to Coffin Spring and another campsite at 2,900 ft. From there it follows the route of the jeep road through Peach Orchard Gap to a campsite on Little Fork Mountain, then through Cherry Log Gap and Panther Gap to Tub Spring. From there the return to the trailhead follows the Chimney Top Trail, or if you have had enough by now, you can take the shorter route via the South Old Mac Mountain Trail. It's downhill most of the way.

—Donald Todd* (updated by David Engebretson)

South Cumberland State Recreation Area

This is a system of natural areas, day-use areas, and other private and public lands in Grundy, Marion, and Franklin counties, linked together by highways and trails. It includes the Savage Gulf, Grundy Forest, Carter, Hawkins Cove, and Sewanee Natural Bridge

*Donald Todd, now a retired biology teacher, led efforts in the 1960s and 1970s to have Morgan State Forest designated a State Natural Area, and, more recently, to protect its boundaries from destructive strip mining. He was also the second president of the Tennessee Trails Association.

State natural areas; the Grundy Lakes and Visitor Center day-use areas; and the Foster Falls and Little Gizzard Creek TVA small wild areas. Also within the system is the Fiery Gizzard State Recreation Trail, which runs mostly across private lands to link the Grundy Forest, Foster Falls, and Little Gizzard Creek areas.

Grundy Forest Day Loop. Length, 1.8 mi.; rating, moderate. The Grundy Forest Day Loop starts to the right behind the trailhead picnic shelter. School branch is crossed within 200 ft. The stream falls 25 ft. just below the crossing. At 0.5 mi. the new CCC campsite for hikers is to the right. This is where the Civilian Conservation Corps boys camped in the 1930s while working on the trails and other projects.

At 1 mi. the trail descends to Little Fiery Gizzard Creek. Soon the Hanes Hole is passed, then Hanes Falls a short distance later. At 1.3 mi. the junction of Little and Big Fiery Gizzard Creeks is passed just before the junction with the Fiery Gizzard Trail. The last 0.5 mile of the Day Loop is the first 0.5 mile of the Fiery Gizzard Trail.

Fiery Gizzard Trail. Length, 13 mi.; rating, moderate to difficult. This is an overnight backpacking trail with sections that make excellent day trips, located in Grundy and Marion counties. The Grundy County trailhead is in the Grundy Forest Natural Area, 6 mi. from I–24 at Monteagle and 1 mi. off TN 56 in Tracy City. The Marion County trailhead is in the Foster Falls Small Wild Area off U.S. Hwy. 41, 7 mi. southeast of Tracy City and 7 mi. north of Jasper.

The trail is named for Fiery Gizzard Creek and Cove, which it follows. The name is said to have come from a story about Davy Crockett burning his tongue on a hot turkey gizzard while camping in the area, but there are other stories just as intriguing. The trail is well known for spectacular scenery that includes waterfalls, deep gorges, sheer rock bluffs, scenic overlooks, spring wildflowers, exceptional fall colors, and dazzling ice formations in winter.

Starting at Grundy Forest, the trail soon descends into the gorge and continues in it until the 500-ft. ascent to Raven Point in the fifth mile. This section is exceptionally spectacular but very dif-

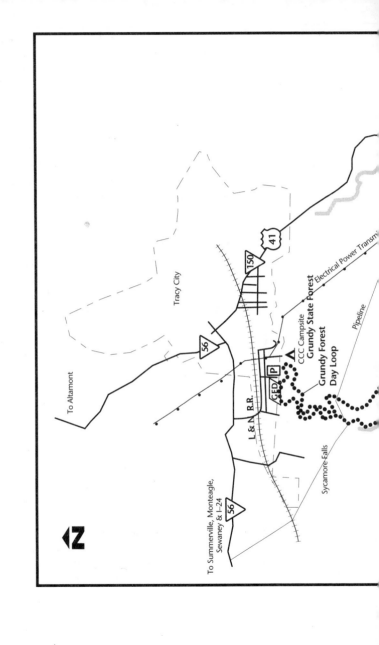

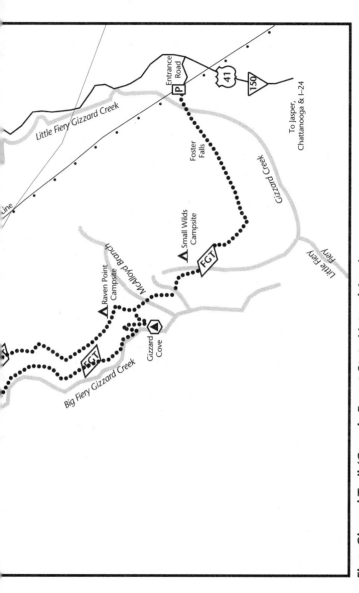

Fiery Gizzard Trail (Grundy Forest State Natural Area)

ficult. The huge trees, rock formations, waterfalls, and cool swimming holes are well worth the struggle across the millions of rocks. There is a campsite on the plateau near Raven Point, but no campfires are allowed. A spur trail leads to the Raven Point Overlook, one of the most beautiful views of the plateau.

The Marion County section begins at Raven Point and runs mostly along the top of the plateau on its way to Foster Falls. The first mile is great, with a nice overlook and crossings of two beautiful streams. The next 3 mi. cut across a recently logged tableland. Abruptly the Laurel Branch Gorge is crossed at mile 4. This rugged gorge is one of the trail's most scenic features.

Soon after the Laurel Branch crossing, there is a campsite that, with the gorge below it, makes up the Little Gizzard Creek Small Wild Area. Campfires are allowed in the small wild area. The last 2.5 mi. to Foster Falls offer some of the best views on the trail as the trail runs along the edge of the escarpment above Little Gizzard Creek, ending at the gorgeous falls. Water can be scarce along the Fiery Gizzard, so it is advisable to carry a canteen. Water from the main stream is unsafe for consumption. The new Father Adamz Campsite is located just before the bridge across Little Gizzard Creek. It is named in honor of the Episcopal minister and Tracy City Boy Scout leader who helped preserve the area near the falls.

The Dog Hole Trail. Length, 2.8 mi.; rating, moderate. This new trail leads from the Raven Point campsite back along the north rim of the gorge and down into Grundy Forest to rejoin the main trail near Sycamore Falls. This is a nice trail with overlooks and other points of interest, offering an easier way to Raven Point and the possibility of walking a loop.

Buggytop Trail. Length, 2 mi.; rating, difficult. This trail provides the only public access to the Carter State Natural Area. The trailhead and parking area are on TN 56 between Sewanee and Sherwood, about 10 mi. south of I–24 at Monteagle. This trail leads to the Buggytop entrance of the Lost Cove Cave. Thomas Barr wrote in *Caves of Tennessee* that Buggytop is "one of the most impressive cave openings in the state." At the base of a 150-ft. limestone cliff, a beautiful cascading creek flows from the opening, which is 80 ft. high and 100 ft. wide. Exploration of the cave is allowed, but taking the monthly guided tour is a good way to get oriented for future trips on your own.

The trail crosses Saddle Mountain to reach the cave. The first section is a rocky climb to the top of the ridge. Then a fairly easy half mile along the crest of the ridge brings you to the sign-up booth where the trail map is displayed. This ridge, known as "The Spur," has several wildflowers in season, including the rare Cumberland rosinweed that blooms in late summer. Just beyond the sign-up booth, the trail descends to the old Lost Cove Road (abandoned) and the clifftop above the cave. Turning right, the trail drops steeply to the cave mouth. This short descent makes the 4-mi. round-trip worthwhile because it's simply spectacular.

⑤ **Stone Door Trail.** Length, 1 mi.; challenge level 1; smooth; foot. The trail starts at the Stone Door ranger station, the western entrance to the Savage Gulf State Natural Area. The trailhead is reached from TN 56 at Beersheba Springs, 25 mi. north of Monteagle and 20 mi. south of McMinnville. This trail is easy, with wide tread and gentle slopes that persons with disabilities can negotiate in wheelchairs. The Stone Door Overlook, at 1,800 ft. elevation, provides a breathtaking view of the 800-ft deep Big Creek Gulf. The cliffs are popular with rockclimbers and rappellers.

The "Great Stone Door," a crevice in the bluff, provided a passage onto the plateau for the Chickamauga Trace Indian Trail.

Big Creek Gulf Trail. Length, 4 mi.; rating, difficult. This trail connects the Stone Door with Alum Gap. It runs through the "gulf" (gorge), making it a very strenuous trail. The exceptional scenery along this trail includes towering sandstone cliffs, giant boulders, the tumbling crystalline waters of Big Creek, and some extraordinary geological phenomena. At the halfway point, a half-mile spur trail leads to Ranger Creek Falls, a 30-ft. waterfall that drops over and disappears under the same limestone bluff. Directly below the Stone Door, a number of springs bring the water back to

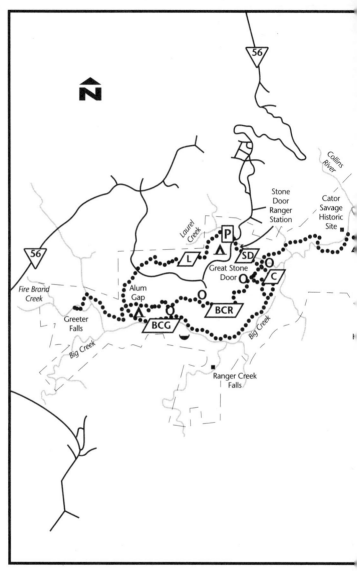

**South Cumberland State Recreation Area
(Savage Gulf State Natural Area)**

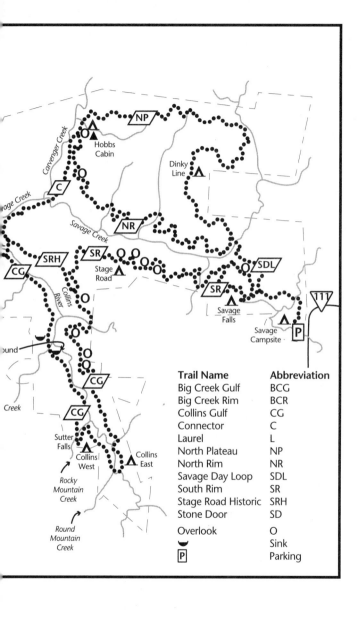

Trail Name   **Abbreviation**

Trail Name	Abbreviation
Big Creek Gulf	BCG
Big Creek Rim	BCR
Collins Gulf	CG
Connector	C
Laurel	L
North Plateau	NP
North Rim	NR
Savage Day Loop	SDL
South Rim	SR
Stage Road Historic	SRH
Stone Door	SD
Overlook	O
◡	Sink
P	Parking

the surface after a 2-mi. underground stretch. The sink that swallows Big Creek is 0.75 mi. past the Ranger Falls spur, just off the trail. Upstream from the sink, the stream flows in its boulder-strewn bed most of the year. This is one of the most interesting trails in the state.

Big Creek Rim Trail. Length, 3.2 mi.; rating, easy. The trail connects Stone Door with Alum Gap campsite. Together with the Big Creek Gulf or Laurel Trails, this is a great trail for a long, interesting day hike or short overnight trip. The trail follows the blufftops with four major overlooks and gently rolling terrain.

Laurel Trail. Length, 2.9 mi.; rating, easy. The trail begins directly behind the Stone Door ranger station and runs to the Alum Gap campsite. The trail crosses numerous moist, fern-filled hollows where a rare white orchid is found sometimes. This trail makes a great return from either Big Creek trail and is the shortest way to the back country campsite.

The Connector Trail. Length, 6.7 mi.; rating, difficult. This trail connects all the Savage Gulf Natural Area trail system. It is all in the gulf and crosses seemingly endless rocky slopes. Although it crosses Big Creek, Collins River, and Savage Creek, there is usually no need to worry about getting wet unless there have been unusually heavy rains. The major streams are forded downstream from the sinks that swallow the entire flow 99 percent of the time. There is a pioneer cabin between the Big Creek and Collins River crossings at the Cator-Savage Historic Site. There is a campsite at the halfway point, directly across from the Collins Gulf Trail junction.

Collins Gulf Trail. Length, 10 mi.; rating, difficult. The trail runs along the rim of Collins Gulf from the junction with the South Rim Trail and the Stagecoach Road at the top of Peak Mountain along a line of cliffs in the middle of the view from the Stone Door, then descends into the gulf. The Collins East campsite is located near the descent into the gulf, where the trail crosses the Collins River on a 100-ft. suspension bridge above a pile of house-size boulders. From there it stays in the gulf. A mile from the boulder crossing, Rocky Point is visible above the trail. A spur trail leads up to Collins West campsite where a new trailhead has been built at the end of 55th Avenue from TN 108 in Gruetli Laager. The trail follows the wall of a cliff below an imposing overhang with Suter Falls, a series of three waterfalls below. Across the creek below the falls, the trail descends to the bottom of the gulf where the Collins River plunges over Pound Falls and disappears into a sink. Horsepound (or Pound) Gulf was the site of a "pound" where stolen livestock were kept during the Civil War. Local guerrilla groups with no fixed allegiance to the South or North stole indiscriminately from both sides. The remoteness and inaccessibility of the gulf made it ideal as both a hideout and a cache for plunder. The largest tributary gulf, Fall Creek, enters below Pound Falls but disappears into a sink before it reaches the trail. There is little water, but great scenery, from here to the junction with the Connector Trail.

The Stagecoach Trail. Length, 1.5 mi.; rating, moderate. The trail is a section of the Chattanooga to McMinnville Stage Road, built mostly by slave labor in 1836. It runs from the Connector Trail up Peak Mountain to the junction of the South Rim and Collins Gulf trails. Near the top there are extraordinary stone walls built by the slaves. This trail is on the National Register of Historic Places.

South Rim Trail. Length, 6 mi.; rating, moderate. The trail follows the south rim of Savage Gulf. It starts from the Savage Day Loop, crosses to the south side of Savage Creek on a suspension bridge, and follows the creek down to Savage Falls. The Savage Falls campsite is at the top of the hill just beyond the bridge. The trail follows the rim 4.5 mi., passing spur trails leading to overlooks, a moonshine still site, and several old-growth trees. The Stage Road campsite is at mile 5, after which the trail crosses Peak Mountain to the junction with the Collins Gulf and Stagecoach trails.

North Rim Trail. Length, 6.3 mi.; rating, moderate. Perhaps the most spectacular trail in the Savage Gulf Natural area, it starts on the back side of the Savage Day Loop and crosses the picturesque Meadow Creek. A half mile past the creek is Meadow Creek Bluff, the first of many striking overlooks. The overlooks get more and more spectacular as the gulf gets wider and deeper. Unlike the South Rim, these views are very near or right on the trail. At an overlook called Tommy Point, one can see the gulf mouth, Peak Mountain, and, in the distance, the Stone Door cliffs. From Tommy Point, the trail turns north and follows the rim of Coppinger Creek, to Hobbs Cabin, where there are a log trail shelter and wonderful pine woods campsites. The junction of the North Rim, Connector, and North Plateau trails is near Hobbs Cabin.

North Plateau Trail. Length, 7 mi.; rating, easy. This trail crosses the plateau north of Savage Gulf, where stately old-growth shortleaf pines tower over the forest. Although generally flat, it crosses the line of hills known as Cagle Knobs. The hollow on the east side of Cagle Knobs contains an outstanding old-growth hardwood forest. The Dinky Line Campsite is 1.5 mi. from the North Rim Trail at Meadow Creek. This section follows the bed of a narrow-gauge logging railroad operated by the Werner Family in the 1920s. The gulf was never logged, while the north plateau was sparsely logged, and the state acquired it in 1973 to preserve the big timber.

Savage Day Loop Trail. Length, 2 mi.; rating, easy. This trail provides access to all the other Savage Gulf trails from the Savage Gulf ranger station, 6 Mi. north of Palmer on TN 399. It has a great overlook of Savage Falls and a grand view down the gulf from Rattlesnake Point. On the back side of the loop is a beautiful old-growth hardwood stand. Pink lady's slipper orchids and mountain laurel decorate the trail in May, along with many other flowers. The first mile is also the last mile, with the actual loop being 2 mi. long. The South Rim Trail starts between the loop junction and the Savage Falls Overlook, and the North Rim Trail starts between Rattlesnake Point and the Loop junction.

Lone Rock Trail. This is a short trail at Grundy Lakes State Park. The Grundy Lakes site was a coal-mining and convict labor operation in the late 1800s, and several historic ruins of mines, buildings, and (most interestingly) the 136 coke ovens are visible along the trail. The whole site is listed on the National Historic Register.

—Contributed by Randy Hedgepath

Short Springs State Natural Area

Busby Falls Trail. Length, 0.8 mi. (one-way). **Machine Falls Trail.** Length, 0.7 mi. (one-way); rating, easy except for steep descent to Machine Falls. This 420-acre jewel, located between Tullahoma and Manchester in southern Middle Tennessee, was officially designated a State Natural Area in 1994. Short Springs is managed by the State of Tennessee's Division of Natural Heritage Natural Areas Program in the Department of Environment and Conservation in cooperation with the Friends of Short Springs, Tennessee Valley Authority, the City of Tullahoma, and the Tullahoma Utilities Board. A rugged area on the edge of the Highland Rim, it contains several waterfalls and an especially rich collection of native wildflowers, some quite rare. The hiker is strongly encouraged to stay on blazed trails because of the fragile ecosystem. The trail system is still under development by the Tennessee Trails Association.

The trail begins at Short Springs Road. From I–24 take exit 111 and turn left onto TN Highway 55 into Tullahoma. Turn right at the traffic light at Anderson Street then right at the second stop sign onto Hogan Road and left onto Country Club Drive. Stay on this road (it changes name to Short Springs Road for 3.7 miles. Parking is at the water tower. While the trail begins at the road, the trailhead and information kiosk are located about 70 yds. from the road to reduce vandalism.

At the information kiosk you will encounter the junction of the Busby Falls Trail and Machine Falls Trail. To do both trails as one large loop, proceed straight on the Busby Falls Trail toward Upper Busby Falls. The trail makes a sharp right turn at Upper Busby Falls and follows the bluff line. There is a short side trail on the left into a mountain laurel thicket where you will see Lower Busby Falls. After rejoining the main trail, the hiker will walk back into a hollow. After crossing the next ridge, the trail intersects with the Machine Falls Trail. Turn left and travel 200 yds. to the edge of the bluff. The trail descends steeply down limestone bluffs for 150 ft. dropping into Central Basin geology. As you descend you may notice the presence of black flaky Chattanooga Shale that delineates Central Basin geology from Highland Rim. At the base of the bluff, turn right and follow the creek upstream to Machine Falls (0.1 mi.), or turn left to walk the loop trail along Bobo Creek (.02 mi.). Both of the trails in the gorge are spectacular for large buckeye and sycamore trees year-round, wildflowers in the spring and early summer, dripping springs off the limestone bluffs in spring and fall, and ice formations in the winter.

After climbing back up the bluff on the return trip, take the first trail on the left to come out at the top of Machine Falls (not a loop). After returning to the main trail, take the second trail junction on the right to return to the trailhead through gently rolling oak and hickory forest.

Future trail development plans include extending the Machine Falls Trail on the other side of the creek up the left side of the ridge. The trail will make a right turn and bring the hiker to the top of Machine Falls. The trail follows the creek upstream and crosses the creek again to intersect with the existing Machine Falls Trail to make a loop.

—Contributed by Arleen Barnett and Brian Bowen

Herb Parsons Lake

Fisherville Nature Trail. Length, approximately 6.5 mi.; rating, easy. This trail is located in Fayette County at Herb Parsons Lake on land managed by Tennessee Wildlife Resources Agency (TWRA). It was originally established and maintained by Boy Scouts of America; however, BSA no longer does this. The Memphis Chapter of Tennessee Trails Association more recently blazed and cleared the trail. There are no maps available. From Memphis go east on TN 57 (Poplar Avenue) through Collierville, Tennessee. Turn north (left) onto Collierville-Arlington Road (TN 205) and stay on this road until you come to Monterey. Turn east (right) on the Monterey-Fisherville Road where there will be sign directing you to Herb Parsons Lake. Turn left and go a short distance to the lake entrance on your right. Monterey-Fisherville Road can also be reached by taking TN 205 south from I–40 (east of Memphis).

Begin the hike by walking in a southerly direction across the dam and following the trail into a grove of pine trees. The trail basically follows the contours of the lake. There are some low areas and creeks through which the trail passes, and it can be wet at certain times of the year. A bridge has been built over the main creek, and the lake is being kept lower than usual, which helps control some of the marshy areas. Along the way you can see loblolly pines and hardwoods such as oak, hickory, dogwood, maple, and river birch. There are turtles, snakes, frogs, and fish in the lake. You can also spot mallards, Canada geese, great blue herons, and an occasional egret. A good variety of raptors, songbirds, small animals, and occasional deer can be seen. The trail is especially good to hike in January, when most of the lake may be frozen; large numbers of ducks and geese concentrate here then. Bring binoculars.

The first 4 miles of trail end at Lakeview Road. Turn left onto Lakeview Road, go a short distance, and turn left again into the woods to complete the last 3 miles of trail. This last section is sometimes used by bow hunters, and there will be a TWRA sign here informing you of this. Hikers should check with the lake office to see when the bow hunters will be having a meet. If they are, you have two choices: You can retrace your steps or continue down Lakeview Road in a northwesterly direction to Fisherville

Road. Turn left here and this will bring you back to the lake office, a distance of 1 mile. If you need further information, the lake-office phone number is (901) 853–0751.

—Contributed by Jerri Bull (updated by Ray Burkett)

Lucius E. Burch, Jr., Forest State Natural Area

This 1,000-acre forest, named for a Memphis attorney, civic leader, and ardent conservationist, extends along the first and second bottoms on the north side of Wolf River in Shelby County just east of Memphis. It contains about 15 mi. of rewarding trails exclusively reserved for hiking, bird-watching, and nature study. It may be reached by taking the Walnut Grove Road (TN 23) exit, the first exit south of I–40 on the south loop of I–240, and proceeding east across Wolf River to the entrance of Shelby Farms Public Recreation Area. Turning right into Shelby Farms from Walnut Grove Road and then taking the first road to the right past tournament soccer fields leads to the trailhead and to a canoe launching ramp on Wolf River.

From the trailhead the upriver segment of the trail system extends in two legs that meet 4 mi. (8 mi. round-trip) upstream at another canoe launching ramp accessible from Germantown Road (TN 177). The downriver segment extends 3.5 mi. (7 mi. round-trip) downstream from the trail head as two successive loops. Both segments are rated easy to moderate. They each pass through four basic ecological communities—river, wetland/swamp, bottomland hardwoods forest, edge.

The river community is comprised of the aquatic life in the river and the plants and animals along the banks. River birch, silver maple, and black willow are the dominant tree species, while the river provides habitat for mink, muskrat, beaver, herons, kingfishers, and several species of ducks.

The wetland or swamp community is dominated by bald cypress and tupelo gums with swamp privet and water elms in the understory. Most of the birds and mammals found in the other communities visit here for breeding or feeding. The wetlands act as natural fish hatcheries and are vital habitat for breeding wood ducks.

The bottomland hardwoods forest community is within the river floodplain but is somewhat dryer when the river is not in flood stage. Dominant tree species are water oak, swamp chestnut oak, and willow oak, with mayapples and spider lily common on the forest floor. Vireos, warblers, flycatchers, and thrushes require these large tracts of forest to survive. Pileated woodpeckers and great horned owls are found here along with such mammals as white-tailed deer, gray fox, bobcat, and raccoon.

The edge community is created where the forest meets field. Many species, both native and exotic, of grasses, herbaceous plants, and shrubs are found here, along with cowbirds, mockingbirds, thrashers, catbirds, and bluebirds. Red fox prefer this habitat as do smaller mammals such as mice, voles, wood rats, and some species of shrews.

Unfortunately, this site—along with most others near cities across the state—is plagued by an invasive exotic plant, common privet, that for more than a century has been used as an ornamental hedge. Like other invasives it produces fruit (berries) prolifically and is spread widely by birds or locally by its aggressive root system. It soon takes over large areas, completely shouldering out native plant communities.

About 35 miles upstream from the Lucius E. Burch, Jr., Forest Natural Area, near LaGrange, is the 6,000-acre Wolf River State Wildlife Management Area which includes within its boundaries the Ghost River State Natural Area. The Ghost River area extends along a 10-mile river corridor of meanders, swamp, and open lake that supports mesic, bottomland hardwoods, and cypress-tupelo swamp forest communities. The river provides a great canoe trail, and while there are no trails presently, a hiking trail system will likely be developed in the future.

Both the Lucius E. Burch, Jr., Forest State Natural Area and the

Wolf River State Wildlife Management Area are important links in the Wolf River Greenway (see chapter 9).

—*Contributed by Larry Smith*

7. Historical Trails

Tennessee's rich cultural heritage may best be experienced by hiking some of her designated Historical Trails. Of the eleven national parks in Tennessee, six (Andrew Johnson, Cumberland Gap, Chickamauga and Chattanooga, Stones River, Fort Donelson, and Shiloh) are specifically national historic parks, military parks, or battlefields, and a seventh, the Natchez Trace Parkway, commemorates an historic old national road. All the national military parks and battlefields have many miles of walking trails, some wheelchair accessible, with interpretive signs detailing significant phases in the development of the historic events. Brochures and maps of each of these parks are available from the National Park Service.

The Tennessee Department of Environment and Conservation manages nine freestanding Cultural Areas across the state, each with either archeological or historic significance. Some, like the Narrows of the Harpeth State Historic Area (a satellite of Montgomery Bell State Park), featuring historic Montgomery Bell Tunnel and nearby Mound Bottom (an important Missisippian temple mound site destined to become a State Archeological Area), have both historic and prehistoric significance.

Some of the best historical trails systems, both state and national, are described here. Note that the first of these systems connects directly with the northern terminus of the Cumberland State Scenic Trail, while the second is within sight of the southern terminus of the CT at Signal Point National Military Park. The other systems described here also connect with, or are near, other state scenic trails, and the Historical Notes in Chapter 4 provide relevant background for the trails described in this chapter.

Cumberland Gap

Here is one of the most significant and scenic spots in Tennessee history. Through it, for centuries, the Warrior's Path linked the tribes of the Midwest with those of the Southeast, and in the late 1700s the Wilderness Road was the major route for settlers coming from Virginia and North Carolina into Kentucky and middle Tennessee. During the Civil War it was held by each side for a time and extensively fortified against an invasion that never came.

Cumberland Gap National Historical Park contains more than 20,000 acres in Kentucky, Virginia, and Tennessee. It encompasses roughly 20 miles of the northeast-southwest ridge called Cumberland Mountain, with the Gap crossing near the lower end of this tract. There are more than 50 miles of hiking trails in the park including the 17-mile Ridge Trail from the Pinnacle on the northeast side of the Gap to the White Rocks overlooking Ewing, Virginia. The Gap itself lies between Kentucky and Virginia, but just below it, at the southeast foot of the mountain, the historic town of Cumberland Gap lies in Tennessee.

In 1996 a four-lane tunnel opened a new highway route beneath the mountain, and the Cumberland Gap was restored to its late-1700s setting. It will become the main trailhead for the park and will connect the Ridge Trail with the Tri-State Trail. Presently underway is a conversion into an accessible trail of an abandoned railroad bed in Cumberland Gap, Tennessee, and its connection through the Cumberland Gap N.H.P. to the remainder of the already converted railway route up Powell Valley through Ewing, Virginia. Completion of this project will provide a superbly scenic 30-mile ridge and valley loop trail between the Cumberland Gap trailhead and the White Rocks near the northern end of the Ridge Trail.

Wilderness Road Trail. Length, 3.5 mi.; rating, moderate. The trail begins near the Iron Furnace in Cumberland Gap, Tennessee, and follows a path close to the original Wilderness Road. After passing through the saddle of the Gap, it continues to the Fort Foote side trail. Here it starts down the mountain to end near the Pinnacle Road 0.4 mi. from the park visitor center.

Tri-State Trail. Length, 1.4 mi.; rating, moderate. This trail begins near the Iron Furnace in Cumberland Gap, Tennessee, also the trailhead for the Cumberland State Scenic Trail, which here coincides with the Tri-State Trail and the Wilderness Road Trail. After leaving the Wilderness Road Trail, the Tri-State Trail passes a Civil War commissary and magazine site, then turns up the mountain to the point on the crest where Kentucky, Tennessee, and Virginia meet, marked by a small shelter with informative plaques. From this point a side trail continues 0.5 mi. along the crest to Fort Farragut, a Civil War artillery emplacement. The Cumberland State Scenic Trail continues from here to the southwest.

For further information, write Cumberland Gap National Historical Park, P.O. Box 1848, Middlesboro, KY 40965-1848, or call (606) 248–2817.

Lookout Mountain

This spot, in Chickamauga and Chattanooga National Military Park, is steeped in history. The national park and an adjoining tract called Reflection Riding have been the scene of many historic events. De Soto followed the Great Indian Warpath through this area in 1540. (Recent historical research strongly suggests that De Soto passed south from the Tennessee Valley down the Conasauga River, well to the east of Chattanooga.) It overlooks the sites of the upper Chickamauga towns wiped out in 1779 by Virginia militia under Colonel Evan Shelby and, again, in 1782 by forces under "Nolichucky Jack" Sevier. The five lower Chickamauga towns lay just west of Lookout Mountain; two of these were destroyed in 1794 by a force of Kentucky and Tennessee volunteers under Major James Ore. Then there was the notable "Battle Above the Clouds" in 1863. Famous landmarks include Sunset Rock, Point Park, Cravens House, and the "Castle in the Sky," a former resort hotel now occupied by Covenant College. There are more than 30 mi. of

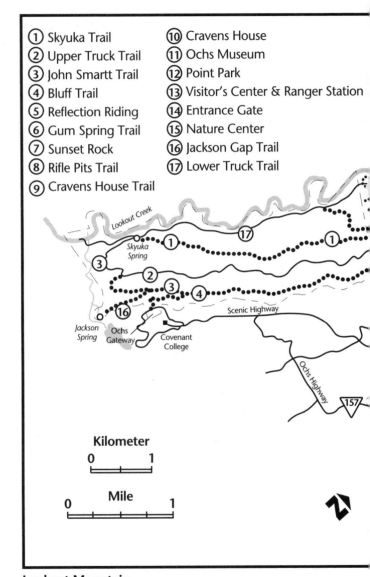

1. Skyuka Trail
2. Upper Truck Trail
3. John Smartt Trail
4. Bluff Trail
5. Reflection Riding
6. Gum Spring Trail
7. Sunset Rock
8. Rifle Pits Trail
9. Cravens House Trail
10. Cravens House
11. Ochs Museum
12. Point Park
13. Visitor's Center & Ranger Station
14. Entrance Gate
15. Nature Center
16. Jackson Gap Trail
17. Lower Truck Trail

Kilometer

0   1

Mile

0   1

Lookout Mountain—
Chickamauga & Chattanooga National Military Park

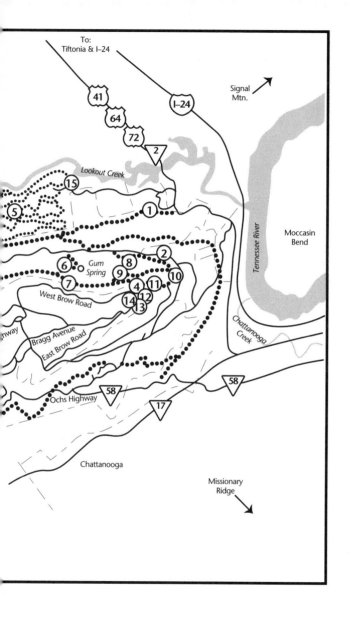

trails in the park, all built by the CCC between 1934 and 1940. U.S.G.S. quads: Chattanooga, 105SE, and Fort Oglethorpe, 106NE.

Bluff Trail. Length, 4.5 mi.; rating, moderate. Many trails branch off from Bluff Trail and are well marked. The hike spreads from Point Park to the Ochs Gateway. From Point Park the trail is reached by metal steps to the left of Ochs Museum. Here the Kentucky Volunteers climbed the mountain to plant their flag after the Battle Above the Clouds; there is a view that commands the broad curves of Moccasin Bend, Signal Mountain, and Missionary Ridge. The first 0.5 mi. of trail gradually descends, following the bed of a narrow-gauge railroad called the Dinky Line. At the junction of the Cravens House Trail to the right, it follows the 1,800-ft. contour, more or less, and Sunset Rock looms into view 0.7 mi. farther. Confederate General Longstreet stood here to direct operation during the struggle for Lookout Valley. Nowadays, people come here to rappel, to hawk-watch, to look at the hang gliders floating down from Raccoon Mountain, or just to sit and gaze at the distant Cumberlands or peaceful Lookout Valley.

The trail is good hiking any time of the year, although in severe winter weather the trails may be closed because of ice (contact the Point Park Visitor Center at 423–821–7786). In winter the icicles hanging from the rocky bluffs make for a photographer's paradise. Wildflowers, shrubs, and ferns are in masses, and lichens cover dripping rocks. The rock formations are extremely interesting, with cavelike openings, overhangs, and several spots where it is not hard to visualize an Indian with a campfire. Metal walkways span slides and areas where it was impossible to carve out a trail from the bluff, and there are natural benches along the way for resting. At the John Smartt Trail junction, veer left and make a 300-ft. climb to the Ochs Gateway parking area. Cars could be parked at Ochs Gateway or at Sunset Rock where there is a walkway up to a parking area on West Brow Road; or at Point Park. Parking space at Ochs Gateway and Sunset Rock is limited, and one-hour parking at Sunset Rock is enforced.

Skyuka Spring Trail. Length, 5.5 mi.; rating, moderate. TN

Hwy. 318 to Skyuka Springs. The trail is highlighted by rock formations, laurel, rhododendrons, ferns, and numerous varieties of trees. Skyuka Spring is named for the Indian Chief Skyuka, whose village was located here. Overnight camping permitted, but a special permit must be obtained at the headquarters at Point Park; fires are not allowed. The spring water that runs into Lookout Creek close by is not safe to drink.

A short distance after leaving Skyuka, there is a fork in the trail and Skyuka Trail bears right. The left fork is a service road that follows the creek into Reflection Riding. This can also be hiked as part of the Scouts' Blue Beaver Trail. This name was taken from the "Beavers in Blue," a phrase coined by the Confederates to describe the activity of the Union soldiers bottled up in Chattanooga in 1863. They were said to be always clearing trees—for fuel, shelter, and fortification. On leaving the spring there is a gradual climb to the 900-ft. level; the trail seems to maintain this elevation (more or less) until nearing the end.

Autumn is the most satisfying time of the year to hike the Skyuka, as the 5.5 mi. from the spring to the trail's end is under a canopy of trees, mainly hardwoods. In the fall, all vie to put forth their brightest reds and yellows with just enough green to contrast. There are many rock outcroppings with interesting erosion patterns. There is a gradual descent near the end on TN 318, a spur off U.S. 64. Cars can be parked at a nearby restaurant.

Cravens House–Bluff–Gum Springs Trail Loop. Length, 4 mi.; rating, moderate. The trail begins at Cravens House, the home of Robert Cravens. The original house, used by generals of both armies, was destroyed after the Battle Above the Clouds and was rebuilt by Cravens in 1866. At the junction of Cravens House Trail and the Bluff Trail, stay to the right and continue to Sunset Rock, past the steps to the marker pointing to Gum Spring, 1 mi. to the right. There is a steep but not too difficult descent of 300 ft.

The Gum Spring Trail dead-ends into the Upper Truck Trail; turn right and follow what seems to be a tree tunnel where bird life abounds. This is really a National Park Service road and is also used as a horse trail. After less than a mile of easy walking, there is an option of continuing on the Upper Truck Trail to Cravens House or making a right turn to return on the Rifle Pits Trail. Along the Rifle Pits Trail there are rock circles and a wall that were no doubt used by the Confederates in battle. Some archeologists say the origin of these stone structures goes back to the woodland culture, a prehistoric period. It is just 1.0 mi. back to Cravens House—a hike of natural, historical, and archeological interest.

The Blue Beaver Trail and the Nolichucky Jack Trail are Scout Award Trails administered by Blue Beaver Trail, Inc., P.O. Box 38, Hixson, TN 37343. They follow generally the trails described in this chapter. Additional information may be obtained by writing to the above address.

—Contributed by Dot Ventress (updated by Charles Spearman)

Natchez Trace National Scenic Trail

The Natchez Trace is one of the best-remembered landmarks from the era of United States expansion into the Old Southwest. For over two decades in the early 1800s, it was the most significant highway in this region and one of the most important in the nation. In places, the Tennessee segment of the Natchez Trace National Scenic Trail follows sections of the original Trace and passes several sites of historical significance.

The southern trailhead lies about a quarter mile northeast of the site of John Gordon's ferry on the Duck River. Gordon, first postmaster in Nashville, began operating the ferry in 1802. A few hundred yards east of the ferry crossing is Gordon's restored home built in 1817-18, mostly under the supervision of his wife while he was away serving as a scout with General Andrew Jackson.

A few miles northeast of Duck River, beside a narrow section of the old Trace still used as a county road, is the now overgrown site of a hand-dug well where Andrew Jackson is said to have stopped on his many trips along the Trace. Local legend has it that two men who operated a stand (inn) here were killed by robbers.

At the Tennessee Valley Divide parking area, the trail crosses Duck River Ridge which was, until at least 1805, the eastern boundary of Chickasaw territory. About 2.5 miles to the north, the trail tops out on Butler Ridge at the Old Trace parking area. Colonel Thomas Butler was in command of the troops working on the trace in the 1801–03 period. A veteran of the Revolution and an ardent Federalist, he was first sent to Tennessee to remove white squatters from Cherokee lands, and in 1799 was commander of the garrisons at Tellico Blockhouse on the Little Tennessee opposite the site of old Fort Loudon and at Southwest Point (Kingston). Camp Butler, mentioned by John Muir in 1867 (see Chapter 4, John Muir Trail) as General Winfield Scott's headquarters during the 1838 Cherokee Removal, was probably named for either Thomas Butler or his nephew, Colonel Robert Butler, who was Andrew Jackson's adjutant-general during the War of 1812 and secretary of the commission that negotiated the Jackson and Chickasaw Purchases of West Kentucky and West Tennessee from the Chickasaw in 1818. The last 1.7 miles of the trail to Garrison Creek, the northern trailhead, follows Butler Ridge on the longest remaining unimproved section of the Natchez Trace in Tennessee. Garrison Creek was named for a nearby U.S. Army post here in 1801–02.

The Tennessee segment of the National Scenic Trail traverses one of the hilliest parts of the Old Trace route and provides some of its best vistas. The Water Valley Overlook across the Parkway from the trail at milepost 411.8 and the overlook at the end of the short spur trail above the Garrison Creek parking area offer particularly rewarding views of wooded hills and pastoral valleys at any time of the year.

This rolling terrain and variety of habitats support a wide diversity of native flora and fauna. White-tailed deer and wild turkey can be spotted anywhere on the trail, and red-tailed hawks and barred owls are often heard or seen. Also heard or seen in the appropriate habitat along the trail, and at the appropriate time of year, are at least fifty other species of breeding birds.

The 1.5 mi. of the trail alongside Burns Branch showcase a striking diversity of native trees, shrubs, wildflowers, and ferns. Walking from the marshy bottom and Ordovician-age limestone bluffs near the Burns Branch parking area to the Mississippian-age cherty ridgetop at the Tennessee Valley Divide parking area, one may find over 200 species of flowering plants and ferns, most of them native. While this is probably the richest native plant habitat in the northern 50 miles of the parkway corridor, it is destined soon to be crossed by a new state highway, I–840. It remains to be seen how well the National Park Service and the Tennessee Department of Transportation can work together to prevent serious degradation of this special place or destructive siltation of Burns Branch itself, a perpetual spring-fed stream here still unpolluted and full of aquatic life.

Some wildflowers to watch for here in each month of the blooming season are:

April

Rue Anemone
Wild Blue Phlox
Purple Phacelia
Jacobs Ladder
Wild Ginger
Bent Trillium
Yellow Corydalis
Trout Lily
Wood Betony
Toothwort (three species)
Foamflower
Star Chickweed
Smooth Rock Cress
False Garlic
Wood Vetch
Yellow Buckeye

Early Meadowrue
Celandine Poppy
Smooth Yellow Violet
White Violet
Green Violet
Common Blue Violet
Mayapple
Spicebush
Bladdernut
Harbinger-of-spring
Round-leaved Ragwort
Sarvisberry
Hepatica (two species)
Leatherwood
Twisted-petal Trillium
Prairie Trillium

May

Purple Rocket
Philadelphia Fleabane
Ox-eye Daisy
Spring Avens
Dwarf Dandelion
Blackberry
Large Houstonia
Jack-in-the-pulpit
Black Cherry
Solomon's Seal
Dolls Eye

White Blue-eyed Grass
Downy Woodmint
Indian Pink
Golden Alexanders
Wild Yam
False Solomon's Seal
Sweet Cicely
Four-leaved Milkweed
White Bergamot
Wild Geranium
Green Dragon

June

Wild Potato Vine
Tall Bellflower
Ruellia
Fringed Loosestrife
Sweet-scented Joe-Pye Weed
Southern Rosin-weed
Large Yellow Wood-sorrel
Wild Hydrangea
White Avens
Black-eyed Susan
Enchanters Nightshade

Hairy Angelica
Coreopsis
Fairy-wand
Indian Physic
Clustered Snakeroot
Ginseng
Honewort
Michigan Lily
Spotted St. Johnsort
Yellow Passion Flower
American Euonymus (Hearts-a-Bustin)

July

Spotted Jewelweed
Tall Meadow Rue
Winged Monkey Flower
Seedbox
Cranefly Orchid
Rose Pink
Thimbleweed

Partridge Pea
Lady's Thumb
Cattail
Pokeberry
St. Johns Wort (three species)
Yellow Passion Flower

August

Mullein Foxglove	Trumpetweed
Brown-eyed Susan	Early Goldenrod
Agrimony	Indian Tobacco
Evening Primrose	Great Lobelia
Pale Jewelweed	Small Wood Sunflower
Cowbane	Tick Trefoil (four species)
False Nettle	Flowering Spurge

September

Late-flowering Boneset	Calico Aster
Mistflower	Wreath Goldenrod
Slender Gerardia	Canada Goldenrod
Virgin's Bower	Woodland Lettuce
Turtlehead	White Snakeroot
Witch-hazel	

Natchez Trace National Scenic Trail. Length, 24.5 mi.; rating, moderate; use, hiking and horseback.

Parkway Milepost	Access Points	Trail Miles
427.6	Garrison Creek Parking Area* (staging area and northern terminus of trail)	0.0
426.2	Old Trace Parking Area	2.1
425.2	Burns Branch Parking Area	1.3
423.8	Tennessee Valley Divide Parking Area	1.4
422.9	Carter Road Staging Area (no parkway access)	1.2
415.6	Highway 7 Staging Area (access via Highway 7 and	8.9

	county road on northeast side of parkway)	
408	Highway 50 Staging Area* (southern terminus of trail) Access via Highway 50 and Totty Lane along west side of parkway)	9.6
		24.5

Comfort stations and drinking water available.

Fort Henry Hiking Trails

These trails are located in Land Between the Lakes (LBL), between Kentucky and Barkley lakes in Tennessee and Kentucky. This 26-mi. system of interconnecting loops closely follows the route of General U.S. Grant's troops in his campaign to capture Fort Donelson during the Civil War. The system starts at the parking lot off Fort Henry-Blue Springs Road (clearly marked by highway signs) and ends at the South Welcome Station on the Trace. To reach the parking lot take Blue Springs Road west from the Trace in LBL or take Fort Henry Road from U.S. 79 (4 mi. east of Paris Landing State Park). In addition to the historical resource, the Fort Henry Trails traverse a variety of hardwood and pine forests along ridges and bottomlands where deer and turkey sightings are common. These trails are located in the Tennessee portion of the Land Between the Lake National Recreation Area, which is a 170,000-acre recreation and environmental education area, operated by the Tennessee Valley Authority. TVA-LBL personnel were assisted by college students, historians, the National Park Service, and two scout troops—Dover Troop 501 and Clarksville Troop 314—in developing this trail system. Trail markings are located at each trail junction and on trailside trees.

The system, which became a national recreation trail in October 1976, is designed so hikers can plan an hour hike or an overnight trip. Camping must be off the marked trails; campfires are permitted except in the periods of high fire danger. The Piney Campground, with full facilities, is nearby, and there are numerous primitive campgrounds in the area. Hikers may register at either end of the Telegraph Trail, which runs from the South Information Center on TN 49 (known as "The Trace") to Fort Henry parallel to Blue Spring Road. Trail maps are available at the South Welcome Station and at Piney Campground. Other trails in the system include Peytona, Tennessee Ridge, Artillery, Devil's Backbone, Piney, Shortfeal Pine, Telegraph Pickett, Pickett Loop, Boswell, and the newly opened Fort Henry Connector that runs from the former site of Fort Henry to the Piney Trail section, making a shorter hike possible.

Shiloh Military Trails

This system of hikes is sponsored by Shiloh Military Trails, Inc., P.O. Box 17507, Memphis, TN 38187, and approved by the Boy Scouts of America. The trails mostly follow roadways in Shiloh National Military Park, the scene of one of the bloodiest battles of the Civil War. The park is located 7 mi. south of U.S. 64 on TN 22 or 14 mi. east of U.S. 45, south of Selmer on TN 142. There are eleven patch-award hikes, including military, historical, environmental, and compass cross-country. Of these, nine range from 10 to 20 miles in length, are rated easy, and are recommended for Scouts 11 years old and up. Two are for younger hikers: the 2-mi. Shiloh Battlefield Trail and the 3-mi. Shiloh Indian Mound Trail. Maps and required reading material may be ordered from the above address. For information call Ken Humphreys, person-to-person at (901) 323–2739. If no answer, write or call Trail Headquarters, Troop 343 Scout Hut, Kingsway Christian Church, 6310 Poplar Avenue, Memphis, TN 38119; (901) 681–0058 (person-to-person).

Also within the park, on top of a 60-ft.-high bluff on the Tennessee River just upstream from the site of Pittsburg Landing, are the remains of a Mississippian period Native American fortified town. Earthen banks mark the lines of inner and outer palisade walls, and a large temple mound still stands in the center of the site with a number of smaller mounds on either side. Erosion by the river at the foot of the bluff is an imminent threat to this important archeological treasure unless extensive stabilization measures are undertaken soon. The site is reached by a 0.5-mi. walk east on a paved road from Riverside Drive just beyond stop 13, Bloody Pond, on the Shiloh Battlefield driving tour.

Nathan Bedford Forrest State Park and Johnsonville State Historic Area

Located 8 mi. northeast of Camden on Kentucky Lake, the park may be reached from I–40 via U.S. 641 to Camden. Turn right onto U.S. 70 and watch for the signs leading to the park.

This area is of unusual historical and geological interest, being the site of a highly irregular conflict as well as containing the highest point of ground in West Tennessee. The Confederate attack on the Union redoubt and supply depot at Johnsonville, replaced by New Johnsonville since the construction of Kentucky Dam, not only was an easy victory for General Nathan Bedford Forrest but is also the only recorded instance in military annals of the defeat of a naval force by a cavalry regiment. Further details of the battle are available at park headquarters.

The park and most of the trail network lie along the wooded west bank of the Tennessee River (Kentucky Lake). It is an area of chert ridges and fertile valleys and abounds in a variety of hardwoods. Also found in abundance are many species of mosses, ferns, wildflowers, and shrubs. Mountain laurel adds its perpetual beauty to the higher ridges. A ranger-naturalist is in residence and is available for consultation. A campground with utility hookups is also within the park.

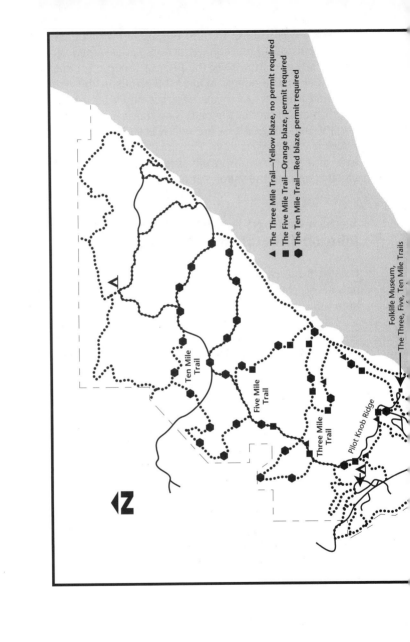

N

▲ The Three Mile Trail—Yellow blaze, no permit required

■ The Five Mile Trail—Orange blaze, permit required

⬡ The Ten Mile Trail—Red blaze, permit required

Ten Mile
Trail

Five Mile
Trail

Three Mile
Trail

Pilot Knob Ridge

Folklife Museum,
The Three, Five, Ten Mile Trails

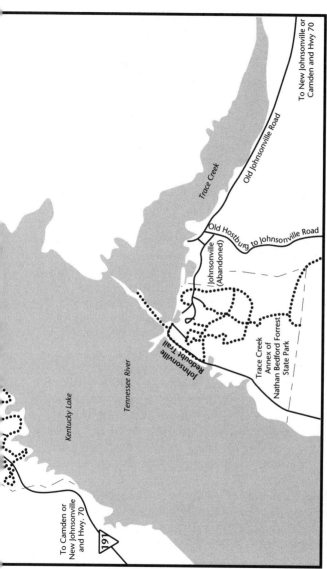

Nathan Bedford Forrest State Park

To New Johnsonville or
Camden and Hwy 70

Old Johnsonville Road

Trace Creek

Old Hostburg to Johnsonville Road

Johnsonville
(Abandoned)

Trace Creek
Annex of
Nathan Bedford Forrest
State Park

Johnsonville
Redoubt Trail

Tennessee River

Kentucky Lake

To Camden or
New Johnsonville
and Hwy. 70

191

Three Mile Trail. Rating, moderate; blazes, yellow. This is a loop trail that begins at the Tennessee River Folklife Center on Pilots Knob. It makes a gradual descent approximately 308 ft. into a hollow and follows the contour of the hollow to exit in a gradual climb to a ridge that leads back to the beginning.

Five Mile Trail. Rating, moderate; blazes, orange. This trail covers most of the old Tennessee Forrest Trail that was sponsored by Boy Scout Troop 343 of Memphis, with patches and medals available for hikers. For further information regarding materials and patches, write to Ken Humphreys, P.O. Box 17507, Memphis, TN 38117.

Ten Mile Trail. Rating, moderate; blazes, red. This trail also begins at the Folklife Center on Pilots Knob, but goes through more of the park. Hardwoods such as oak, hickory, yellow poplar, sycamore, river birch, beech, and cherry are in evidence. There are several varieties of fern and moss in the hollows along streams, and shrubs and wildflowers abound. Mountain laurel and flame azalea bloom in the spring. There are small mammals such as fox, raccoon, and squirrel, as well as deer. Since the park is located near the Tennessee River Flyway, migrating ducks and geese may be seen in season. For brochures, maps, or information call (901) 584–6356 or write Nathan Bedford Forrest State Park, Eva, TN 38333.

Johnsonville Redoubt Trail. Length, approximately 4 mi.; rating, moderate. This trail is located in the Trace Creek Annex of Nathan Bedford Forrest State Park, across the Tennessee River from Pilot Knob. Access is from U.S. 70 in New Johnsonville, where a sign points north to the Johnsonville State Historic Area. The trail goes by sections of Old Johnsonville to historic sites such as redoubts, rifle pits, cemeteries, home sites, and the old railroad turnaround and railroad bed.

Reynoldsburg, located 4 mi. northeast at the mouth of Dry Creek, was the Tennessee River crossing point of Glover's Trace, which in the late 1700s ran from Nashville down most of Trace Creek from present McEwen to Waverly and then down Dry Creek. Settled around 1800–1805, Reynoldsburg in the 1830s became a stop on the Nashville-to-Memphis stage line, which mostly followed the old Glover's Trace.

Johnsonville (named for Andrew Johnson, military governor of Tennessee from 1862 to 1865) had been a steamboat landing at the mouth of Trace Creek prior to the Civil War. It became a major Union Army supply depot when the Nashville and Northwestern Railroad was completed in May 1864.

After abandoning Atlanta in September 1864, General John Bell Hood, now in command of the Army of Tennessee, moved west into north Alabama. By late October he was preparing to invade Tennessee, while General William Tecumseh Sherman had ceased chasing him and was returning to Atlanta to begin his "march to the sea." Meanwhile, General Forrest's cavalry corps were in West Tennessee where on November 4, hoping to sever the Tennessee River section of Sherman's supply line from Louisville to Atlanta, they attacked the Union riverport depot at Johnsonville Landing. In less than twenty-four hours Forrest's troops destroyed four Union gunboats, four transports, seventeen barges, and over $8 million worth of supplies and took 150 prisoners, at a cost to his force of two killed, nine wounded, and two guns lost. For more information call (615) 535-2789 or write to Johnsonville State Historic Area, Denver, TN 37054.

Fort Pillow State Historic Area

Located on the Mississippi River at the first Chickasaw Bluff, this is where Fort Prud'homme was built by the French in 1682 (*see* Chapter 4, Chickasaw Bluffs Trail). To get there, turn west off U.S. 51, 9 mi. north of Covington near Henning on TN 87; proceeding 17 miles, turn right onto TN 207, which leads to the park entrance. Trail maps are available at the visitor's center. There are picnic facilities and a good campground.

Here in late 1861 and early 1862, Confederate engineers completed fortification of the First Chickasaw Bluff, the most formidable of four forts they built on the bluffs to thwart an apparently imminent Union invasion via the Mississippi River. The steamboat channel ran so close under the bluff here as to be within musket range of the fort, while passing gunboats were open to plunging fire from the fort's guns and could scarcely elevate their own sufficiently to return fire. In the 1860s the river channel lay where Cold Creek Chute Lake lies today, about 1 mi. east of the present channel. At Slip-in Overlook there is a panoramic view, one of the most beautiful in West Tennessee, where changes in the river since the Civil War are identified.

When the fort was abandoned by the Confederates in May 1862, the Union Army occupied it immediately and held it for two years to prevent its recapture and the cutting of Mississippi River traffic. When the advance brigade of General Nathan Bedford Forrest's cavalry corps approached before dawn on April 12, 1864, 550 Union soldiers held a redoubt they had built on the high point of the bluff overlooking the mouth of Cold Creek. They also occupied four lines of huts immediately south of the redoubt and a long rifle pit extending from 200 yds. south to 100 yds. east of the redoubt. Much of the 3-mi.-long outer breastworks, built by the Confederates as the fort's landward defense line, looked down on the Federals' redoubt, but there were only a few Federal pickets posted there. All but two of them were captured by Forrest's advance brigade just after dawn.

By 9:00 A.M., Forrest's main force moved up toward the redoubt. When they captured the outer line of huts, the general called a truce to offer the Union commander the chance to surrender honorably with all his men to be treated as prisoners of war. The Union commander refused, and the redoubt was stormed and taken with heavy Union casualties. In the process, the fort was effectively destroyed for further use by either side.

Today, the original breastworks remain in good condition and are followed in many places by the trail system. The Union redoubt of 1864 has been restored after extensive archeological study, and interpretive signs relate information about the battle.

Fort Pillow S.H.A. is also a Wildlife Observation Area designated by the Tennessee Wildlife Resources Agency. It provides habitat for deer, turkey, and many other species of animals and, especially, migratory birds. Mississippi kites can often be viewed from the bluffs during the summer. Fifteen miles of hiking trails guide the hiker over the breastworks and battle site, while the hilly terrain, hardwood forests, and interpretive signs identifying wildlife species and habitat provide many opportunities to study and enjoy the park's natural setting.

Fort Pillow Historical Trail. Length, 10 mi.; rating, moderate. For information about trail patches, contact Ken Humphreys, Historical Hiking Trails, Inc., P.O. Box 17505, Memphis, TN 38187. The trail starts on the road near the Inner Breastworks, elevation 400 ft., and runs generally northwestward following the breastworks, then passing over several points of land believed to have been used by Confederate sharpshooters in the Battle of Fort Pillow. The trail crosses a ravine by way of a swinging bridge, then heads up the slope past the area where the Union army occupied cabins, huts, and tents. It follows the bluff northeastward past the reconstructed main redoubt, which was held by Union troops.

The Historical Trail (blazed in red) and Historical Trek (blazed in yellow), coinciding to this point, continue generally eastward to reach Crutcher Lake Road entering the park from Anderson-Tully State Wildlife Management Area, just across Cold Creek to the north. Here the Historical Trek turns right to parallel the road southeastward, while the Historical Trail crosses the road and continues northeastward along the blufftop to a point where the Outer Breastworks approached Cold Creek; it then follows the Breastworks remnants, first eastward, the southward.

After crossing the road again, the trail follows the main east-west portion of the Outer Breast works for about 1.5 mi. to Fort Pillow Lake. There is a beaver dam on the left below the dam that forms the lake. Crossing the dam and following the road uphill to the northwest, there are more breastworks parallel to the road on the left. The trail turns left through a break in the breastworks and

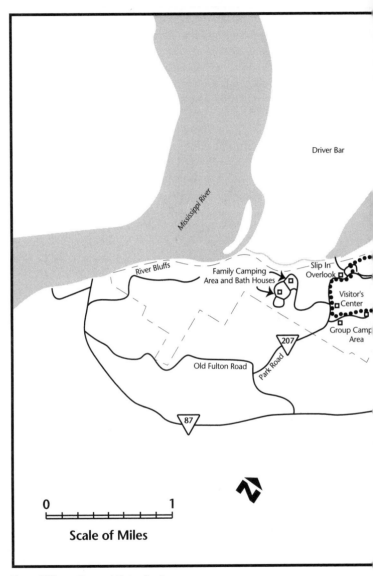

Fort Pillow State Historic Area

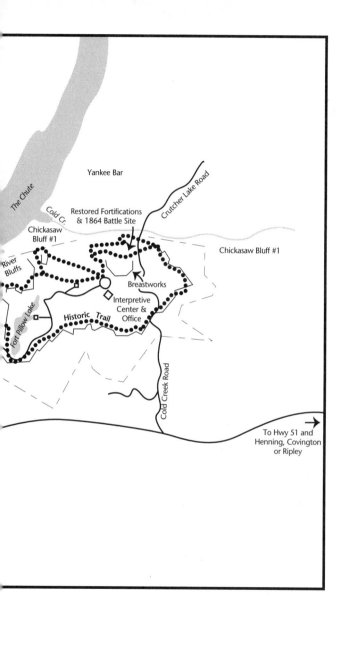

Yankee Bar

The Chute

Cold Cr.

Crutcher Lake Road

Restored Fortifications
& 1864 Battle Site

Chickasaw
Bluff #1

Chickasaw Bluff #1

River
Bluffs

Breastworks

Fort Pillow Lake

Historic Trail

Interpretive
Center &
Office

Cold Creek Road

To Hwy 51 and
Henning, Covington
or Ripley

follows a ridge, then drops into a low area above the beaver pond, elevation 270 ft. Now it goes up a steep hill to the top of a ridge, elevation about 380 ft., and follows the top of the ridge, past the Group Camp and the Visitors' Center, to the road. Here the trail turns right and follows the road about 0.5 mi. to the Slip In observation point. This is the upper end of the first Chickasaw Bluff, which "slipped in" to the Mississippi River in 1907, blocking the Cold Creek Chute. The elevation is about 420 ft., and the river is at 210 ft. An industrial plant is visible on the Arkansas side of the Mississippi River immediately upstream, and Osceola, Arkansas, 7 mi. upriver to the northwest, can be seen on a clear day.

Again, the trail follows the road downhill around a U-turn and leaves the road to go uphill to the northwest to the top of a bluff, then northward to the west leg of the Outer Breastworks, turning east along more breastworks, which were the connecting link between the outer works and the inner fortified hills. The trail now descends to a dirt road, goes left about 400 ft., then north (right) up the side of one of the fortified hills along more breastworks. It goes to the edge of the bluff, parallels the edge for a short distance, passes the end of more breastworks, and travels downhill to another dirt road. The trail follows the road a short way, then turns left up the next hill and follows more breastworks around the top of the hill to the edge of the bluff. It runs east along the bluff, then downhill and generally eastward to a point overlooking the ravine that was crossed on the first leg of the trip. From here the trail runs south, then east, ascending a steep, wooded ridge to the Inner Breastworks, and follows it to the starting point.

Two other trails are the **Fort Pillow Historical Trek,** a 5-mi. loop suitable for younger hikers, and the one-way **First Chickasaw Bluff Trail,** a 5-mi. segment of the Chickasaw Bluffs State Scenic Trail, which has an adequate campsite 1 mi. from the south end. The southwest trailhead for the latter is at the townsite of old Fulton at the end of TN 87, and the northeast half of it coincides with the Historical Trail as far as Crutcher Lake Road, which is the northeast trailhead of the First Chickasaw Bluff Trail. All three Fort Pillow trails offer nice patch awards.

8. Trails on Other Federal Lands

Great Smoky Mountains National Park

♿ **Sugarlands Valley Nature Trail.** Length, 0.5 mi. loop; challenge level 1; smooth. Located 0.5 mi. south of the Sugarlands Visitor Center on Newfound Gap Road, this fully accessible paved trail is designed to provide the visitor with a taste of what the 500,000-acre national park has to offer. The trail passes a stone chimney, a stone wall, and the West Prong of the Little Pigeon River. At the trail entrance, the hiker can pick up a large print brochure that is keyed to numbered posts. The printed material is supplemented by four tablet exhibits and twelve tactile exhibits, which consist of raised pictures such as leaves and depressed letters. Exhibits point out that the Sugarlands Valley, which now appears to be an undisturbed forest, was once home to a hundred families, two churches, three schools, two hotels, a post office, two tubmills, and several sawmills. The area had been farmed and logged for a hundred years before the park was established. Against the backdrop of a regenerating cove hardwood forest along the trail, the visitor learns of the great diversity of trees, fishes, and salamanders that now inhabit the park and make this area worthy of its International Biosphere Reserve designation.

—Contributed by Harold Draper

Tennessee Valley Authority Small Wild Area

The TVA has set aside fifteen tracts of land to be preserved as small wild areas. Two are on the Cumberland Plateau, and the rest are on TVA reservoir land. They vary in size from eight to 300 acres, and each contains unique natural features, such as caves, waterfalls, and springs. Trails were developed by YCC and YACC crews, and there are five national recreation trails in these areas. The River Bluff Trail on the Norris Dam Reservation was dedicated as a national recreation trail on June 10, 1976. The Lady Finger Bluff Trail on Kentucky Lake received state and national recreation trail designation on April 13, 1978. The Hemlock Bluff Trail was designated a national recreation trail on November 27, 1981. We describe these three trails and TVA's newest small wild areas and trails, Big Ridge and Whites Creek.

Hemlock Bluff National Recreation Trail. Length, 6.5 mi.; rating, moderate. This trail, entirely on TVA property, provides a scenic hike along steep ridges and bluffs with numerous views of Norris Lake. The trailhead, with three parking spaces, is located in Union County, Tennessee, at the Loyston Point Recreation Area, on the road to the boat ramp. Exit I–75 10 mi. northwest of Knoxville onto TN 61 and go northeast 4 mi. to Park Road, then north 5 mi. on Park Road to Ridge Circle Road, then east on Ridge Circle Road 2 mi. to Loyston Point Road, and then northeast 3 mi. to Hemlock Bluff N.R.T. Loyston Point also has a campground, picnic area, and swimming beach.

From the parking area the trail briefly descends, then climbs through a hardwood forest and soon crosses a gravel road (closed to traffic). It is a good idea to note this intersection, since this road is part of the return trip. After passing the road, the trail descends through hardwood and pine forests and reaches the lake edge after about 0.5 mi. The trail immediately climbs steeply to a ridge, levels out on a contour, and then climbs again to a ridgetop at about 1 mi. from the trailhead.

The trail descends steeply from the ridge, then turns sharply and follows the lake edge along a small embayment. A wildlife food plot is visible to the right of the sharp turn. This point is about 1.5 mi. from the trailhead. The terrain becomes less steep as the trail follows the lake edge for about 1 mi. When the terrain again becomes steeper, the trail begins a series of switchbacks up to a high ridgetop. The ridgetop is about 3 mi. from the trailhead.

The trail follows the ridgetop, and after about another 0.5 mi., the first hemlocks become visible to the left. The small grove of hemlocks, which gives the trail its name, is visible on both sides of the trail for several hundred yards. At 4 mi. from the trailhead, the trail descends through a pine forest. At 4.5 mi., the trail passes old homesites along an old road in a grove of cedar and pine trees, then passes rock outcrops. At 5 mi., the trail descends into a small gully and makes a sharp turn at the end of it. It then ascends to a gravel road.

Continue by turning right on the gravel-and-grass road, which passes wildlife openings and food plots. After about a mile, the road climbs to a hilltop. When reaching the hilltop, start looking for the trail crossing while walking along the ridge. Turn left to return to the parking area for a total hike of about 7 mi.

—Contributed by Harold Draper

River Bluff Trail. Length, 3.1 mi.; rating, easy. To get there take the first left turn off U.S. 441 after passing the overlook across the Norris Dam from the visitor's center. The road will fork immediately. Take the left fork down the hill to the parking area at the trailhead, elevation 1,000 ft. This loop trail passes through three distinct forest regions. From the parking lot, the trail first passes through a pine plantation that was decimated by southern pine bark beetles in the 1970s. This area is characterized by young dogwoods, redbuds, American beech, and maple. Pine trees killed by southern pine bark beetles are slowly decomposing into the soil and providing nutrients for successional hardwoods. Take the left fork of the trail, descending gradually toward the Clinch River at 840 ft.

The lower part of the trail near the river is famous for wildflowers in the spring. In April, yellow adder's tongue (also called trout lily), trillium, bloodroot, twinleaf, and toothwort bloom in profusion along with a few bright yellow celandine poppies. Ferns grow in the shade of a towering limestone bluff on the right, and equisetum (also called scouring rush) grows along the riverbank on the left. Canada geese are often seen and heard in this section of the river. Trout fishermen in waders ply their skills in the river during low flows. Near Hibbs Island and the low water dam (also called a weir), the trail begins a long gradual climb. Dutchman's breeches, phlox, and twinleaf are prominent spring wildflowers in this section of the trail.

The upper region of the area is drier, less protected, and usually warmer than the lower part of the trail. Squaw root, ginger, toothworts, and mayapples are found on these drier sites. Near the top, 1,100 ft. elevation, the trail passes an old chestnut tree trunk, all that remains of a noble giant that was stricken by the blight of the 1920s. A bench provides opportunity to enjoy a moment of solitude and to catch your breath. The trail levels out and follows the crest of the ridge. Tulip poplars have reached tremendous size and age here. Many show signs of lightning strikes and have broken tops. They provide cavities and roosts for owls, woodpeckers, flying squirrels, and raccoons. The descent back to the original trail passes through some remaining Chinese chestnut trees that were planted for wildlife mast after the American chestnut blight.

Flower patterns change with the seasons, from the yellow and white of spring flowers to the blue and purple of asters and Joe Pye weed in the fall. You can hike the River Bluff Trail over and over and always find something new. A free brochure and spring wildflower key is available by writing TVA, Wildlife and Natural Heritage Resources Section, Norris, TN 37828.

—Contributed by Judith Bartlow

Whites Creek Trail. Length, 2.5 mi.; rating, moderate. The Whites Creek Trail provides a scenic loop along ridgetops overlooking Watts Bar Lake. Most of the trail traverses public lands in the TVA Whites Creek Small Wild Area, but part of the loop uses service roads on lands managed by Bowater Southern Corporation. Forests are mixed pine and hardwoods and pine plantations. Access to the trailhead is from U.S. 27 at milepost 30 in Rhea County, Tennessee. This milepost is 8 miles south of Rockwood and 7 miles north of Spring City. At the crossroads, turn southeast onto the paved Roddy Road. After 0.6 mi., the road becomes gravel and ends at the TWRA Whites Creek boat ramp about 1.0 mi. from U.S. 27.

The trail begins along the lakeshore to the right of the boat ramp. Follow the wooden walkway and white blazes into the woods. After about 0.5 mi., a sign announces the Whites Creek Small Wild Area, 176 acres, after the trail crosses a small creek. The trail then climbs steeply on rock steps to arrive at a ridgetop at about .75 mi.

At the ridgetop, turn sharply left to begin the loop. The trail follows the TVA-Bowater boundary (marked by red paint on trees) for a short distance, then leaves the boundary to wind across the tops of several small knolls. These provide good views of the lake from 120 to 150 feet above the lake level. After the third knoll, the trail descends sharply to the right, crosses two small gullies, and climbs to another ridge at the TVA boundary. The trail follows this ridge for several hundred yards, then descends and leaves the Small Wild Area (designated once again by a sign). After crossing a gully, the trail climbs to a road, enters a pine plantation, and follows the road for a short distance to an intersection with another road. Turning right, it follows a road up a valley to the ridgetop, where it turns sharply right and enters a hardwood forest. After a few minutes, the loop is complete. Turn left to return to the parking area and trailhead.

Big Ridge Trail. Length, 1.3 mi.; rating, easy to moderate. Not to be confused with Big Ridge State Park. This area is near Chattanooga, Tennessee. Take State Highway 153 north across Chickamauga Dam. Take the first right after crossing the dam onto Lake Resort Drive. Then take the first left into the North Chickamauga Creek Greenway. Walk the paved greenway beside North Chickamauga Creek. At 0.5 mi. the Big Ridge Trail turns off into the woods at the trailhead sign. The first part of the trail is an old woods road that led to a homesite at the top of the ridge. The trail follows a gentle grade through second growth hardwood forest of chestnut oak, red oak, hickory, and persimmon. It turns left when it reaches the ridge and continues along the ridge with backward views of Chickamauga reservoir and Chickamauga dam. The homesite is visible as a patchy clearing on top of the ridge. All that remains are a stone cistern and June blooming day lilies. The trail meanders through the woods on top of the ridge and enters an old-growth forest as it begins the downhill section of the loop. Some of the trees in this section are estimated at 200 years old. Note the thick loose soil underfoot that characterizes these undisturbed forests. Largest trees in this section include tulip poplar, white oak, American beech, sugar and red maples, sassafras, and buckeye. Early spring wildflowers are false Solomon's seal, Solomon's seal, toothwort, spring beauty, larkspur, trillium, bellwort, doll's eyes, and bloodroot. This section of the trail generally follows the contour and returns to the main trail. Turn right and in a few hundred yards you will be back on the greenway.

This trail was constructed by two Boy Scouts as Eagle Award projects and is maintained by Boy Scout Troop 223. The 207-acre TV Small Wild Area has been designated an urban wildlife sanctuary by the National Institute for Urban Wildlife.

—Contributed by Judith Bartlow

Fiery Gizzard Trail. See Chapter 6 for description of the section in Foster Falls S.W.A.

Lady Finger Bluff Trail. Length, 2.5 mi.; rating, moderate. This trail lies in the small wild area of the same name at the mouth of the Lick Creek embayment of Kentucky Lake. To get there, turn right (north) off U.S. 412/TN 100 just west of Linden onto Creek Road, and follow the signs. This was Tennessee's twelfth national recreation trail and the nation's 115th. From the parking area the trail winds around the head of a small cove, crossing the inlet on a footbridge, then traveling over a low hill to the main shoreline near water level through hardwood timber. Spring flowers along the trail include blue phlox, star grass, wood sorrel, shooting star, and red trillium. On dedication day, April 13, 1978, a jack-in-the-pulpit had pushed through the trail tread at one point. The trail curves right to follow the main body of the lake a short distance, swinging right up Stocking Hollow, named for a narrow embayment shaped like the foot and ankle of a stocking. It curves left around the "heel" and follows the shoreline to the head of the embayment, then turns left across a footbridge and turns back left uphill.

Climbing a sharp rise on native stone steps, the trail reaches a fork, the beginning and end of a loop over Lady Finger Bluff, shaped like a lady's finger. It curves right at the top to follow the edge of the bluff northward about 200 ft. above the surface of the Tennessee River, the "narrows" of Kentucky Lake. A section of the Tennessee National Wildlife Refuge lies across the river. There are several vantage points for views of the lake and the surrounding countryside. Skeletons of gnarled cedars, resembling the famous bristlecone pines of the West, stand at the edge of the bluff. After 0.3 mi. the trail curves right again and runs back downhill to the end of the loop, backtracking to the trailhead. A free brochure is available by writing TVA as noted above. (See River Bluff Trail description.)

Obed Wild and Scenic River

Added to the National Park System by Congress in 1976, sections of four streams course within this watershed. Cutting deeply into the sandstone of the Cumberland Plateau, the Obed and its tributaries have carved spectacular gorges as much as 500 ft. deep, dotted with huge boulders and rimmed by overhanging bluffs. With its variety of slopes and aspects, the area supports a rich diversity of plants and animals and a mixture of forest types.

Much of the river system flows through Catoosa Wildlife Management Area under state jurisdiction. It provides habitat for more than one hundred breeding bird species, including the rare red-cockaded woodpecker, as well as bobcat, mink, fox, and white-tailed deer. The clear swift water supports populations of bass, muskellunge, bluegill, and catfish. The Catoosa Area is a favorite of deer, turkey, and small game hunters during managed hunts and/or open seasons. Obed River, Daddy's Creek, and Clear Creek are popular with experienced white-water canoeists and kayakers.

Hiking opportunities within the Obed Wild and Scenic River area are presently offered mostly on old logging roads in Catoosa Wildlife Management Area, which are closed during managed hunts (call TWRA at 615–781–6500). The General Management Plan for Obed Wild and Scenic River calls for development of a trail system. The options among routes and trail-use possibilities— hiking, horse, mountain bike—are under study. An inventory and assessment of existing trails in the Obed WSR has been completed as phase 1 of a coordinated trail plan being developed by the NPS. It is likely that phased development of the system, with much reliance on private volunteers, will be proposed. A first step might be a 2-mi. or so addition to a trail from Lilly bridge to the Lilly Bluff overlook. The addition would run from the overlook along the south rim of Clear Creek gorge to an overlook above the junction of Clear Creek and the Obed. The next phase might be a loop of 20+ mi. up the north rim of the Obed from Clear Creek, then north across Catoosa (and private land to be acquired) to the south rim of Clear Creek at Barnett bridge and back down Clear Creek to Lilly bridge. Another future possibility is a trail of 20+ mi. along the south rim of the Obed from Nemo Bridge to the Devils Breakfast Table (here coincident with the Cumberland State Scenic Trail) and on to Adams bridge. The Obed Wild and Scenic River Visitor Center is in Wartburg on U.S. 27, 22 mi. north of I–40. For information write: Manager, Obed Wild and Scenic River, P.O. Box 429, Wartburg, TN 37887; Manager, Catoosa Wildlife Management Area, 216 East Penfield, Crossville, TN 38555.

Nemo Trail. Length, 2.5 mi.; rating, moderate. This trail begins at a parking area on the west side of the Emory River at Nemo bridge. The bridge is located on Catoosa Road about 6.0 mi. southwest of Wartburg. The trail was built by T.V.A. in the mid-1980s. It leads upstream along the river's left (facing upstream) bank, gradually working its way up to the bluff line and following along the top of the bluffs on the south side of Obed River until it enters an old logging road and descends to the Obed at Alley Ford. It features interesting geological formations along the bluffs, winter glimpses of the Obed, and an abandoned coal mine well into the process of reclamation by nature. (See Chapter 4, Cumberland Trail.)

Big South Fork National River and Recreation Area

This 105,000-acre mostly forested preserve lies about two-thirds in Tennessee and one-third in Kentucky, along the north-flowing Big South Fork of the Cumberland River. It was set aside for outdoor recreation focused on the river system and its deep rugged gorges. Besides the sheer scenic beauty of its seemingly endless cliffs and rock houses, natural arches, and waterfalls, it is a prime locale for white-water canoeing and rafting, fishing and hunting, and horseback and mountain bike riding. There are also over 170 miles of trails reserved exclusively for hikers, including over 40 miles of the John Muir State Scenic Trail (see Chapter 4) and almost 40 miles of the 260-mile-long Sheltowee Trace National Recreation Trail. The Bandy Creek Campground and Visitor Center is located on Bandy Creek Road off Tennessee 297 about 14 miles west of Oneida and 24 miles east of Jamestown.

An easy, but extremely interesting trail not described here, the 3.7-mile Oscar Blevins Loop Trail, starts at the Bandy Creek Visitor Center. It features a variety of evidences of man's relationships with this land from prehistoric times to the recent past, and nature's responses, as discussed in an interpretive booklet available at the visitor center. Another booklet describes thirty species of native trees found in the Big South Fork gorge and identified by numbered posts along the easy 2-mile (4 mi. round-trip) Angel Falls Trail starting at Leatherwood Ford. (see below for location). A third booklet interprets the natural and cultural history revealed by the landscape at fourteen posts along the nearly .5-mile (3.0 mi. round-trip) Gentleman's Swimming Hole Trail at historic Rugby, started in the 1880s by author Thomas Hughes as a colony for unemployed sons of English gentry. Rugby is located on TN 52, 18 mi. east of Jamestown, and 6 mi. west of Elgin.

Twin Arches Loop Trail. Length, 5.9 mi.; rating, difficult. From Bandy Creek Visitor Center go west on TN 297 to TN 154, turn right, and go 1.8 mi. on TN 154. Turn right onto Divide Road and go 1.3 mi. to a fork. Take left fork, Divide Road, for another 2.7 mi. to another fork. Take right fork, Twin Arches Road, and follow it 2.4 mi. to the Twin Arches trailhead.

Twin Arches is one of the most popular destinations in BSFN-RRA and the loop trail also passes a primitive campsite at an old abandoned farmstead and Charit Creek Lodge, a hostel for backpackers and horse trail riders. From the trailhead the Twin Arches Trail leads 0.7 mi. out a narrow ridge, down two sets of steep stairs, and along the base of the bluff to the North Arch, a natural bridge.

The Twin Arches Loop Trail passes under the North Arch (93-ft. span, 51-ft. clearance) and travels just over 1.5 mi., first along the bluff line past several huge rock shelters, then descending to Station Camp Creek. Here a field, a lone chimney, a spring, and a nearby cemetery mark the site of the Jacob (Jake) Blevins farm of the 1800s, abandoned in the 1930s. Proceeding down Station Camp almost a mile, the trail joins a gravel road and quickly reaches a bridge over Charit Creek, with Charit Creek Lodge just beyond. The original building underlying part of this structure may date back to the early 1800s, and the site itself is reputed to have been a station camp of "long hunters" in the 1760s. The long hunters were skilled woodsmen and marksmen, mostly from Virginia and North Carolina, who came across the mountains in small groups on horseback and spent many months at a time (sometimes more than a year) exploring the Cumberland River watershed. Finding an area they liked, they set up a station camp and hunted until the game became scarce or until enough animal pelts had been collected to make the return from the "long hunt" profitable.

From the lodge the trail ascends steeply 1.1 mi. back to the base of the arches. From here a short trail to the left leads under the South Arch (135-ft. span, 70-ft. clearance); a stairway between arches leads to the top of the bluff and back across the top of the North Arch; while the Twin Arches Loop Trail continues .25 mi. to the right back to the North Arch where the Twin Arches Trail returns 0.7 mi. to the trailhead.

Honey Creek Loop Trail. Length, 5.6 mi.; rating, difficult. Turn west off U.S. 27 onto TN 52 at Elgin, then right onto a paved country road less than 0.5 mi. from U.S. 27. Follow Burnt Mill Bridge signs just over 4.0 mi. to Burnt Mill Bridge. Cross the bridge and continue about 3.5 mi. to the Honey Creek parking area on the right.

One of the most beautiful of the BSFNRRA trails on a yard-by-yard basis, this rugged little 5.6 mi. loop trail on the Big South Fork of the Cumberland River does not have the large, spectacular attractions of some of the other trails. It does have much to offer, however: a number of small waterfalls, intriguing rock formations, rock houses used by Indians for temporary shelter during hunting trips, massive boulders jumbled in creek beds, and a wide variety of Cumberland Plateau vegetation. The trail follows natural gorges around a small mesa of managed timberland and is an excellent example of what can be done with a relatively small amount of land with proper study and usage. Most of the trail lies within a block of 109 acres originally set aside as a Bowater Pocket Wilderness; yet the feeling of isolation is virtually complete once the hiker leaves the road and parking area. *Note:* This was the most rugged of all the trails covered while doing research for this guidebook.

Honey Creek Overlook provides a spectacular view of the Big South Fork from a vantage point some 250 ft. above the river and is wheelchair accessible.

The Sheltowee Trace National Recreation Trail. Length,

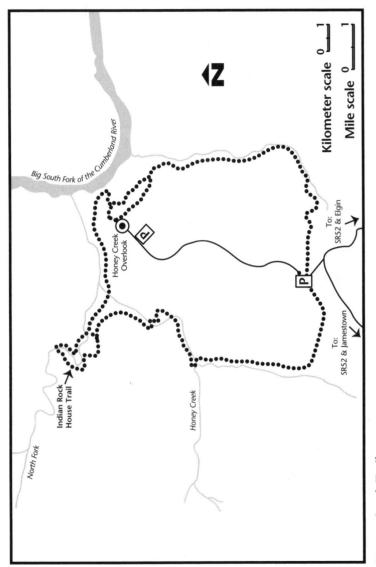

Honey Creek Trail

about 260 mi.; rating, moderate to difficult. It starts at the Hidden Passage Trailhead in Pickett State park and coincides with the first 5 miles of that trail and with the first 9.5 miles of the John Muir Trail. (The John Muir Trail, 70% of which is in BSFNRRA, is described in Chapters 3 and 4.) The John Muir Trail branches off to the right about a mile before the Sheltowee Trace leaves BSFNRRA to enter Daniel Boone National Forest in Kentucky. From here the trace continues 59 miles to Cumberland Falls State Park and almost 200 miles farther northeast to end near the Licking River in Cowan County, Kentucky. Much of the Trace north of Cumberland Falls lies on roads, and some of it is open to horseback and off-road vehicle use. Extended hikes on the Sheltowee Trace should be carefully planned only after receiving up-to-date information from the U.S. Forest Service, Stearns Ranger District, P.O. Box 429, Whitley City, KY 42653 and from Big South Fork National Recreation Area, P.O. Box 630, Oneida, TN 37841.

♿ **Leatherwood Ford Walkways.** Length, 0.25 mi.; challenge level 2; smooth; foot. This loop beside the Big South Fork River begins at a large trailhead gazebo at the south end of the paved parking area. Accessible rest rooms and public telephone are nearby. From the gazebo the 8-ft.-wide paved trail initially drops toward the river on a 16 percent grade for about 50 ft. Here the loop trail turns to the right, downstream, while the trail ahead continues about 200 ft. down a 10 percent grade to the riverside and then across a 300-ft. planked low-water automobile bridge originally built by the WPA. The loop trail goes about 200 ft. downstream, generally level, then again drops on a 16 percent grade for about 30 ft. to an 8-ft.-wide boardwalk. The boardwalk extends another 200 ft. downstream past several riverside observation decks with benches. It then turns away from the river and climbs on a 12 percent grade for about 40 ft. to the paved return leg of the loop which winds back to the trailhead on short up and down grades ranging up to 10 percent. There are cross slopes up to 10 percent in places on the paved trail.

The Leatherwood Ford area is highly scenic and particularly rich in its variety of trees, shrubs, and herbaceous plants. The historic ford itself is named for a locally abundant deciduous shrub with flexible branchlets and tough bark used by native Americans to make bowstrings and baskets.

Leatherwood Ford is on TN 297, 3 mi. east of Bandy Creek Campground.

♿ **John Muir Trail.** Length, 0.25 mi.; challenge level 2; fairly smooth; foot. This 4-ft.-wide hard-packed gravel trail starts at the Leatherwood Ford gazebo. Passing under Leatherwood Ford Bridge it leads upstream through northern hardwood (beech-maple) forest with hemlocks, white pines, and yellow birches adding to this northern character. Several rest stops with benches encourage enjoyment of the forest and river. This section of the trail, improved for wheelchair use by the Telephone Pioneers of America, ends at two house-size boulders typical of local gorge streambeds.

♿ **East Rim Overlook Trail.** Length, 400 ft.; challenge level 2; smooth; foot. An 8-ft.-wide paved trail leads from the paved parking area down two switchbacks on an 8 to 10 percent grade through woods of white, red, and chestnut oaks, red maples, and Virginia pines. At the rim of the gorge, a railed wooden platform offers a superb view of the Big South Fork 500 ft. below. Across the river upstream is the mouth of North White Oak Creek gorge. Leatherwood Ford is around the bend downstream. The parking area for this trail is at the end of East Rim Road, which goes west from TN 297 about 1.5 mi. southeast of Leatherwood Ford Bridge.

Corps of Engineers

Bearwaller Gap Hiking Trail. Length, 6 mi. one way; rating, moderate; elevation change, 300 to 400 ft. This trail is located on Corps of Engineers land surrounding the Cordell Hull Dam and

Reservoir, U.S.G.S. quad 321SW, Carthage. To get to the trail from I–40, take exit 258 toward Carthage. You may take TN 263 to the Overlook trail entrance or take TN 85 to the Defeated Creek Park trail entrance.

The trail runs from the recreation area to Tater Knob Overlook and is marked with international markings, 3-by-6-in. white painted blazes. It is a unit of both the Tennessee and national recreation trail systems. Map brochures are available at the Cordell Hull Resource Manager's office.

Many years ago when the black bear was still common in Tennessee, the bears were often found "wallering" in a patch of woods that offered cool shade and moist earth. The local people have named one of these gathering places "Bearwaller Gap." It is said that the depressions still visible around the gap are all that remain of the days when the bears came here to wallow. Ascending the first hill from Defeated Creek Recreation Area, one might observe turkey vultures in the large trees. They are found frequently along this part of the trail.

The trail environment includes many forest types found in Middle Tennessee, including the cedar glade community, unique to the central basin of the state. Hardwood forests in this area are dominated by oaks and hickories; associated species include maple, tulip poplar, ash, dogwood, and redbud. At a point near the Defeated Creek entrance to the trail, a rock outcropping overlooking the trail contains fossils of animals that lived in this area about 300 million years ago when it was under 40 to 60 ft. of ocean. Not far from this outcropping, there is an old stone quarry from which materials were taken for construction of the old Lock 8, completed in 1924. All that remains of the quarry is one steel drilling rod protruding from the rock. It often provides a lookout station for turkey vultures.

A primitive campsite is located at Two-prong, which is a forked embayment of the lake. There is a spring here, but the water should be purified before drinking. Between Two-prong and the overlook there are many traces of man's early settlement in the area, including old wagon roads, stone fences, and large haystack-shaped piles of stones removed from the fields and pastures to make the land more usable. The Bearwaller Gap Trail is an excellent place to observe wildflowers in the spring, summer, and fall. Some of these are mayapple, red trillium, columbine, cardinal flower, jack-in-the-pulpit, wild geranium, wild phlox, violets, prickly pear, bloodroot, and false garlic. At the overlook end of the trail, the hiker may ascend Tater Knob for an excellent view of Cordell Hull Lake and Dam, the Horseshoe Bend Area, and the Defeated Creek Recreation Area.

—Contributed by David Stidham (updated by Todd Yann)

Twin Forks Trail. Length, 20 mi.; rating, easy. The trail is located on the East and West forks of Stones River and the backup of J. Percy Priest Lake, where the two rivers join. The trail is on land managed by the U.S. Army Corps of Engineers in Rutherford County. The eastern access is at Walter Hill Dam and Recreation Area on U.S. 231, about 26 mi. south of I–40 at Lebanon or 5 mi. north of Murfreesboro. U.S. 231 is a link in the Trail of Tears State Scenic Route, described in Chapter 4. The trailhead is located on the south side of Stones River by an old dam and reservoir in the Walter Hill Park and Picnic Area. There is a second access point at the East Fork Recreation Area, at mile 14 off Central Valley Road, which turns west from U.S. 231 near the trailhead at Walter Hill Park. The western terminus is at Nice's Mill Dam on Sulphur Springs Road. The trail is now considered to be mainly equestrian by the Corps as this usage has become dominant.

In 1976, the Murfreesboro Chapter of the Tennessee Trails Association took on as their project the building of a trail along the Stones River on Corps of Engineers property, a plan the Corps sanctioned. The original idea was a trail of approximately 14 miles from Walter Hill to the East Fork Boat Landing, and a connector trail of 8 miles, on the West Fork from Nice's Mill to East Fork Boat Landing. The two sections of trail would connect at the confluence of the two rivers, making a linear trail of about 22 miles. There were to be two trails for each route, one more inland for horseback trail riders and one closer to the river for hikers. The TTA group built the hiking trail from Walter Hill to East Fork in the 1970s, and it was used by hikers and by horseback riders. A second trail for equestrian use was never built, as riders simply found it convenient to use the hiking trail. The 8-mile connector section from Nice's Mill to East Fork was flagged but TTA never worked on it.

The 8-mi. section of the trail from the East Fork Area to Nice's Mill is used primarily by horse traffic. There are unloading facilities for horse trailers, parking lots, a picnic shelter, and numerous picnic tables scattered in the shade of maple and oak trees at the East Fork Recreation Area. To reach the western trailhead, park on the south side of the river and proceed west along the stream and under the highway bridge. This section follows the line of the river and is marked with white blazes for several miles.

Travelers on the Twin Forks Trail are exposed to a richness of flora and fauna characteristic only of riversides. There are more diverse forms of life here than in any other type of environment. The trail wanders through stands of water-tolerant trees such as cottonwood, yellow poplar, sycamore, and black willow. On the slopes above, a mature hardwood forest composed of hickories, oaks, and maples fights for survival on thin soil with exposed limestone outcroppings. The outcroppings provide good den sites for groundhogs, foxes, bobcats, and skunks—as well as lizards and snakes. The snakes found here include the king, blue racer, garter, and eastern milk snake. There are very few poisonous snakes, but don't rule out the possibility of encountering a copperhead or a timber rattlesnake. Please resist the temptation to kill a snake or disturb in any way any of the plants or animals here; they are essential components of a complex, but rapidly disappearing, ecosystem that you are invading.

Birds of all kinds can be seen. The bright flashes of the colorful warblers, bluejays, and cardinals are in sharp contrast to the plainly garbed sparrows, thrushes, towhees, and bobwhite quail. As the hiker proceeds down the trail, the kingfishers, great blue herons, and black-crowned night herons croak, irritated at being disturbed from their fishing. Less disturbed are the flycatchers in the upper story of the woodlands—phoebes, pewees, and king-birds—capturing flying insects. Between the deeper pools, tracks in the soft mud or an occasional crawfish claw indicate where raccoon and mink hunt at night.

If the crawfish escapes the mammalian predators, the backward swimmer must dodge smallmouth and red-eye bass. Farther downstream, where the river gets deeper, there is room for catfish, bream, white bass, rockfish, and carp. The riffles where the raccoon and mink now hunt once witnessed a more dramatic confrontation for survival. The armies of the Confederacy and the Union met a few miles upstream from the terminus of the trail at Nice's Mill. Here, on the West Fork of Stones River near the city of Murfreesboro, a fierce battle (Battle of Stones River) took place, beginning December 31, 1862, with 23,000 casualties. It was the bloodiest single day of the war in Tennessee. The shallow ford at this point was bloody and muddy from the crossing of men, horses, cannons, and equipment as the battle lines were being drawn.

Both armies suffered massive casualties, and on January 2, 1863, the confederate forces began to retreat, leaving the Union to claim a costly victory. If you are in this area, a visit to the Stones River National Battlefield will provide more information on this battle and a chance to hike on the historical trails there.

—Contributed by Bertha Chrietzberg

Land Between the Lakes National Recreation Area

This is a 170,000-acre public outdoor recreation and environmental-education area in western Tennessee and Kentucky containing more than 135 miles of trails in both states, with about one-third of them in the smaller Tennessee portion. Since part of the Tennessee Valley Authority's function is to demonstrate natural resource management and development of recreation facilities, there has been experimentation with various tread materials on the trails. At the campgrounds, bike trails and some hiking trails are paved with asphalt. Bark, gravel, and, more recently, wood chips have been tried as tread-surfacing materials. The 0.5-mi. Songbird Walk at Piney Campground is designed for visitors to observe wildlife, particularly songbirds, and has special plant groups, bird houses, and feeders in a gently sloping field with scattered trees and shrubs. This is a demonstration of wildlife management practices that can be duplicated in a suburban backyard. The main north/south road through LBL, TN 49, is entered on the Tennessee side from U.S. 79, 2.5 mi. west of Dover.

North-South Trail, Tennessee Section. Length, 65 mi. with 20 mi. located within the Tennessee portion; rating, easy to moderate. The trail starts at the information center on "The Trace," TN 49, and runs northward past the Buffalo Range to the Kentucky line. It continues through Kentucky to the north visitor's center. Backwoods camping is allowed for anyone securing a backwoods camping permit, which is good for one year and costs $10 per person. Select campsites away from the marked trail.

The trail is marked by white metal strips. Maps are available at the information center or by writing Land Between the Lakes National Recreation Area, 100 Van Morgan Dr., Golden Pond, KY 42211, or calling (502) 924–2000. The trail runs southward from the center parallel to The Trace for about 1 mi., then turns westward for about 2 mi. before turning south again. It winds along the ridge between the Cumberland and Tennessee River watersheds, the Tennessee Valley Divide, for about 6 mi. to the road to Ginger Bay on Kentucky Lake; crossing this road, no. 205, it turns left and follows it about 2 mi. to a buffalo pasture on The Trace. Crossing The Trace, the trail goes south about 3 mi. to cross road no. 211 and another 4 mi. to cross road no. 221 just past a metal overnight camping shelter. Another 6 mi. south along the trail brings you to a yellow-blazed connector trail leading off to the right to the Fort Henry Trail system described in Chapter 7. Staying to the left leads

2 mi. to the trailhead at the south welcome station.

⑤ **The Pawpaw Path.** Length, approximately 0.7 mi. This is a demonstration project, as are many of the facilities in the Land Between the Lakes. Brandon Spring Group Camp, the site of the trail, is not open to the general public, being used for recreational and environmental education, but interested persons can visit the trail by contacting Operations Department, Land Between the Lakes, 100 Van Morgan Dr., Golden Pond, KY 42231, telephone (502) 924–5602. Brandon Spring is located on Lake Barkley and road 226, about 3 mi. north of the southern boundary of LBL.

The Pawpaw Path gets its name from a small group of pawpaw trees at the south end of the loop. This tree is a member of the custard-apple family occurring in the West Indies. It grows in moist locations in the lower Midwest and the South, though many trees were destroyed when bottom-lands were cleared for agriculture. It has a deep red blossom in spring and bears an elongated yellow fruit with a pleasant aroma, pulpy flesh, and large seeds. The fruit ripens in September and is so highly prized that people seldom allow it to get completely ripe on the tree. It is often called the North American banana because of its shape, but it does not peel like a banana. Most foresters are not familiar with the pawpaw, since it is fairly rare and has no commercial importance.

The Pawpaw Path is actually two loops, the shorter being an asphalt-paved trail about 200 yds. long and fairly flat to accommodate wheelchairs. The longer loop, about 0.5 mi., has a sawdust tread and gentle grades that require moderate effort by heart patients and people who have some difficulty walking. Both loops lie in a shallow basin with a small stream running lengthwise down the middle through open woods. Intersections are designed to "channel" hikers to the right, so that they follow the trail in a clockwise direction. Signs interpret the objects of interest along the trail, telling about the trees and their uses and calling attention to old foundations. A special feature of each loop is tree identification and interpretation. As with the paving, signage is somewhat deteriorated and scheduled for refurbishing by mid-1998.

Trees along the trail include the dogwood, white ash, sweet gum, black gum, oak, hickory, red cedar, wild black cherry, sassafras, tulip, hackberry, beech, and pawpaw. There are ferns, poison ivy, deer browse plants, and wild grapes. The sawdust path leads to the right at about 50 yds. from the beginning of the paved loop. There are benches along the way so that tired walkers can rest and enjoy their surroundings. Footbridges span the brook at the upper end of each loop, and the sawdust path merges with the paved trail just before the bridge at the lower end. The Pawpaw Path is intended to serve as a model for park planners, reception directors, and environmental educators.

9. Urban Trails and Greenways

Some of the more challenging, and many of the most interesting, hiking trails in Tennessee are in urban parks. Those described here lie either in sizable natural areas in major cities or within protected greenway corridors, most often along natural features such as ridges and streams or man-made routes such as roads, railways, or utility rights-of-way.

Each of the natural areas of the major cities—Bristol, Kingsport, Knoxville, Chattanooga, Nashville, Jackson, and Memphis—is associated with a nature center featuring a museum and various related facilities for environmental education, ecological research, and ecosystem restoration. Extensive programs of classes, field trips, and projects for volunteers are offered by each nature center, and hiking their trails is a nice way to experience much of the physiographic and ecological diversity of Tennessee.

In the past three decades, many cities in Tennessee developed trails in greenways along the rivers or streams important to their historic growth. Notable in this regard are the greenway systems with multi-use trails in Kingsport, Knoxville and Knox County, Sevierville, Maryville-Alcoa, Chattanooga and Hamilton County, Cookeville, Murfreesboro, Smyrna, Nashville, Brentwood, Ashland City, Clarksville, Jackson, Collierville, Germantown, and Memphis and Shelby County. Each of these localities has a master plan calling for extension of its greenway and/or riverwalk system. In 1996, through the Governor's Bicentennial Greenways and Trails Program, twenty-five smaller communities across the state received planning grants, especially for projects that connect existing trails and greenways. These and many other communities are proceeding to establish urban trail systems to meet the needs of walkers, joggers, bicyclists, those with physical disabilities, older citizens, and other special populations.

Meanwhile, several grass-roots efforts to create regional greenways are underway. The Watauga River Greenway in upper East Tennessee will link historic sites of national importance such as Rocky Mount, the first seat of government of the old Southwest Territory, with Fort Watauga and Sycamore Shoals State Park. The Great Smoky Mountains Regional Greenway will connect communities from Knoxville to Gatlinburg and Newport with a multi-use trail system offering an alternative entryway to the nation's most visited national park. The work of the Cumberland Trail Conference was described in Chapter 2. The Cumberland River Task Force hopes to link Land Between the Lakes, Clarksville, Ashland City, and Nashville, primarily via an inactive rail line alongside the Cumberland River. The Wolf River Conservancy seeks to protect the entire 90-mi. corridor of that stream from Memphis to the headwaters in north Mississippi, to restore water quality and natural ecosystems, and to provide a canoe trail and hiking trails. The 177-mi. Mississippi River Trail bike route was described in Chapter 4 (see Chickasaw Bluffs Trail), while the Mississippi River Greenway from Canada to the Gulf is being initiated, it is hoped, by construction of a 5-mi. Chickasaw Bluff segment along the Memphis waterfront with funds from state and federal grants, private developers, the Chickasaw Conservancy, and the City of Memphis.

Bristol: Steele Creek Park

There are about 25 miles of hiking trails, rated easy to difficult, in this 2,196-acre municipal park. To reach the park take U.S. 11W east from I–81 and go 2 mi. to intersection of U.S. 11W with TN 126. Proceed southwest on TN 126 about 1.5 mi., following signs to the main drive entering the park on the left. The park extends along the Beaver Creek Knobs, a forested ridge that starts near Blountville and thrusts northeastward into Bristol's urban heart. This ridge is bisected by the gorge of Steele Creek dammed at the southeast park boundary to back the 54-acre Steele Creek Park Lake up to the northwest park boundary. The park's main recreation area centers around the lake's northern end, where a boat dock and a new Nature Center are located, and it includes two main trails: Lakeside Trail and Tree Walk. Also starting in the main recreation area are trails leading into the two more remote sectors of the park, Slagle and Trinkle hollows. All trailheads are reached via the main park drive which loops about 1 mi. through the main recreation area.

ⓖ **Tree Walk.** Length, 0.25 mi.; challenge level 2; smooth; multi-use. The trailhead is located near the Pines Picnic Area at the eastern end of the main park drive loop. This 8-ft.-wide paved trail extends from the picnic area to the footbridge across Mill Creek at the head of the lake and features interpretive signs identifying the species of many large old native trees here. It winds along the creek on rolling grades mostly under 5 percent but up to 10 percent for short distances. At the footbridge it joins the Lakeside Trail (see below), which from this intersection extends as an 8-ft.-wide paved trail 0.2 mi. up Mill Creek to a paved parking area on Broad Street just off TN 126 about 1 mi. east of the main park drive entrance. This parking area offers the best wheelchair access to the Tree Trail and Lakeside Trail.

ⓖ **Lakeside Trail.** Length, 2 mi.; challenge level 2; smooth to rough; multi-use. This hard graveled trail is the most intensively used trail in the park. It is wide enough to accommodate walkers, joggers, bicyclists, and wheelchair users and extends from the head of the lake to the dam. From its junction with the Tree Walk, this 8-ft.-wide trail drops on a 13 percent grade for about 20 ft. to a 90-ft. railed footbridge (boardwalk) across Mill Creek. From the end of the bridge the trail becomes a level 12-ft.-wide hard graveled road with cross slopes up to 5 percent or so in a couple of spots. Cobbles protruding an inch or two from the road surface in places can mostly be avoided by wheelchairs. There are several benches along this 1.8-mi. section on the grassy strip between the trail and the lake. The steep forested slope on the other side of the trail shades most of the route during the morning hours. Along the way there are great views of the wooded knobs and slopes of the gorge, the lake, and the open landscaped area around the head of the lake.

Slagle Hollow Northeast Access Trail. Length, 1 mi.; rating, difficult. This trail starts across the lake from the boat dock and leads into a complex of trails in the southwest sector of the park centered around Slagle Hollow, which is a registered State Natural Area. The park's master plan calls for trail planning, reconstruction, and improvement to emphasize hiking usage and reduce uses inimical to the preservation of the area's sensitive ecology. In the summer many species of neotropical migrant birds can be seen and heard along this trail.

Hidden Hollow Trail. Length, approx. 1 mi.; rating, difficult. This falls within the Trinkle Hollow Boundary Area, which includes the entire section of the Beaver Creek Knobs lying northeast of the lake. It is unspoiled, ecologically significant, and has relatively few trails compared to Slagle Hollow. The Hidden Hollow Trail extends from the Lakeside Trail near the head of the lake through a shady secluded hollow up to the highest elevation in the park at the power line cut.

♿ **Nature Center.** Length, 0.22 mi.; challenge level 2; smooth to fairly smooth; foot. The center provides interpretive displays for park visitors and conducts programs on the park's natural history. From its paved parking area just off the main park drive, an 8-ft.-wide paved trail leads 500 ft. down a 10 percent grade to a lakeside boathouse. From there a 3-ft.-wide level hard gravel path follows a narrow strip of land across an arm of the lake 400 ft. to the beginning of an 8-ft.-wide railed boardwalk which extends the remaining 300 ft. across the lake to the Slagle Hollow trailhead.

Flatridge Trail. Length, approx. 1.5 mi.; rating, strenuous. It leaves the Hidden Hollow Trail near the bottom and climbs more directly by a number of switchbacks to the same high point, then leaves the power line cut to drop steeply down a ridge to join the Lakeside Trail near the middle of the gorge.

For more information write: Bristol Leisure Service Department, P.O. Box 1189, Municipal Building, Bristol, TN 37621.

Kingsport: Bays Mountain Park

There are 25 miles of hiking trails in this 3,000-acre nature preserve, with the many individual trails and loops varying in rating
from easy to difficult. There are also 10 miles of unpaved roads
designated for mountain bike use. The park, operated by the City
of Kingsport, is located just southwest of the city, in Sullivan
County west of I–81 and just off Reservoir Road

Nestled between Holston River Mountain on the northwest
and Bays Mountain on the southeast, the park encompasses these
ridges and their protected basin, which contains a forty-four-acre
lake. Trailhead for the hiking trail system is a the lakeside Nature
Center. There is a $3.00-per-car admission charge for parking and
$1.50 charge per person for planetarium and nature programs.
Write Bays Mountain Park, 853 Bays Mountain Park Road,
Kingsport, TN 37660 for trail map and information.

♿ **Native Animal Habitats Trail.** Length, 0.5 mi.; challenge level 2; fairly smooth; foot. This 6-ft.-wide asphalt trail is accessed from the lower level of the Nature Center. It winds through
a waterfowl aviary and amidst river otter, bobcat, white-tailed deer,
raccoon, and gray wolf habitats, some of which have ramped elevated walkways for better observation of the animals. The lake and
dam are also accessible by this short trail.

Cumberland Gap: Cumberland Gap Historic Trail

Construction is planned in 1998 in the Town of Cumberland Gap
for a new walking/hiking trail that will be completely handicapped
accessible. Approximately 1 mile of trail will be constructed utiliz-
ing an abandoned railroad corridor that provides an overlook of
the town and a marvelous view of the Pinnacle (the highest point
within the Cumberland Gap National Historic Park). A remaining
railroad trestle provides a shaded resting point for hikers under a
replicated covered bridge pavilion. The trail has parking at both

ends, with a visitor's museum at the northern side of the trail next to a scenic trout stream (fishing is not allowed).

Plans are underway to connect this trail with the starting point of the Cumberland Trail within the Cumberland Gap National Historic Park (see Chapter 7).

For more information, contact the Town of Cumberland Gap at (423) 869-3860.

—Contributed by Alison Brayton

Knoxville: Ijams Nature Center

Ijams is an eighty-acre city park, bird sanctuary, and community nature center, located on the banks of the Tennessee River in south Knoxville.

On the original twenty-acre tract, easy foot trail loops totaling more than 1 mi. in length wind through mature woods, across meadows and streams, around sinkholes and a pond, and past fern banks and the bluffs overlooking Fort Loudon Lake. An abundant variety of wildflowers, grasses, and native trees and shrubs, along with the aquatic habitats, support a diverse animal population and over forty breeding bird species. Besides the central Serendipity Trail loop, there are the Discovery Trail loop, the Fern Walk, the Pine Succession Trail, and others.

Ijams has a new 14,000-sq.-ft. Nature Center located on sixty acres on the lake adjacent to its original twenty-acre site. In front of this facility is a 0.25-mi. accessible trail soon to be extended to 1.0 mi. and connected with 4.0 mi. of paved trail looping through the adjacent 331-acre Eastern State Wildlife Management Area of the Tennessee Wildlife Resources Agency.

The City of Knoxville plans to link its extensive and growing greenway system with Ijams and Eastern State W.M.A. (located at the junction of the Holston and French Broad rivers) to create the beginning of the Great Smoky Mountains Regional Greenway, stretching up the French Broad and Little Pigeon rivers through Sevierville, Pigeon Forge, and Gatlinburg into the National Park.

To reach Ijams from downtown Knoxville, just follow the green signs from the south end of Gay Street Bridge east on Sevier Avenue and Island Home Avenue. For further information write: Ijams Nature Center, P.O. Box 2601, Knoxville, TN 37901.

ⓑ **Serendipity Trail.** Length, 0.3 mi.; challenge level 2; fairly smooth; foot. This 4-ft.-wide paved trail loops completely around the broad-topped knoll occupied by the old nature center and its country garden setting. On most of the loop, the lower slope is beautifully forested, and many of the native trees adjacent to the trail are identified with Braille markers. On a bluff at the apex of the loop, a railed deck with benches overlooks Fort Loudon Lake, and across the trail there is an organic garden. A little farther on a butterfly garden is on the inside of the loop, and limestone sinkholes lie in the forest below. This delightfully varied trail has 10 percent cross slopes in places, one grade at 8 percent for about 70 ft., and a couple of 12 percent grades for about 30 ft. It is to be renovated in 1998 and will connect with the new trail at the new Nature Center to complete a 1.0-mi. loop that meets ADA requirements and accesses a major portion of the park.

Norris City Watershed

There are more than 20 miles of interconnecting trails in this large wooded area maintained to protect the City of Norris water supply. Some of these are jeep roads; others are for foot traffic only. Unlicensed off-road vehicles and "dirt bikes" were barred from the watershed in 1987 at the insistence of the city's liability insurance carrier. Most trails are open to mountain bike and horseback riders, although some trails are restricted. All are good hiking trails. Camping is not allowed, but Norris Dam State Park, nearby, has two good campgrounds. Three very good loop systems are described below.

Cliff Trail–Reservoir Hill–Observation Point–Grist Mill Loop. Estimated distance, 2 mi.; rating, difficult. Most of the Cliff

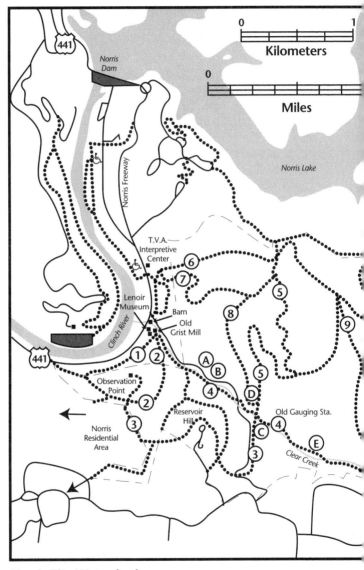

Norris City Watershed

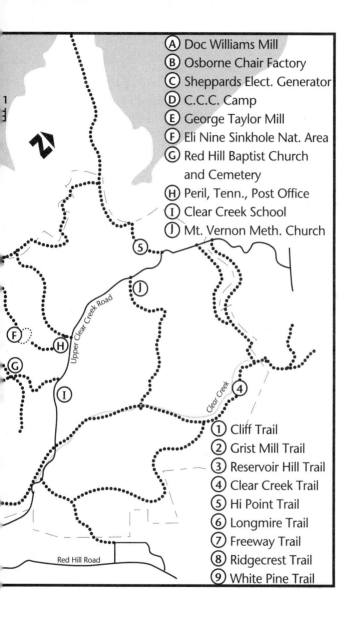

(A) Doc Williams Mill
(B) Osborne Chair Factory
(C) Sheppards Elect. Generator
(D) C.C.C. Camp
(E) George Taylor Mill
(F) Eli Nine Sinkhole Nat. Area
(G) Red Hill Baptist Church
    and Cemetery
(H) Peril, Tenn., Post Office
(I) Clear Creek School
(J) Mt. Vernon Meth. Church

Upper Clear Creek Road

Clear Creek

Red Hill Road

(1) Cliff Trail
(2) Grist Mill Trail
(3) Reservoir Hill Trail
(4) Clear Creek Trail
(5) Hi Point Trail
(6) Longmire Trail
(7) Freeway Trail
(8) Ridgecrest Trail
(9) White Pine Trail

and Grist Mill trails are on Tennessee Valley Authority (TVA) or Norris Dam State Park land and are not maintained by the City of Norris. Much of this loop of trails is unmarked. The trailhead for both the Cliff and Grist Mill trails is in the state park behind the Lenoir Museum on U.S. 441 at about 900 ft. elevation. After about 50 ft. from the beginning of the trail, Cliff Trail turns right onto an unmarked, narrow foot trail. The foot trail follows the face of a cliff overlooking U.S. 441 and the Clinch River up a moderate slope to about a 1,000-ft. elevation. Plants growing along the trail include Solomon's seal, bloodroot, dwarf-crested iris, and heartleaf. Through heavily wooded terrain, hikers can catch glimpses of the Clinch River below and hear the roar of the weir dam. As the trail curves left around the end of the bluff, the roar of rushing water gives way to the serene sounds of open woodland: the trill of birdsong and the trickle of stream and miniature waterfall. The trail winds uphill past the tiny waterfall on the right, follows the waterway, and branches to the left past a hemlock tree on the right to a shelf at about 1,000-ft. elevation. The trail turns left onto a narrow foot trail that winds through open woods where it intersects with Reservoir Hill Trail at about 1,200 ft. (Hikers should avoid the old roadway to the right which goes through private property.)

Reservoir Hill Trail to the left leads to the Observation Point loop, the major reward of this hike! Take either the left or right fork to loop the 1,380-ft. peak, which provides views of a big bend in the Clinch River and Norris Dam upstream to the right. The Clinch River Bridge on I–75 may be visible in the distance to the left. Deer are likely to be spotted in the open woods along the trail. The octagonal pavilion at Observation Point is a popular rendezvous for local recreationists. Originally constructed by the CCC in the 1930s, it was destroyed by vandals but was rebuilt by a group of Norris residents and the Norris Watershed Board in 1994. A picnic table is provided near the pavilion.

After completing the loop, follow Reservoir Hill Trail only a short distance and turn left between twin oaks onto the Grist Mill Trail. This intersection is marked. The trail follows an old, un-

252

kempt road down a gentle slope, crosses a power line, and turns left beside the line. At another old road about 300 yds. downhill, the trail turns left about 0.3 mi. from the starting point. Hikers might spot a ruffed grouse near the old Grist Mill, on the right, a landmark for visitors to the Norris Dam area.

Clear Creek–Reservoir Hill–Grist Mill Loop. Length, approximately 3 mi.; rating, moderate to difficult. This loop starts at the wheel of the Grist Mill, crosses two small wooden bridges, and follows the mill race about 200 yds. to a spring. Lower Clear Creek Road and the creek are below on the left. The trail follows a shelf along the side of a steep hill through a stand of young trees and passes a rock outcropping and an open spot under the TVA power lines. At 0.2 mi., a side trail with steps leads down to a picnic table by the stream. As the trail curves left across the end of a small ravine, another small bridge provides an easy crossing of a wet-weather stream flowing to Clear Creek from the right. The trail continues up Clear Creek past a park bench, a good place to sit and observe nature and marvel at the handiwork of the CCC who built the retaining walls of hand-cut stones to hold the downhill side. The trail passes another bench overlooking a small rock dam and pond, then follows the path of an old millrace. Before continuing, notice the beginning of the old millrace. Water was fed from the millrace and across the creek in a wooden flume to Williams Mill (1890–1915). At the other end of the millrace, the trail turns left across Lower Clear Creek Road to a footbridge, then turns to the right and passes a group of abandoned fish hatchery tanks and another dam where the roar of a refreshing waterfall can often be experienced; a picnic table is by the pond on the left. The trail passes a marshy area on the right and crosses a small wet-weather stream flowing through a culvert to intersect with a jeep road, High Point Trail.

At High Point Trail, turn right across the wooden bridge. Just past the bright blue pumping station, and before reaching Lower Clear Creek Road, Reservoir Hill Trail leads off to the left and parallels the road up a gradual slope 0.3 mi., where it then crosses the road. It climbs the hill on a switchback trail to a brief level stretch, past a sinkhole on the left, and crosses a marked jeep road—Reservoir Hill Circle Trail. The trail now leads up a long slope past an old picnic shelter on the left and up a steep, straight path to the top of Reservoir Hill, 1,360-ft. elevation. The beautiful craftsmanship of a stone wall is evident as you approach a short, steep side trail to the overlook and the underground reservoir. The Reservoir Hill overlook (also accessible by car from the City of Norris) is one of two elevated views on the Norris Watershed of Norris Dam, the Clinch River Valley and the Cumberland Mountains beyond (the other is Observation Point).

Return to the trail that leads to the left downhill about 0.3 mi. under big oak trees, following a long ridge past a footpath on the right. It crosses a power line right-of-way to a junction with a trail leading left downhill to the Norris residential area. The Reservoir Hill Trail, however, continues uphill, crossing another power line and curving to the right in second-growth timber. The loop takes the right fork at the next intersection, the Grist Mill Trail. This trail completes the loop back to the Grist Mill. Continuing straight leads to Observation Point Shelter (see above).

Clear Creek–White Pine–Ridgecrest Loop. Length, approximately 4.4 mi.; rating, moderate. This portion of Clear Creek Trail and the lower portion of White Pine Trail are restricted to foot traffic because of their ecological sensitivity. The loop starts from the bright blue pumping station parking area off Lower Creek Road. Cross a wooden bridge and turn right on the trail up the left side of Clear Creek. An old weir and stream gauging station is easily spotted 200 yards from the start, and water seeps from the hillside on the left another 200 yards up the trail. A large drain and "kissing" tree to the left and a concrete post on the right mark the site of the George Taylor mill (1880–1910). The trail parallels the old millrace as the hills on either side flatten and stepping-stones cross the creek. The trail turns up along the right side of the creek, then makes a slight rise, and continues past a large spring inside a fenced concrete structure to the White Pine Trail 100 yards beyond. (To the right, the White Pine Trail follows an access road

0.3-mi. to Upper Clear Creek Road.)

This loop turns left on White Pine Trail and crosses Clear Creek—much smaller now—and follows a spring branch on the left through a thicket of honeysuckle and multiflora rose into thick woods. It passes two old gauging weirs at springs on the left. The creek has a solid rock bottom in places here. After 100 yds. the trail levels off briefly, crosses a thicket in an open area, and then crosses the spring branch, continuing up a gentle slope past a tiny spring on the left. The flow from a second spring, up the hill, runs down the trail. Springs water the valley floor, encouraging lush growth of plants in the open areas. In the next open spot, Japanese wineberries grow, descendants of a TVA agricultural venture in the 1930s. White blossoms in spring are followed by fuzzy red calyxes that close up around the developing berries. The salmon-colored fruit bursts forth in late June, deepening in color as it ripens. The berry leaves a unique yellow-orange cone when picked. The juicy, slightly tart berries are prized by local residents for making jelly.

Farther up the slope, the waterway dries. At 2 mi. from Clear Creek, the trail intersects with Raccoon Run Trail. White Pine Trail follows it to the right across a grassy glade, past a wildlife watering hole on the left, then uphill to open woods. The trail then climbs a long slope and intersects with High Point Trail. (About 0.1 mi. to the right are Longmire Trail and High Point at 1,460 ft. elevation on the border of Norris Dam State Park. A trail from the pinnacle leads to the left 0.5 mi. to the cabin area of the park.) This loop follows High Point Trail to the left about 0.2 mi., to the Freeway Trail, which turns sharply right up the hill at about 1,400 ft. elevation. Temporary roads have been bulldozed to the right in an old timber sale area to allow access for firewood cutting and fire protection, but are less obvious now. At about 0.2 mi., Ridgecrest Trail cuts off to the left.

The downhill Ridgecrest Trail follows an old roadbed with short detours around windfalls. It follows the crest of the ridge down into mixed pine-hardwood forest, becoming steeper on the toe of the ridge. Detouring around old foundations left by CCC Camp TVA-8,

Company 297, the trail leads left to High Point Trail. The starting point at the pumping station is 200 yds. downhill to the right.

—*Contributed by Dan Thomas*

Oak Ridge

Besides the North Ridge Trail described here, Oak Ridge now has four other greenways with hiking trails totaling more than 7 mi. in length.

North Ridge Trail. Length 7.75 mi.; rating, moderate to difficult. The NRT follows the north side of Black Oak Ridge along the northern border of the city of Oak Ridge through designated Greenbelt, from Reservoir Road to Endicott Lane. The trail was built in the early 1970s by Tennessee Citizens for Wilderness Planning, a local conservation group that was organized by William L. and Liane Russell. The NRT was the first trail inside a city, the second in Tennessee, and thirty-sixth in the nation, to be designated a National Recreation Trail. The NRT is marked with white blazes. Eight access trails are marked with blue blazes. (See individual descriptions below.)

The western terminus of North Ridge Trail is located at the intersection of Mississippi Avenue and Outer Drive (Access 1), which is 1.4 mi. west of Illinois Avenue, a major traffic artery. From its terminus on the ridgetop the NRT descends gradually via Reservoir Road for 0.23 mi. following TVA transmission lines, then turns right to climb a short ramp and enter the woods. The NRT follows the 1,100-ft. contour for 1.1 mi. through open woods before dropping a little to cross TN 62. While crossing the four-lane highway, the hiker should bear slightly left (northwest) in order to more readily locate Old Batley Road (asphalt). The NRT follows the latter down to its junction with Illinois Avenue Access Trail (Access 2).

The NRT almost immediately leaves Old Batley Road to follow a side valley uphill for 0.2 mi. to pass underneath TVA power lines. The trail drops steeply down to a major valley with a small stream.

Here is the junction with North Walker Access Trail (Access 3). The NRT passes through extensive limestone rock outcropping while sharply ascending and descending. In so doing, it runs close to the edge of the Oak Ridge Greenbelt, passing about 75 ft. from a private residence. In the next major valley the NRT crosses Key Springs Road. (Access 4). Less than a mile farther on is the junction with Orchard Lane Access Trail (Access 5).

After passing more extensive rock outcrops, NRT turns left and follows an old woods road for 0.2 mi., then turns right to ascend again. In the next major valley, the NRT turns left up Georgia Access Trail (Access 6), then merges with the red-blazed Delaware Loop for a short distance while crossing an all-weather stream. From here it is only 0.3 mi. sharply uphill to Delaware Access Trail (Access 7). Three major ridge climbs later, the NRT ends at Endicott Lane (Access 8).

Access Trails to North Ridge Trail

Access 1, Reservoir Road. The trailhead at the western terminus of North Ridge Trail is marked by a steel barricade located between residences at 852 and 862 West Outer Drive. Reservoir Road (an old dirt road) and Mississippi Avenue (paved) meet at their intersection with West Outer Drive. From the trailhead, North Ridge Trail (NRT) follows Reservoir Road downhill (north) for 0.2 mi., then turns right and enters the woods via a short ramp.

Distance along NRT to the next exit: 1.7 mi.

Access 2, Illinois Avenue. Length, 0.2 mi.; rating, difficult. The blue-blazed Illinois Avenue Access Trail begins behind a convenience store at 400 North Illinois Avenue (corner of West Outer Drive and North Illinois Avenue). It runs steeply downhill alongside a deep ravine for 0.2 mi. to its junction with the NRT on Old Batley Road (paved).

Distance along NRT to next exit: 0.5 mi.

Access 3, North Walker Lane. Length, 0.3 mi.; rating, moderate. This blue-blazed access trail begins near the end of North Walker Lane, off West Outer Drive. A Greenbelt Area sign marks the trailhead between residences at 109 and 117/119 North Walker Lane. North Walker Access Trail descends for 0.3 mi. to its junction with the NRT in the bottom of the valley.

Distance along NRT to next exit: 1.5 mi.

Access 4, Key Spring Road. Length, 0.4 mi.; rating, easy. Key Springs Road is a paved connector from Outer Drive to TN 61 in the valley north of Oak Ridge, and begins between residences at 220 and 224 Outer Drive. It is 0.4 mi. down Key Springs Road to its crossing of the NRT.

Distance along NRT to next exit: 0.8 mi.

Access 5, Orchard Lane. Length, 0.2 mi.; rating, difficult. The trailhead for the blue-blazed Orchard Lane access trail is near the intersection of Orchard Lane and Orkney Road. A trail sign is posted behind a steel barricade, between residences at 122 and 126 Orchard Lane. Orchard Lane access trail follows an old and badly-eroded evacuation route and descends for 0.2 mi. to the NRT.

Distance along NRT to next exit: 1.0 mi.

Access 6, Georgia Trail. Length, 0.4 mi.; rating, easy. The trailhead (a short length of pavement) is located between residences at 96 and 98 Outer Drive. The blue-blazed Georgia Access Trail gradually descends along an old gravel road for 0.4 mi. to its junction with the NRT.

Distance along NRT to next exit: 0.3 mi.

Access 7, Delaware Access Trail. Length, 0.4 mi.; rating, moderate. The blue-blazed Delaware Access Trail starts at a city pumping station located on Outer Drive, near its junction with Delaware Avenue. This is also the trailhead for the Delaware Loop (red-blazed). It is 0.4 mi. from the trailhead to the NRT.

Distance along NRT to its terminus: 1.9 mi.

Access 8, Endicott Lane. Endicott Lane is the eastern terminus of the North Ridge Trail. Its trailhead is adjacent to a residence at 103 Endicott Lane, and is marked by an NRT trail sign and NRT's white blazes.

—Contributed by Ken Warren

Chattanooga: Reflection Riding and the Chattanooga Nature Center

A network of hiking trails, rated easy to moderate, lies within the 300-acre Reflection Riding nature preserve. It starts at the Chattanooga Nature Center and climbs in successively longer loops up the east side of Lookout Creek Valley. **Susan's Curves Trail,** 1.3 mi., **Bradford Williams Trail,** 3.5 mi., and the **Park Border Trail,** 4.2 mi., all wind through predominantly oak forest with scattered pine groves, around deep gorges, across rock fields, and among moss-covered boulders; all these trails offer occasional vistas of the valley. The Park Border Trail also connects with the Skyuka Trail on Lookout Mountain (see Chapter 7). The Great Indian Warpath and the Cisca and St. Augustine Trail crossed Reflection Riding, and in 1863 the Battle of Lookout Mountain began here.

A 3-mile loop for cars starts at the nature center. It features a wide variety of wildflowers in each blooming season, and most trees and shrubs are identified along with many historic points of interest. Walkers find excellent birding here in the early morning hours along wooded areas bordering fields near the creek. The Lookout Creek canoe trail anchored by the Chattanooga Nature Center stretches 5.7 mi. from the Tennessee River across the state line into Georgia. A nominal admission charge permits access to the nature center and Reflection Riding.

To reach the Chattanooga Nature Center, exit I–24 at Tiftonia, go east on U.S. 41 2 miles, turn right on Lookout Mountain Parkway, TN 318, and then right onto Garden Road, which ends at the Center.

Write to The Chattanooga Nature Center, 400 Garden Road, Chattanooga, TN 37419.

♿ **Woodland Walkway.** Length, 55 ft.; accessible; smooth; foot. The nature center is fully accessible. This 6-ft.-wide paved trail starts at the center's paved parking area and leads into the bottomland hardwood forest of Lookout Creek. It passes a wildlife exhibit area where injured creatures such as foxes, hawks, and owls are held in pens because they are unable to survive in the wild.

♿ **Wetland Boardwalk.** Length, 2,000 ft.; accessible; smooth; foot. This 6-ft.-wide railed boardwalk extends the Woodland Walkway across the forested floodplain of Lookout Creek. It passes a creek-side shelter ideally positioned for quiet observation of wetland wildlife.

♿ **Drive-through Trail.** Length, 0.75 mi.; challenge level 1; fairly smooth; auto and foot. Starting at the nature center parking area, this level part of the 3-mi. hard-packed gravel road loop has mostly pastoral farmland on one side and the bottomland forest of Lookout Creek on the other.

Chattanooga: Tennessee Riverpark

♿ **Riverwalk.** Length, 2.0 mi.; accessible; smooth; multi-use. The Tennessee Riverpark is reached by taking the first exit from TN 153 south of Chickamauga Dam onto TN 58 and taking the first road to the right into the park. This 8-ft.-wide paved trail extends downstream from a parking area below Chickamauga Dam 0.75 mi. to another parking area at the Riverpark headquarters and food concession building. There are accessible rest rooms, telephones, and picnic shelters at each end and two shelters with benches and emergency telephones along the trail. Extensions of the trail at each end past the parking areas and loops through picnic areas add another 1.25 mi. to its length. Most of the route is shaded by large native riverbank trees, and the trail offers panoramic views of the river. Near the lower end parking area, a paved railed 6-ft.-wide ramp descends about 300 ft. on a 7 percent grade to a railed fishing pier that extends 50 ft. over the river beneath the DuPont Parkway Bridge. Long-range plans call for a connector trail via this bridge between the Riverpark and the North Chickamauga Creek Greenway.

⑤ **Bluff Walk.** Length, 1.5 mi.; challenge level 1; smooth; multi-use. This second phase of the Tennessee Riverpark was completed in 1997 and lies almost 6 mi. downstream from the first, described above. It begins at Ross's Landing Plaza at the corner of Chestnut Street and Riverfront Parkway in downtown Chattanooga. In 1815 John Ross established a landing, warehouse, and ferry here. A 6-10 ft.-wide paved and railed trail extends upriver on both sides of the Parkway from the Tennessee Aquarium at the Plaza to an outdoor amphitheater beneath Walnut Street Bridge. It then climbs via a series of accessible paved, railed switchbacks past the Bluff Furnace historical site to the Hunter Museum on the blufftop. The trail then continues through the Bluff View Arts District—an eclectic community containing a bed and breakfast, several unique restaurants and coffee houses, and interesting art boutiques. An overlook is cantilevered out over the Tennessee River offering panoramic views of Maclellan Island and the riverfront. Further eastward the riverwalk passes the Portera Sculpture Park, where commissioned art pieces are displayed for sale and/or enjoyment. Two handsome pedestrian bridges cross Georgia Avenue to connect the riverwalk into and through the historic Battery Place neighborhood. The riverwalk currently terminates at the Battery Place and Mabel Street intersections. From this terminus you can easily access the campus of the University of Tennessee at Chattanooga. The final riverwalk segment linking out to the completed handicapped-accessible Rowing Center segment is scheduled for completion in 1998.

The historic 107-year-old steel-truss Walnut Street Bridge can be accessed from the south shore on Walnut Street where on-street parking is generally available. It can also be accessed on the North Shore from Frazier Avenue, a unique older district now undergoing a revival with new clothing stores, fly-fishing shops, coffee houses, and art boutiques. Formerly a two-lane automobile span, the bridge is now a 1,600-ft. linear park offering many inviting rest spots with superb views of the city's dramatic river and mountain setting.

A phased master plan calls for extending the park and trail system along the entire south shore of the river stretching from Ross's Landing and the Tennessee Aquarium* for 10 mi. to the Chickamauga Dam. The remaining 6-mi. stretch along the south shore is planned for completion during the year 2000. Additionally, the new eight-acre Coolidge Park is being planned for the north shore on riverfront property between the Walnut and Market street bridges. Handicapped-accessible entry is by pedestrian-only alleys leading from Frazier Avenue. This new public park will contain a historic carousel, a multi-purpose pavilion, public rest rooms and security station, supportive parking, water features, and a variety of public art in addition to handicapped-accessible trails and open space. The riverwalk along the north shore will include river overlooks, a performance stage, and pathways providing river access. This new park is planned for completion by early 1999. Later phases will develop the riverpark out to Moccasin Bend, where it will end in a broad loop opposite the north end of Lookout Mountain.

—*Contributed by Jim Bowen*

Chattanooga: North Chickamauga Creek Greenway

♿ **Greenway Trail.** Length, 0.35 mi. one-way, 0.7 mi. roundtrip; challenge level 2; smooth; multi-use. The North Chickamauga Creek Greenway, and the trail, extend about 1.5 mi. along the east

*The fully ADA accessible Tennessee Aquarium offers a wonderful underwater view of the state's unique aquatic biodiversity. Through the Aquarium's living exhibits, the visitor progresses along the entire Tennessee River from its headwaters near the peaks of the Unaka Mountains, through the upper, middle, and lower Tennessee Valley and beyond, into the Mississippi River and, ultimately, the Gulf of Mexico, encountering the successive changes in aquatic, and typical streamside, habitats. A tour of the cultural history of the region will also interest every hiker.

side of the creek from near Chickamauga Dam through a hardwood forest and loblolly pine plantation to Greenway Farm. To reach the greenway parking area, exit TN 153 just north of Chickamauga Dam onto Lake Resort Drive and go east about 0.2 mi. to the greenway entrance on the left. Accessible rest rooms and emergency telephone are located at the parking area and there is a paved ramp for launching canoes or small boats on the creek. This 8-ft.-wide paved trail starts at the north end of the parking area and proceeds upstream paralleling the creek. First crossing a slightly arched 70-ft. railed bridge, it climbs steadily through second growth hardwood forest at grades up to 8 percent for 200 ft., or so, and up to 10 percent for shorter distances. Cross slopes reach 6 percent at several points. At 0.35 mi. from the trailhead, the Lower Loop Trail branches off to the right and returns 0.35 mi. to the trailhead. At 0.5 mi. the Big Ridge Trail turns off to the right into the TVA small Wild Area (see Chapter 8). The Greenway Trail continues straight ahead another 0.2 mi., where it ends as a paved trail by making a 0.2-mi. loop. From near the end of the loop, an 8-ft.-wide gravel trail continues 0.6 mi. over the top of a high bluff (with a good view of Lookout, Elder, and Signal mountains) to Greenway Farm, a city/county-owned facility. Unassisted wheelchair use of the Lower Loop Trail and the last 0.35 mi. of the paved part of the Greenway Trail is not recommended because of grades up to 17 percent on the former and up to 21 percent in a tight turn on the latter.

In 1993, the Friends of North Chickamauga Creek Greenway (FNCCG) was incorporated to: promote establishment of a greenway along all 26 mi. of the Creek (such a plan for the lower 8 mi. already had been adopted by the city), including a hike/bike trail for the lower 8 mi.; encourage sound land use throughout the watershed; promote preservation of natural and cultural resources; and help provide funding and facilitate citizen involvement. Since then, the city acquired over 220 acres along the lower 8 mi. TVA designated 200 acres within the corridor as a Small Wild Area, the DuPont Company designated 200 acres of its land at the mouth of the creek as a Wildlife Sanctuary, and Bowater designated 1,095 acres in the gorge on the upper part of the creek as a Pocket Wilderness and developed 9 mi. of hiking trails (see Chapter 10). FNCCG is working with the city and the Trust for Public Lands to acquire more parcels and easements for the greenway and with the Conservation Fund and a number of federal and state agencies to identify sources of pollution in the watershed and to restore and protect the water quality.

Chattanooga: South Chickamauga Creek Greenway

A Governor's Bicentennial Greenways and Trails Program grant funded the planning and design of a 22-mi. 10-ft.-wide asphalt multi-use trail extending along South Chickamauga Creek from the Chattanooga-Chickamauga National Military Park to the Tennessee Riverpark. There is presently a 4-mi. 8-ft.-wide gravel nature trail along the creek, surrounded by open land and wetlands, extending from Brainerd Road to Shallowford Road atop the Brainerd levee.

Murfreesboro: Murfreesboro Greenway

⑥ **Stones River and Lytle Creek Greenway Trails.** Length, 4.5 mi.; accessible; smooth; multi-use. The Stones River Greenway officially opened in the fall of 1996, and in the fall of 1997 the extension of a greenway along Lytle Creek was added. The 4.5 mi. of greenway was then officially designated the Murfreesboro Greenway. This is a 12-ft.-wide paved strip to be used by walkers, joggers, bicyclists, roller bladers, and wheelchairs users, and the Stones River also has designated canoe trails. The greenway is open from dawn to dusk and is patrolled by policemen on bicycles. It offers area residents and visitors an opportunity to enjoy a quiet river or creekside experience in an area rich in Civil War history. The southern terminus is located at Fortress Rosecrans, and the northern end connects with the Artillery monument of Stones River National Battlefield. This section of the trail is 3 mi. in length. Construction has begun on a trail to connect with the main Battlefield Park and should be completed in 1998. Wayside exhibits are planned to interpret Civil War history along the trail. Some exhibits are already in place—at Fortress Rosecrans, the Bragg monument, Redoubt Brannan, and the Artillery monument. The shallow ford area of the Stones River near the Bragg monument was the scene of one of the greatest battles of the Civil War.

The Lytle Creek section of the Greenway branches off the Stones River Greenway on the bridge near Fortress Rosecrans. It is 1.5 mi. in length and its destination is Cannonsburgh. It passes under Broad Street following Lytle Creek. Interesting plants and wildlife abound in this area, and wildflowers are found from early spring until late fall. Labels have been placed by the trees on the northern end of the river trail. Park benches are conveniently placed, and, at the Bragg monument, there is a shelter with rest rooms. There are also areas along the trail where one might stop and fish. These trails go through the heart of Murfreesboro. The Lytle Creek section actually goes under downtown Broad Street at two bridges and continues on to the interesting log village of Cannonsburgh. There is, of course, no charge for visitors in any of these areas. Plans call for future extension of the greenway several miles to Black Fox Spring, a historically (see Chapter 1, Black Fox Trail) and ecologically significant wetland. Preservation of the site has been spearheaded by the private citizens' Black Fox Wetlands League, and interpretive trails and boardwalks are planned.

The trails may be accessed in a number of places. There is ample parking at the northern terminus of Thomspon Lane, the Bragg Headquarters on the Old Nashville Highway, the southern terminus of Old Fort Parkway at Fortress Rosecrans, and at the Cannonsburgh area of the Lytle Creek section. The best access points for newcomers to find are the Fortress Rosecrans entrance and the Thomspon Lane entrance. Enter Old Fort Park from Old Fort Park Parkway, the street that enters Murfreesboro from exit 78 of I–24. Drive back to Fortress Rosecrans, near the golf course. A short interpretive trail of Fortress Rosecrans is directly in front of you as you enter the parking lot, and the Murfreesboro Greenway begins to your left. There is a very large parking area off Thompson Lane at the Northern terminus. From I–24, take exit 78 onto Old Fort Parkway, and take an immediate left onto Thompson Lane. After you cross the big intersection with Broad Street, the parking lot will be about one-eighth of a mile farther on your right, before the Stones River Bridge.

—Contributed by Bertha Chrietzberg

Nashville: Percy and Edwin Warner Parks

There are 12 mi. of hiking trails maintained by the Warner Park Nature Center in the 2,681-acre Warner parks in the southwest quadrant of Metro Nashville. There are also 10 mi. of bridle paths and 30 mi. of paved roads, 6 mi. of which are closed to motorized traffic. This is the state's largest city park entirely within city limits. It is home to a wide variety of native plants and plant communities typical of the outer Central Basin and to many species of raptors, songbirds, and neotropical migrants, including nesting cerulean warblers. Its forested core, 80 percent of the total acreage, is a registered State Natural Area, predominantly oak-hickory with pockets of mixed-mesophytic and patches of red cedar. To get to the parks, go south on TN 155 from exit 204 on I–40 to Harding Road, U.S. 70S. Turn right and go to the junction with TN 100. Take the left fork (TN 100) 3 mi. to the Warner Park Nature Center, on the left past Old Hickory Boulevard, for maps and trail information.

The Percy Warner Park trailhead parking lot is in the Deep Well picnic area on TN 100, 1.5 mi. from U.S. 70S. The two trails here are the 2.5-mi. Warner Woods Trail, blazed in white, and the 4.5-mi. Mossy Ridge Trail, blazed in red; both are rated moderate. The trails pass through mature woods with huge oaks, tulip poplars, sassafras, sugar maples, hickories, and many others. Wildflowers abound spring through fall, and there are many species of ferns, mushrooms, birds, and animals.

There are two trailheads in Edwin Warner Park, one at the nature center and another, the Natchez Trace trailhead, at the parking area 0.1 mi. from the Woolwine entrance to the park (on TN 100) along the entry drive to the nature center. The interior road system can be accessed directly from the Natchez Trace trailhead and the system of dirt footpaths can be accessed from the nature center. These two trailheads are connected by a 0.25-mi. segment of an old (c.1800) road that was one of several that led from Nashville to the north end of the Natchez Road built by the U.S. Army in 1801–02 from the Tennessee River in Alabama to Garrison Creek in Williamson County, TN (see Chapters 4 and 7).

Just beyond the park boundary, 0.4 mi. west of the Natchez Trace trailhead along this old road, lies Devon Farm and the brick farmhouse begun about 1795–96 by John Davis. Davis possibly followed the original Chickasaw (later, Natchez) Trace to first reach this spot and later improved it to a wagon road to his farm. It was later extended across the Little Harpeth River and the Big Harpeth and on to join the Natchez Road. Davis came to Nashville in 1788 from Pasquotank County, North Carolina, and almost immediately joined the company of scouts, and became a fast friend, of Captain John Gordon, who began operating a ferry on the Natchez Trace at Duck River around 1802.

Hikers can access the Percy Warner Park trails from the nature center via a 1.0-mi. easy connector trail. Trails are marked with colored arrows on posts at intersections. Three trails are self-guided, with interpretive booklets available at the trailhead. These are the Nature Loop, coded yellow, length 0.75 mi., rated moderate; the Owl Hollow Loop, coded orange, 0.3 mi., rated easy; and the Little Acorn Trail, an easy 150-yd. loop coded green. The Hungry Hawk

Trail, coded purple, is an easy 0.3-mi. loop featuring a bird blind, a wildlife tracking station, and a wildlife observation platform. A booklet and "purple packs" continuing materials to help young hikers observe the wildlife may be checked out from the nature center. Light green arrows lead to an amphitheater nestled in a clearing. The Harpeth Woods Trail, a 2.5-mi. loop, coded blue and rated moderate, may be started from either trailhead. Hikers can enjoy a variety of forest types and especially large beech, oak, and red cedar trees. Cross an old rock quarry, see fossilized evidence of life forms of 400 million years ago, and enjoy a preserved section of the historic Natchez Trace.

—*Contributed by Deb Beazley*

♿ **Interior Road System.** Length, 5 mi.; challenge level 2; smooth; multi-use. This former scenic drive system of 16-ft.-wide paved roads in Edwin Warner Park is permanently closed to motorized traffic. It was resurfaced in mid-1993 to a 10-ft. width leaving 6 ft., or so, of the old pavement to eventually deteriorate to a soft track. The system consists of: a 2-5-mi. main loop that winds at midslope completely around the forested hilly spine of the park; a 0.6-mi. interior loop around a high point with a scenic view of the Harpeth Valley; a 0.14-mi. connector road across the main loop; and four roads from 0.2 to 0.4 mi. long connecting the main loop with the park perimeter.

One exterior connector road on the south side of the park starts from a gate at a parking lot near picnic area 4, which has accessible rest rooms. Another exterior connector road on the north side of the park begins at the Natchez Trace trailhead paved parking area just inside the TN 100 (Woolwine) entrance to the park. All gates barring auto access to the interior road system have 4-ft.-wide unobstructed openings.

The exterior connector roads and the interior road system all have grades mostly 5 percent or less but also have long stretches (up to 300 ft.) from 6 percent to 8 percent and many shorter segments (up to 50 ft.) from 9 percent to 13 percent. Cross slopes throughout the system are often over 3 percent, and in the numerous sharp turns commonly range from 10 percent to 14 percent.

An especially scenic section of the main loop lies 0.6 mi. east of the Natchez Trace trailhead where the road follows a contour around the north end of a spur off the park's central spine. The steep slope above is in mature hardwood forest and the lesser slope below, mostly open meadow. Around the end of the spur, mossy stonework of the WPA-era extends along both sides of the road. Here the road enters a deep wood on both sides where large gnarled beech trees cling to almost precipitous rocky slopes. Where the wood ends on the lower slope, a large accessible observation deck at the edge of a meadow overlooks the nature center and the valley of Vaughn Creek.

⚅ **Riverbend Road.** Length, 0.2 mi.; accessible; fairly smooth; multi-use. This 16-ft.-wide paved half-loop, closed to motorized traffic, begins at the picnic area 5 parking lot just off the main Edwin Warner Park Drive from the Vaughn Road entrance. It follows the inside of a bend in the Little Harpeth River with the wooded riverbank on one side and closely mowed open woods and meadow on the other. This is a good spot for early morning wildlife watching. Snapping turtles, banded water snakes, raccoons, muskrats, and green and great blue herons are often seen along the river. King-fishers regularly work the bend, and red-tailed hawks often soar over the meadow. Squirrels, bluebirds, and a variety of other songbirds can usually be seen or heard.

Nashville: Shelby Bottoms Greenway and Nature Park

This 810-acre bottomland just 2 miles from the center of downtown Nashville was farmed for many generations but remained undeveloped since almost all of it lies in the 100-year floodplain. Soon after Mayor Philip Bredesen established the Metro Greenway Commission in 1992, the tract was bought by the city for protection of its outstanding natural features and for development of Metro's first large-scale greenway project. For two decades, a local resident, Mark Hackney, had catalogued and written about the champion trees, rare plants, and wildlife diversity of Shelby Bottoms, and, together with Dr. Robert Kral, professor of botany at Vanderbilt University, had made known these unique values to the mayor and the community.

Seasonal and permanent wetlands (including beaver ponds) and fragments of bottomland hardwoods forest remain on the site, and it has long been a favorite area for Tennessee Ornithological Society and Audubon Society field trips. Sixty-three species of trees have been recorded, including five of state-champion size and one national co-champion, along with 178 species of birds, and one federally listed, and several state listed, rare plants. The site extends 3.5 mi. along the Cumberland River's north bank from Shelby Park through Cooper Creek, which enters the Cumberland opposite Two Rivers Park.

Phase One of the greenway was completed in 1997, opening 150 acres immediately adjacent to Shelby Park and providing a large parking area and 3.5 mi. of trail including a 1.5-mi. 10-ft.-wide asphalt paved loop and 0.9 mi. more of the paved trail with four mulched trails looping off the paved loop and 0.9 mi. extension. The paved extension runs upstream along the river. In Phase Two, scheduled for 1998–99, development will be extended 2.5 mi. farther along the river to Cooper Creek, with more mulched trails looping inland off of it.

The Shelby Bottoms Greenway is reached by exiting I–24/65 at the Shelby Avenue off-ramp and proceeding 1.5 mi. east to the Shelby Park entrance at the end of Shelby Avenue, then following the main park drive past the lake and ballfields to, and along, the riverside to the greenway entrance beneath the Louisville and Nashville Railroad trestle. Parking and the trailhead shelter are just beyond the entrance.

    ⓑ **Shelby Bottoms Greenway Loop Trail.** Length, 1.2

mi.; accessible; smooth; multi-use. From the trailhead shelter the trail leads 500 ft. south to a junction with the riverside segment coming from the right. Turning left and crossing a 100-ft. bridge spanning a ravine, the trail follows the top of the wooded riverbank 600 ft. to an overlook and river observation deck with a view of an historic water treatment plant (on the National Register) on the far bank. Continuing upstream another 1,400 ft. to a junction, the riverside trail extends upstream, while the loop trail turns left away from the wooded riverbank and crosses an open early successional field 400 ft. to reach a boardwalk leading 150 ft. through a wooded seasonal wetland. The paved trail comes to an elevated sheltered observation deck 350 ft. beyond the boardwalk. This is an outstanding vantage point for seeing and hearing raptors, woodcock, plovers, sandpipers, and many other marsh and field birds and neotropical migrants. The seasonal open wetland immediately to the west is soon to be impounded with a water-level control mechanism that will permit creation of appropriately timed mudflats to attract a large variety of wading species and shorebirds.

The trail continues northwest around the upper end of the shorebird habitat, then southwest and, passing a wooded wetland on the right, returns to the trailhead shelter 0.5 mi. from the elevated observation deck.

As mentioned in Chapter 5 (Tennessee Bicentennial Mall State Park) the process for completing a greenway downriver linking Shelby Bottoms via Shelby Park, Shelby Avenue, Shelby Street Pedestrian Bridge, and Riverfront Park and Greenway to the Bicentennial Mall is well underway. More visionary, but nevertheless being seriously considered, is an extension of the greenway across the river from Shelby Bottoms to Two Rivers Park and the mouth of Stones River, then up that historically rich stream past Andrew Jackson's boatyard (where craft for the Lewis and Clark expedition of 1804 were built) and his race track at Clover Bottom, and around both shores of J. Percy Priest Lake to eventually connect with the Stones River segment of the Murfreesboro Greenway.

Ashland City

⑤ **Cumberland River Bicentennial Trail.** Length, 4.0 mi.; 2 mi. of challenge level 1; 2 mi. of challenge level 2; smooth; multi-use. This scenic riverside rail-trail can be accessed on Chapmansboro Road (west of Ashland City) from Sycamore Harbor, which is the accessible end; or from Mark's Creek, which is not wheelchair accessible due to still incomplete bridges. This scenic trail lies between the Cumberland River with its adjacent wetland areas and inland cliffs and meadows. With a riot of wildflowers along its shoulders, the trail is topped with crush and run on all but the restored bridges, which are beautifully planked. A medley of waterfowl, songbirds, reptiles, and mammals can be seen year-round on this path that once saw CSX trains running between Nashville and Clarksville. Future plans for the trail include running it back into Ashland City, connecting it with several city parks and then circling back to rejoin the trail at the Mark's Creek access. The longer-range vision is for its extension upstream to Nashville and downstream to Clarksville.

—Contributed by Margo Farnsworth

Clarksville: McGregor Park

⑤ **Cumberland Riverwalk**. Length, 1,700 ft.; accessible; smooth; foot. This 12-ft.-wide paved trail extends along the landscaped bank of the Cumberland River from a playground to a boat ramp with adjacent parking areas at both ends. Along the trail are picnic areas and three river overlooks. Construction of a 700-seat amphitheater built into the riverbank as well as a rivermaster's house featuring an accessible Cumberland River interpretive center has begun and is to be completed by late 1998. Current plans call for extending the walk another mile through the fringe of downtown Clarksville to Valleybrook Park. Long-range plans are to connect the Valleybrook terminus with a converted rail-trail for over 80 mi. through Ashland City and Nashville to Murfreesboro. McGregor Park is located in Clarksville on Riverside Drive (U.S. 41A Bypass) which extends from U.S. 41A on the north to the junction of TN 12 and TN 13 on the south.

Jackson: Cypress Grove Nature Park

Cypress Grove Nature Park features an elevated boardwalk that winds 4,800 ft. through an unspoiled 165-acre cypress forest. Dominant trees in this wetland are white ash, red maple, sweet gum, bald cypress, and water tupelo; jewelweed and cardinal flowers are prominent. There are also open ponds and open meadows in the park that, along with the forest, support a wide variety of wildlife. Cypress Grove is the initial element of a long-range plan for establishing a greenbelt on the three sides of the city encompassing parts of the Forked Deer River bottomlands and also uplands. The park is located on U.S. Hwy. 70 about 1.5 mi. west of the interchange of the U.S. 45 Bypass and U.S. 70 on the west side of Jackson. For information about the park and its special classes, write to Cypress Grove Nature Park, 400 S. Highland Avenue, Attn: Park Naturalist, Jackson, Tennessee 38301.

    ⑤ **Boardwalk.** Length, 4,800 ft.; accessible; smooth; foot. About 80 percent of the trail system is a 6-ft.-wide railed elevated boardwalk. The Jewelweed Trail is an 800-ft.-long unelevated boardwalk, 4 ft. wide and unrailed. The only significant grades in the system are 100 ft. at 8 percent from the parking area to the nature center and 40 ft. at 10 percent where the Jewelweed Trail first leaves the main boardwalk. Sensitive fern and royal fern are prominent along the Jewelweed Trail. There is also an 800-ft.-long Aerie Trail that leads from the Boardwalk Trail to the Raptor Center where injured non-releaseable hawks, falcons, owls, and vultures are cared for and on display. From the railed observation deck at Killdeer Pond, one sees black willows, cattails, bulrushes, and, in late summer, blooming meadow beauty and water primrose. Cypress Knee Loop circles an area thick with these protuberances, and it provides benches and a shelter. An observation deck and a tower on Wood Duck Lake offer good places to watch songbirds, waterfowl, wading birds, owls, and raptors. Overall this is a delightful trail at any season for the sights, sounds, and smells of typical West Tennessee cypress-tupelo swamps.

Savannah

This is a short but historically significant greenway, as yet only partially finished. The area abounds in Native American sites dating from the Woodland and Mississippian periods (see Chapter 7, Shiloh Military Trails). At Savannah there were large towns where a major trail along the Tennessee River met one from the Pinson Mounds site. Family groups led to the area in 1816 by Colonel James Hardin to settle his father's land grant found fourteen mounds here, some up to 30 feet high and covering a half-acre. In 1818 Hardin County was created, and in 1827 the site of David Robinson's ferry was chosen as a new county seat by virtue of its location on the river and its accessibility to citizens west of the river. Robinson's wife is credited with naming it Savannah after her hometown in Georgia. Robinson built a Federal-style brick home atop one of the ancient mounds overlooking his ferry and in 1842 presented it as a wedding gift to his daughter Sarah and her husband, William Cherry.

Savannah's strategic location on the river, and on roads running east to west and north to south, was highlighted when the river route and the southernmost of the overland routes taken by the Cherokee crossed here in the late 1830s during their removal from East Tennessee. In March 1862, General U.S. Grant headquartered himself here at the Cherry Mansion, and from here on April 6 he hurried by dispatch boat to the sound of guns coming from Pittsburg Landing 9 miles upstream, where his army of 40,000 camped around Shiloh Church was being assaulted by a larger Confederate force under General Albert S. Johnston.

While the prosperous planters in Hardin County were slave-holders, some prominent citizens, including merchant William Cherry, were pro-Union, and the county was one of only three in West Tennessee that voted against secession in 1861. After the war everyone, including the county's freed blacks, struggled to adjust to new conditions. By the 1880s the African American community was developing leadership in business, education, and religion. One of the young leaders was Alec Haley who ran a ferry at Savannah landing. His son Simon Alexander Haley was one of the first African Americans mobilized for service in the army in 1918 and he later became a college professor and father of author Alex Haley Jr.

The Tennessee River Museum, a focal point for the Savannah Historic Trail, presents an excellent series of displays unfolding the region's history, including paleontology, archeology, Civil War operations in the area, steamboating on the river, and musseling—featuring the gear and boats used and a typology of species found here in the world center of mussel diversity (see Preface).*

ⓢ **Savannah Historic Trail.** Length, 1.0 mi.; (2.0 mi. round-trip); rating, easy. In 1994 Savannah received a challenge cost-share grant from the National Park Service to fund interpretive exhibits at key sites along a proposed Tennessee River Historical Walking Trail on the waterfront. The city received a Symms National Recreational Trails Fund grant in 1996 to build the trail. Initially an 800-ft. ADA-accessible River Trail loop was built in the newly created Wayne Jerrolds Park just south of the Harrison/Mc-Garrity Bridge over the river. The trail features an overlook and a wayside exhibit telling of the Trail of Tears river and overland routes. From the parking area a 0.6-mi. walk (or drive) along River-side Drive and Main Street leads to the Tennessee River Museum at 507 Main Street. Also, the River Overlook and historical wayside ex-

*The historical background above was taken from a book published by the Museum in 1996—*On the Banks of the River, a History of Hardin County Tennessee* by Tony Hays.

hibit were built, telling of the nearby Savannah mounds, Cherry Mansion, Alec Haley's ferry crossing, and the Savannah cemetery, the burial place of some of Grant's men killed at Shiloh and also of Alex Haley Jr.'s father and mother, "Queen." This segment of the historic trail is connected to the Tennessee River Museum by a 1,200-ft. walk (or drive) along Main Street past a Grant Headquarters Monument and "The War Comes to Savannah" wayside exhibit.

These historic trail segments above and below the Harrison/McGarrity Bridge were to be linked by a 700-ft. riverwalk but, to date, right-of-way has not been granted by one of the landowners involved.

Memphis: Lichterman Nature Center

The Lichterman Nature Center is an environmental education facility and wildlife sanctuary operated by the City of Memphis Park Commission and by Memphis Museums, Inc. Located in east Memphis, Lichterman Nature Center was the first nature center in the nation to be accredited by the American Association of Museums. Its sixty-five acres contain 3 mi. of trails that cover a variety of habitats, including a ten-acre lake, forest, and a field, which support a diversity of plant and animal life. The Lichterman Nature Center's Wildlife Resource Center cares for select native wildlife and has mid-South animals on display. The education staff serves the community through extensive education programs instructing classroom groups and visitors about the environment in an outdoor setting.

In February 1994, fire destroyed the center's historic 8,000-square-foot log interpretive center. The Adirondack-style building was built in 1927 by Memphis entrepreneur Clarence Saunders, and was listed on the National Register of Historic Places. It had opened in 1983 as an education center and museum.

The Nature Center is now looking to the future and has recently completed an extensive master plan that includes a new visitor center, renovated native wildlife habitats, redesigned entrance, wildlife gardens, teaching stations, and rental areas. The new Nature Center envisions itself as a model facility where adults and students can have an exciting, first-hand experience with the natural world.

Non-member admission fees to the center are $2.00 for adults and $1.00 for students and senior citizens. To reach the center take the I–240 loop in east Memphis to the Germantown/Poplar Avenue East exit. Go east on Poplar Avenue, and turn right onto Park Avenue. Then go west to Lynnfield Road and turn left. The entrance is on the left before you reach Quince Road. For further information write to The Lichterman Nature Center, 1680 Lynnfield Road, Memphis, TN 38119.

—Contributed by Larry Pickens

10. Trails on Private Land

A number of the trails described in this guidebook cross private land but were built by state personnel and volunteer organizations. The trails described in this chapter were built by private companies or land trusts on their own lands.

BOWATER POCKET WILDERNESS TRAILS

Bowater, Inc. owns more than 350,000 acres of timberlands in Tennessee. In 1967 Bowater adopted an open-land policy and published maps of three of its tree farms to be used by outdoor recreationists. The largest recreation complex is on the Piney River Tree Farm near Spring City. It includes the Piney River Picnic Area, Stinging Fork Falls Pocket Wilderness, Newby Branch Forest Camp, and the Piney River and Twin Rocks trails.

The company then decided to set aside small areas of unique character and outstanding scenic value, accessible only by foot trails. The first of these "pocket wildernesses," Virgin Falls, was dedicated in 1970. In 1969 the first trail was developed at Stinging Fork Falls, later included in a pocket wilderness. There are now five of these areas in Tennessee, and all are state-registered natural areas. Their trails are all restricted to foot use only.

An attractive booklet, complete with maps, on Bowater recreation opportunities may be obtained by writing to the Public Relations Department at Bowater Incorporated Woodlands Division, Calhoun, TN 37309-0188.

Bacon Ridge Pocket Wilderness

This, the newest Bowater Pocket Wilderness, is a 264-acre working tree farm with ninety-one acres of natural hardwoods forest and the rest in pine plantations of three ages—four, six, and thirteen years. It was set aside in 1995 as an outdoor classroom for forestry, wildlife, and conservation education. It is located in the Valley and Ridge physiographic province and encompasses a typical valley and ridge. It also lies right on, or very close to, the route taken by John Muir from Kingston in Roane County to Philadelphia in Loudon County on this "Thousand Mile Walk to the Gulf" in 1867 (see John Muir Trail in Chapter 4).

The trail gives hikers a first-hand view of how a commercial forest is managed—planting, nurturing, and clear-cutting. It also shows the effects of surface mining on forested lands. Hematite-rich Silurian-age rocks surface in the valleys of this province, and the area is dotted with old hand-dug iron ore pits and crisscrossed by wheelbarrow trails and railroad grades.

Bacon Ridge Trail. Length, 3.4 mi.; rating, moderate. This loop trail features a series of twenty-two numbered stops on its self-guided tour and can take up to three and a half hours to complete. To reach the trailhead follow TN 58 about 6 mi. south from Kingston and turn left onto TN 72. Go 2 mi., just past Midway High School, and turn right onto Dogtown Road, which within 0.5 mi. passes the Bacon Ridge Trail parking area turnoff to the right. From the trailhead at the parking area, the trail first goes north skirting the east, and then north, edges of a natural stand of Virginia pines; it then proceeds northwest into a large six-year-old plantation of loblolly pines to reach, at 0.4 mi., the start of the main loop. Turning right, the trail goes northeast to soon cross Turkey Hollow Creek and then proceeds north, still in the six-year-old pines. At 0.85 mi. a trail branches off to the left, but the main trail, graveled to this point, continues north to a corner of the pine plantation where the graveled surface ends.

The trail continues north through a natural hardwoods forest. Doubling back to the southwest it descends through a belt of four-year-old loblolly, then switchbacks into the natural hardwoods in Turkey Hollow reaching, at 1.5 mi., the north end of the trail that branched off at 0.85 mi. This trail to the left leads 0.2 mi. up Turkey Hollow back to the graveled trail, thus offering a shorter return to the trailhead (2.5 mi. round-trip). The main trail, to the right, crosses Turkey Hollow Creek, switchbacks out of the Hollow, and continues west through the hardwoods. Native species to be found here include American chestnut saplings, yellow poplar, sweetgum, white oak, and red oak.

Turning north, the trail enters a thirteen-year-old plantation of loblolly and climbs to the top of Bacon Ridge. Hardwoods forest, here dominated by chestnut oaks, extends from the ridgetop down the west-facing slope. The trail follows the ridge south-southwest and at about 2.0 mi. it continues south with hardwoods on the right slope and a four-year-old loblolly plantation to the left. Still on this dividing line, the trail turns east to switchback off the ridge and enter natural hardwoods again just before reaching the end of the main loop at 2.9 mi. and retracing the initial 0.4 mi. to the trailhead.

Piney River Tree Farm

The general area contains three Bowater trails, two of which start from the Piney River Picnic Area. To reach these trailheads, turn west off U.S. 27 onto TN 68 in Spring City, then left onto Shut-In Gap Road at the western edge of town. It is about 1 mi. to the picnic area. Pennine USGS quad, 118NW.

Twin Rocks Nature Trail. Length, 2.5 mi.; rating, moderate. This short trail winds up a narrow ridge formed by a horseshoe bend in Piney River. Starting at the picnic area (about 850 ft. elevation), it parallels the Piney River Trail a short distance, then breaks away to climb through a dry rocky area covered with oaks and hickories. It winds around the north face of a steep slope through dense laurel to an intersection with the return trail, which drops off the ridge to the west. The trail to Twin Rocks continues along a narrow backbone carved out of the rest of the ridge by the Piney. Panoramic views of the Great Valley of the Tennessee and Piney River Gorge are spectacular along the ridge, especially from the top of Twin Rocks, 1,360 ft. elevation. Ruffed grouse and other birds common to the region are often heard along the trail. The return trail intersects with the Piney River Trail for the return to the picnic area.

Piney River Trail. Length, 10 mi.; rating, easy/moderate. This trail was dedicated as a national recreation trail April 22, 1978; 230 people registered for the dedication hike and received the official trail patch. For more than two decades it has been under consideration as a segment of an extension of the Cumberland State Scenic Trail south from Brady Mountain (see Chapter 4). Starting at the picnic area at 850 ft. elevation, it winds up the hillside to about 1,100 ft. following the contour. Twin Rocks Nature Trail branches off to the left as the Piney River Trail rounds the end of the ridge. At 0.8 mi. a side trail leads downhill to the river. One-half mile farther it crosses a branch, holding closely to the contour. After the second branch the trail leads downhill to the 102-ft. suspension bridge across the river, 3 mi. from the picnic area.

Across the bridge, the trail turns upriver on the bed of an old narrow-gauge Dinky railroad that was used to mine and log the area beginning in 1909. The hiker can still see an occasional rail, a broken axle, an old mine site, and remnants of the old grade. Spots along the creeks—Hemlock Falls, White Pine Cascades, Raining Bluffs Falls, Wonder Log Falls—add a great deal of beauty to the trail experience. A 20-ft. creosoted bridge runs over Pine Branch, and a 50-ft. steel bridge crosses Rock House Branch. One-half mile up Rock House Branch, named from the overhanging rocks that provide shelter from the elements, is a tiny pool called the "bath tub." The stream has carved a deep basin in solid rock, not much larger than a bathtub, 7 ft. deep.

Up Duskin Creek from Rock House Branch, there is a 50-ft. steel bridge across a slide area. At Big Cove a mixed hardwood forest has grown in the moist soils, rich from clear-cutting in the

Dinky Line days. Picking its way around a bluff, the trail passes an old mine tipple and its waste pile on the right. Beyond, another 50-ft. steel bridge crosses to the south side of Duskin Creek. (All materials for the bridges were flown in by helicopter to avoid destruction of the sites.) A short distance upstream the trail crosses a road and turns north to the Newby Branch Forest Camp. It is 6 mi. back by road to the Piney River Picnic Area. The one-way hike from Piney River Picnic Area to Newby Branch Forest Camp takes five to six hours.

Stinging Fork Trail. Length, 3 mi.; rating, moderate. The last of the trio in the Piney River Tree Farm, this trail was built in 1969, the first trail on Bowater property. The parking area is on the right, 4 mi. from the picnic area on Shut-In Gap Road. The soft needles from a managed pine plantation cushion the hikers' feet as the trail meanders toward the edge of Stinging Fork Gorge. It follows the edge through thickets of huckleberry bushes and laurel. The huckleberries are ripe and abundant in early summer, and the laurel is in bloom. A spur trail leads down a narrow point to a rocky promontory called Indian Head Point, where there is a view of the rugged Stinging Fork Gorge. The main trail drops down to a series of steps and switchbacks to Stinging Fork Creek below the falls. A short trip up the creek finds Stinging Fork Falls, a 35-ft. waterfall and cascade located in a very picturesque setting. At present the trail just runs in and back, but future plans include completion of a loop near the end, into and out of the gorge.

—Contributed by David Rhyne and Clarence Streetman

Laurel-Snow Pocket Wilderness

Laurel-Snow Trail. Morgan Springs USGS quad, 110SE. Length, 8 mi.; rating, moderate. This trail is located near Dayton, Tennessee, site of the famous "monkey trial" of the 1920s, when high school science teacher John T. Scopes tested the Tennessee law prohibiting the teaching of the theory of evolution in the public schools. The trial attracted Clarence Darrow for the defense and William Jennings Bryan on the side of the fundamentalists. Bryan College was established in Dayton as a memorial to the "silver-tongued" politician. The corner drugstore where Scopes and friends worked out the idea of the test case is still there. The store has been remodeled, but the old-fashioned soda fountain tables were retained.

To get to the Laurel-Snow trailhead, turn west off U.S. 27 just north of the Rhea County Hospital onto Walnut Grove Road, then left onto Back Valley Road, then right onto Richland Creek Road, following the signs for a total distance of about 2 mi. from U.S. 27 to the pocket wilderness parking area. This was the first national recreation trail in Tennessee and the first in the nation to be designated on private land by the U.S. Department of the Interior. From the parking area at about 850 ft. elevation, the trail follows an old nineteenth-century railroad bed up Richland Creek Gorge and past an old mine tunnel on the right. It crosses a 50-ft. bridge over Laurel Creek at 1,100 ft. and forks, the east leg going to Laurel Falls, some 80 ft. high, and to Bryan Overlook with its view of the Tennessee Valley at 1,700 ft. elevation. The west leg goes up the other side of the gorge to Buzzard Point, which provides a view of the Tennessee Valley and Dayton. Doubling back on this leg across a spur of the Cumberland Plateau, the trail winds down to Snow Falls, a small waterfall in an extremely rugged gorge on Morgan's Creek.

A few remnants of the early twentieth-century mining operation remain, such as railroad ties, bridge foundations, a closed air shaft, and rock retainer walls. For the most part, though, the area has returned to its natural wild state, with little evidence of man's use during the past seventy years. Just south of the parking area are some old coke ovens almost covered with vegetation.

While the trail is not classified as difficult, covering it in its entirety is a good day's workout. The round trip on the Laurel Falls option alone is 5 mi. and requires three hours, while that on the

Snow Falls option is 6 mi. and requires four hours. It is a popular outing spot for Bryan College students, who affectionately refer to the area as "the pocket."

—Contributed by David Rhyne

Virgin Falls Pocket Wilderness

Virgin Falls Trail. Length, 8 mi.; rating, difficult. Lonewood USGS quad, 332SE. This trail is located 8 mi. south of De Rossett off U.S. 70 between Crossville and Sparta. Follow Eastland Road 5.9 mi. and turn right onto Scott's Gulf Road at the Chestnut Mountain Wilderness sign. Proceed 2 mi. to the Virgin Falls parking area on the right, located on the Caney Fork River in White County, Virgin Falls was the first Bowater's pocket wilderness trail to be opened, with a formal dedication hike in May 1970. This is a single trail with a loop at the end. It is recommended that six to eight hours be allowed for the full round-trip. The access trail leaves the parking area at about 1,750 ft. elevation, passing mostly through typical Cumberland Plateau second-growth timber. It follows down a branch to Big Branch Falls at 1,700 ft. and drops on down to cross Big Laurel Creek at 1,540 ft. The trail follows the right side of the creek downstream.

At 1,500 ft., a side trail leads to the right to the Caney Fork Overlook Loop, rising along the hillside to 1,700 ft., where there are views of the Caney Fork River Valley to the south. The overlook trail drops back to the main trail at 1,300 ft. The main trail veers to the right along the 1,300-ft. contour to cross a branch, then turns left along the hillside, and drops to 1,100 ft. The spur trail to Big Laurel Falls is to the left. At Big Laurel Falls the creek disappears underground beneath a 30-ft. waterfall. An overlook near Big Laurel Falls provides a view of Caney Fork Valley with no signs of humans visible. The main trail now runs westward along the side of a steep bluff overlooking the Caney Fork River about 0.5 mi., then turns north up Little Laurel Creek at the beginning of the Virgin Falls Loop. The trail drops gradually along the side of a ravine for about 0.3 mi. to Sheep Cave where a stream emerges. It crosses Little Laurel Creek at about 1,000 ft. elevation, doubles back south, then curves west across a point to Virgin Falls.

At Virgin Falls, an underground stream surfaces on the side of a sinkhole, runs over a flat rock surface for 50 to 75 ft., then drops 110 ft. over a cliff, disappearing into another cave at the bottom. This is a year-round stream. Sheep Cave is geologically similar except the stream is smaller. The caves have been mapped, and information on them is available from the Tennessee Division of Geology. Leaving the falls, the trail continues southward around the head of a ravine, winding down to Little Laurel Creek at about 880 ft. elevation. A designated backpack camping area is located off the trail to the right. The main trail continues eastward, climbing back to about 1,050 ft. to complete the loop. From here backtrack on the main trail to the parking area.

—Contributed by David Rhyne

North Chickamauga Pocket Wilderness

Opened to the public in June 1993, this 1,100-acre pocket wilderness contains two trails and features mature forest, interesting rock formations and spectacular vistas, wildflowers and wildlife, old coal mines, and an abandoned moonshine still. The parking area is located off U.S. 27 on Montlake Road just beyond the city boundary of Soddy-Daisy and just before Montlake makes a hairpin curve to begin the ascent of Walden Ridge. The entrance area features picnic facilities and handicapped accessibility to North Chicamauga Creek. Chattanooga USGS quad, 105SE.

The Hogskin Branch Loop Trail leads northwest from the parking area and is 1.5 mi. round-trip. The Stevenson Trail extends along the north slope of North Chickamauga Creek from the northwest end of the Hogskin Branch Loop. Including the northern leg of the Hogskin Branch Loop, the Stevenson Trail is about 4 mi. long or 7.8 mi. round-trip. Both trails are rated easy to moderate, and a primitive camping area is located near the end of the Stevenson Trail.

TENNESSEE RIVER GORGE TRUST

The Tennessee River Gorge provides over 25,000 acres of relatively undisturbed and highly diverse habitat for many threatened or endangered plant and animal species. The gorge is home to American ginseng, Carey's saxifrage, and Tennessee leafcup, each considered threatened or of special concern in the state, as well as large-flowered skullcap, a federally endangered plant. Rose gentian, until discovered in the gorge in the early 1980s, had not been seen in Tennessee since 1895.

The high wooded slopes of the gorge also have proven to be an ideal setting for reintroduction of the osprey, or fish hawk, to Tennessee. In all, ten federally endangered species of birds, including the bald eagle and peregrine falcon, are found here. Raccoon Mountain overlooking the gorge is a favorite spot for birders watching hawk migrations.

Historically, the gorge has played an important role in the settling of the Chattanooga area. Indian habitation sites on Williams Island date from 8,000 B.C. to A.D. 1800, and a fortified town was there at the time of DeSoto's passing through East Tennessee in 1540. Years later, pioneer families, traders, flatboat oarsmen, and steamboat captains fought the violent currents of Tumbling Shoals and the Suck. The gorge thus embodies the cultural heritage of this region.

The 1980s brought more threats to the essential character of the gorge than any previous period, as Chattanooga and Hamilton County rapidly expanded. Early in the decade, a group of local citizens concerned with the rapid unplanned development of the gorge sought help from The Nature Conservancy to maintain its natural integrity. The Conservancy established a land-use plan, and an independent local organization, The Tennessee River Gorge Trust, was chartered to oversee and maintain this program. Working closely with landowners to assure responsible development and preservation of natural values, the Trust uses various protection techniques including conservation easements, gifts and bequests of land or reserved life estates or lease backs, and outright purchase of land.

The Trust has long been a supporter of the Cumberland Trail and is active in helping maintain the Tennessee River Gorge Segment. Besides the trail system described below, the Trust has created hiking trails on Williams Island State Archeological Area and elsewhere in the gorge.

Pot-Point Trails

Pot Point, in Marion County, is owned by the Tennessee River Gorge Trust. Named for a rapid that once dominated the Tennessee River at this site, Pot Point rises 1,200 feet from the river to the bluff line of the mountain. The area consists of 490 acres of thick, hardwood forests and rolling meadows along a spectacular river bend. Pot Point is home to Chattanooga's first biological field station: a renovated 1830-era log cabin that has existed since the earliest settlement of the area.

Pot Point Trail. Length, 3.0 mi.; rating, moderate. The 3-mi. Pot Point Trail begins and ends at the historic Pot House. Marked with blue blazes, the trail loops through every habitat and landform that the Grand Canyon of the Tennessee has to offer at this midpoint of its journey through Walden's Ridge. The Pot House is located on River Canyon Road 4 mi. from the Suck Creek Bridge on TN 27 in Marion County, just twenty minutes west of Chattanooga. Parking is situated above the road overlooking the Pot House Biological Field Station.

The trail entrance can be accessed from either the Pot House or just to the south of the parking lot. The upper trail section of 1.3

mi. is moderate to difficult and climbs the canyon walls to a point just below the Cumberland Plateau escarpment. This section is highlighted by beautiful scenic vistas, especially in the fall and winter. A mature forest of oaks, hickories, and other assorted hardwoods surrounds the trail. Spring wildflowers along this section can be spectacular. A campsite is located off the upper section near a spring that provides water year-round.

The lower 1.7-mi. section of the trail follows an easy to moderate path along the Tennessee River through bottomland forests, fields, and wetlands. This section of trail is characterized by open fields and some of the best panoramic views of the area. Wildlife is seen on the lower trail at all times of the year and is dominated by birds of all kinds, including bald eagles, osprey, and numerous songbird species. Deer are seen frequently and often swim the Tennessee River in plain sight of the lower trail.

The Pot Point Trail is open to the public year-round, with permission from the Trust. For complete information, contact the Tennessee River Gorge Trust offices at Suite 104, 25 Cherokee Boulevard, Chattanooga, TN 37405; telephone (423) 266–0314. The trail crosses River Canyon Road and care should be taken when crossing.

Ⓑ **Pot Point Boardwalk.** Length, 400 ft.; accessible; smooth; foot. This wooden boardwalk is located in the heart of the Tennessee River Gorge. The boardwalk begins at the Pot Point Biological Field Station, meandering through bottomland forest, offering views of the Tennessee River and many species of native plants. A wide variety of birds can also be seen from the boardwalk.

—Contributed by Jim Brown

WESTVACO: KEEL SPRING NATURE TRAIL

Governor Don Sundquist dedicated this, the first of Westvaco Corporation's system of nature trails in Tennessee, in May 1996 as the official kickoff of his Bicentennial Greenways and Trails Program. Located in the northwest corner of the Western Highland Rim, this beautiful little trail and preserve showcases the forest and small stream ecosystems typical of that physiographic province. More than a place to hike and enjoy the outdoors, these trails are designed to educate visitors about the region's ecology and the company's ecosystem-based approach to sustainable forest management.

The spring was named for a local resident, W.L. Keel, an employee of Ayer Lord Tie Company, the former landowner. Westvaco acquired a 4,000-acre tract here in 1984 to be managed as timberland but set aside 225 acres of stream and uplands around the spring for its nature trail. The preserve is located in Stewart County on Leatherwood Road, 4 mi. south of Dover. As the crow flies, it is only 3 mi. south of both Land Between the Lakes National Recreation Area and Fort Donelson National Military Park, 6 mi. west of Cross Creeks National Wildlife Refuge, and 5 mi. northwest of Stewart State Forest. These public lands, together with those of a few private owners along Tennessee Ridge, such as Westvaco, form an almost continuous greenbelt containing habitats ranging from the Cumberland River bottoms to the forested top of the Cumberland/Tennessee Valleys watershed divide.

Keel Springs Nature Trail is exclusively for foot use. An excellent interpretive brochure keyed to twenty-three marked stops along both loops of the trail is available by writing or calling Westvaco Corporation, P.O. Box 1206, Paris, TN 83242; (901) 642–6500.

Yellow Poplar Loop Trail. Length, 0.5 mi.; rating, easy. The first 0.1 mi. of the trail from the parking area along the stream to the Outdoor Classroom is paved and rated: accessible, smooth, foot. The remainder of this lower loop is woodland footpath that crosses the west fork of Lick Creek several times. (It was across the icy backwaters at the mouth of the swollen Lick Creek just east of Dover that General Nathan B. Forrest led his cavalry, each horseman carrying an infantryman behind him, before daylight on February 16, 1862, to escape Fort Donelson's surrender to General U.S. Grant later that day.)

About 200 ft. along the accessible section, a wildflower garden is reached where such natives as bloodroot, wild sweet William, wild geranium, dwarf crested iris, Virginia bluebell, jack-in-the-pulpit, green dragon, cardinal flower, butterfly weed, spider lily, and black-eyed Susan can be found blooming in season. Where the paved trail ends at the Outdoor Classroom is an annual breeding bird survey point. Louisiana waterthrush, barn swallows, northern rough winged swallows, and eastern phoebes are often seen here along the stream, which itself is alive with fish, crayfish, snails and other crustaceans, and insect larvae.

Another stop on the unpaved part of the lower loop reveals the geology of the area, including the uses made by Native Americans of the siliceous cherts embedded in the local Mississipian period Warsaw limestone. Others tell of the value to wildlife and man of the yellow poplar (the Tennessee state tree), black walnut, white ash, and the lowly goldenseal. Particularly interesting is an explanation of the making of charcoal throughout these forests in the early to mid-1800s to support iron ore furnaces scattered over this part of the Western Highland Rim (fourteen in Stewart County alone). All these forests were clear-cut at some time during the period to feed this thriving industry (see Mongomery Bell State Park in Chapter 5).

White Oak Loop. Length, 0.6 mi.; rating, moderate. This upper loop of the trail mostly passes through a mixed hardwoods forest typical of the area. Natural and manmade changes and their ecological effects on the forest can be observed at the numbered stops. The composition, growth patterns, and wildlife values of the forest understory species, such as dogwoods, maples, beech, and gum, are observed at one stop. Others show the natural regeneration of oak-hickory forest; a plot planted to provide a winter food source for turkey, deer, quail, rabbits, and other wildlife; a loblolly pine plantation and the bird and animal species it attracts at successive stages of growth; and a wildlife pond and the species it supports. The evidence of past logging practices from an old logging trail is discussed at one stop, while another tells how good forest roads are built today. A picnic area is at the top of the ridge.

11. Trails Organizations

Tennessee Trails Association. Organized in 1968, this statewide association is dedicated to the development of a state trails system. There are three types of membership: individual, supporting, and student. The association works with the Department of Environment and Conservation on right-of-way acquisition, trail development, and trail maintenance, and it sponsors the Adopt-a-Trail program. There are monthly membership activities, and TTA publishes a monthly newsletter. Five or more members in one location may form a local chapter. Present chapters are: Nashville, Memphis, Murfreesboro, Clarksville, Cumberland Mountain, East Tennessee, Plateau, and Upper Cumberland. For information, write to Tennessee Trails Association, P.O. Box 41446, Nashville, TN 37204.

Smoky Mountains Hiking Club. Organized in 1924, this is the oldest and largest independent trail club in Tennessee. SMHC has published an annual handbook since 1927 and has been affiliated with the Appalachian Trail Conference since 1928. The club sponsors thirty-five to forty hikes a year, plus two slide shows and other social events, and publishes a monthly newsletter. It maintains more than 100 miles of the Appalachian Trail. For more information, write to them at P.O. Box 1454, Knoxville, TN 37901.

Tennessee Citizens for Wilderness Planning. The group was organized in 1966. It is a conservation activist organization that includes trails in its overall program. It sponsored the building of the North Ridge Trail in Oak Ridge (described in Chapter 9) and oversees the maintenance of this trail, in cooperation with the City Parks and Recreation Department and local scout troops. It has an agreement with TVA and Hiwassee Land Company to maintain the Whites Creek Small Wild Area

Trail on Watts Bar Lake. It maintains the Cedar Barrens Natural Area, including an interpretive trail, in Oak Ridge. For information contact Liane B. Russell, Newsletter Editor, 130 Tabor Road, Oak Ridge, TN 37830, (423) 482–2153.

Tennessee Eastman Hiking and Recreation Club. The group is made up of employees of Tennessee Eastman Company. The club maintains 115 miles of the Appalachian Trail and helped establish the Trail of the Lonesome Pine. For information, write to the club in care of Tennessee Eastman Company, P.O. Box 511, Kingsport, TN 37662.

Historical Hiking Trails, Inc., and **Shiloh Military Trails, Inc.,** P.O. Box 17507, Memphis, TN 38187-0507. They publish *Hiking Trails of America* jointly with Boy Scout Troop 343 of Memphis "for Boy Scouts, Girl Scouts, and other youth groups." The organizations sponsor patch awards for nineteen trails, seventeen of them in Tennessee, and publish materials about Shiloh National Military Park, Memphis Historical Trail, and other places of historical interest. Ken Humphreys is responsible for the success of many of the projects sponsored by these groups. Award sponsors for other trails in Tennessee are listed in *Hiking Trails of America.*

Tennessee Parks and Greenways Foundation. Formed in 1997 through a merger of the Tennessee State Parks Foundation and the Conservation Fund's Tennessee Greenways Program, this organization's long-term goal is to preserve the beautiful character of the state by helping create a green infrastructure with state parks as the crown jewels. Call Kathleen Williams at (615) 386–3171 for more information.

Governor's Council on Greenways and Trails. Chartered by Governor Don Sundquist in the fall of 1997, the Council consists of representatives from a diverse group of people interested in greenways and trails including walkers, hikers, equestrians, bikers, motorized trail users, greenway and natural resource protection advocates, the general public, and industries that support conservation of natural resources. The make-up of the Council has changed somewhat since late last year. The Council emphasizes making Tennessee's trails accessible to all user groups, including persons with disabilities. Nonvoting representatives from various state, federal, and nonprofit agencies also sit on the Council with a view toward creating a statewide network of organizations working toward a common vision of greenways and trails in Tennessee. For information write or call Tennessee Department of Environment and Conservation, Recreation Services Division, 401 Church St., Nashville, TN 37243-0439; (615) 532–0748.

Tennessee Chapter of the Sierra Club, P.O. Box 52641, Knoxville, TN 37950-2641. Groups are located in the Tri-Cities, Knoxville, Chattanooga, Cookeville, Nashville, and Mamphis. Each group has monthly meetings, and a year-round program of outings and activities related to environmental protection. The Cherokee Group (Chattanooga) maintains a section of the Cumberland State Scenic Trail in Prentice Cooper State Forest.

The Nature Conservancy of Tennessee, 50 Vantage Way, Suite 250, Nashville, TN 37228; T**he Tennessee River Gorge Trust, Inc.** Suite 104, 25 Cherokee Blvd., Chattanooga, TN 37405; and **The Southern Appalachians Highlands Conservancy** P.O. Box 4092 CRS Station, Johnson City, TN 37602. Each of these organizations is engaged in preserving biodiversity and protecting ecologically significant natural areas in, respectively, all the physiographic provinces of Tennessee in their regional and global contexts; the Grand Canyon of the Tennessee River in Hamilton and Marion counties; and the Highlands of Roan in Carter County and adjacent North Carolina counties. Each group works in partnership with government and private landowners to assure protection of such areas on their lands, and each also acquires and manages such areas when no other means to assure protection are available. Finally, each has a program of outings and ecosystems-protection projects for its members and supporting volunteers.

References

The titles listed below may be of interest to the region's hikers.

Arnow, Harriette Simpson. *Seedtime on the Cumberland.*

Bierly, Michael Lee. *Bird Finding in Tennessee.*

Brandt, Robert S. *Tennessee Hiking Guide.*

———. *Middle Tennessee on Foot: Hikes in the Woods and Walks on Country Roads.*

Brewer, Carson. *Hiking in the Great Smokies.*

Coleman, Brenda D., and Jo Anna Smith. *Hiking the Big South Fork.*

Homan, Tim. *Hiking Trails of the Joyce Kilmer-Slickrock and Citico Creek Wilderness Areas.*

Horn, Stanley F. *The Army of Tennessee.*

Lewis, Thomas M.N., and Madeline Kneberg. *Tribes That Slumber.*

Manning, Russ. *The Historic Cumberland Plateau—An Explorer's Guide.*

Manning, Russ, and Sandra Jamieson. *Best of the Big South Fork.*

———. *The Best of the Great Smoky Mountains National Park.*

———. *South Cumberland and Fall Creek Falls.*

Miller, Robert A. *The Geologic History of Tennessee.*

Murless, Dick, and Constance Stallings. *Hikers Guide to the Smokies.*

Myer, William Edward. *Indian Trails of the Southeast.*

Skelton, William N. *Wilderness Trails of Tennessee's Cherokee National Forest.*

Williams, Samuel Cole. *Early Travels in the Tennessee Country* (out of print).

About the Author

Evans Means was a journalist for fifty years. An outdoor conservation writer with numerous published articles, he is the founder of the Southeastern Outdoor Press Association (SEOPA) and a past president of Outdoor Writers Association of America (OWAA). Outdoor editor at the *Oak Ridger* (Tennessee) for four decades, Means also managed to pursue a career in electrical engineering and write two plays. He originated the Cumberland Trail in 1965 while president of the Clinch and Powell River Valley Association. The trail was chosen as the pilot project for the Tennessee Trails Association, which Means cofounded in 1968.

He was the first recipient of the Tennessee Trails Award, presented by the Tennessee Trails Association in 1979. He received the Z. Carter Patten Award, the highest honor given by the Tennessee Conservation League, and was made a life member of SEOPA in 1981. He was awarded honored life membership in the Tennessee Outdoor Writers Association in 1983. He received the Ham Brown Award, the highest honor bestowed on a member of OWAA, in 1982. He was the first recipient of the Tennessee Trails Association Lifetime Recognition Award in 1992.

About the Editor

Bob Brown is a trustee of The Nature Conservancy of Tennessee. He was the first president of the Tennessee Trails Association and currently serves on the Governor's Council on Greenways and Trails, the Metropolitan Nashville Greenway Commission, and the board of directors of the Friends of Warner Parks. He is a longtime member of several of the organizations listed in Chapter 11.